Praise for *Living Corporate Citizenship*

"*Living Corporate Citizenship* provides a useful roadmap for companies that are moving along the path towards greater corporate responsibility. Through lively case studies, the book illustrates just how managers can successfully lead their companies into living up to the nine principles of the Global compact and provides a helpful analysis of the aray of responsibility initiatives that emerged in recent years."

Sandra Waddock
Professor of Management, Carroll School of Management,
Senior Research Fellow, Center for Corporate Citizenship,
Boston College

"The UN Global Compact is an enormously important corporate citizenship initiative with participation from business, the UN, labour organizations and NGOs. For those people who are interested in how the Global Compact has evolved in its first few years this well researched book is a crucial source of information and learning."

David Bell
Head of People, Pearson Group
Member of Advisory Group to the UN Secretary General on the
Global Compact

"In essence, *Living Corporate Citizenship* explores the relationship between globalization and corporate citizenship and provides a useful guide to the UN Global Compact and other key international initiatives. For anyone trying to understand the corporate social responsibility and corporate citizenship agendas, this book offers useful case studies, thoughtful reflection and sound guidance."

Dr Vernon Jennings
Vice President Ethics and Social Responsibility,
Stakeholder Relations, Novo Nordisk A/S

"This is must reading for anyone wishing to keep up with the rapidly changing, and increasingly important, challenges of corporate citizenship."

John Gerard Ruggie
Kirkpatrick Professor of International Affairs, Harvard University

"This book illuminates the emerging convergence of the debate on and practice of global corporate citizenship. This is a must read for everybody dealing with this important subject."

Georg Kell
Senior Advisor to the UN Secretary-General

"Finally we have a book on corporate citizenship that is neither spin nor a punt for the 'the one right way'. Steeped in rich experience and scholarship, this level headed but passionately written piece of work may well mark the coming of age of the corporate citizenship movement. This is also an indispensable handbook for business leaders in the developing world who struggle to comprehend the complexities of corporate responses to the multiple global crises that so threaten the environments within which business operates. Either read this book, or remain bewildered by the meaningless babble that dominates discussion about this crucial subject."

Professor Mark Swilling
Sustainability Institute, University of Stellenbosch

Living
Corporate
Citizenship

FT Prentice Hall
FINANCIAL TIMES

In an increasingly competitive world, we believe it's quality of thinking that will give you the edge – an idea that opens new doors, a technique that solves a problem, or an insight that simply makes sense of it all. The more you know, the smarter and faster you can go.

That's why we work with the best minds in business and finance to bring cutting-edge thinking and best learning practice to a global market.

Under a range of leading imprints, including *Financial Times Prentice Hall*, we create world-class print publications and electronic products bringing our readers knowledge, skills and understanding which can be applied whether studying or at work.

To find out more about our business publications, or tell us about the books you'd like to find, you can visit us at
www.business-minds.com

For other Pearson Education publications, visit
www.pearsoned-ema.com

Living Corporate Citizenship

Strategic routes to socially responsible business

McINTOSH, THOMAS, LEIPZIGER

AND COLEMAN

 **Prentice Hall**
FINANCIAL TIMES

An imprint of **Pearson Education**
London ■ New York ■ Toronto ■ Sydney ■ Tokyo ■ Singapore ■ Hong Kong
Cape Town ■ New Delhi ■ Madrid ■ Paris ■ Amsterdam ■ Munich ■ Milan ■ Stockholm

PEARSON EDUCATION LIMITED

Head Office:
Edinburgh Gate
Harlow CM20 2JE
Tel: +44 (0)1279 623623
Fax: +44 (0)1279 431059

London Office:
128 Long Acre
London WC2E 9AN
Tel: +44 (0)20 7447 2000
Fax: +44 (0)20 7447 2170
Website:www.business-minds.com

First published in Great Britain in 2003

© McIntosh, Thomas, Leipziger and Coleman 2003

The right of Malcolm McIntosh, Ruth Thomas, Deborah Leipziger and Gill Coleman
to be identified as Authors of this Work has been asserted by them in accordance
with the Copyright, Designs and Patents Act 1988.

ISBN 0 273 65433 0

British Library Cataloguing in Publication Data
A CIP catalogue record for this book can be obtained from the British Library.

10 9 8 7 6 5 4 3 2 1

Typeset by Northern Phototypesetting Co. Ltd, Bolton
Printed and bound in Great Britain by Biddles Ltd, Guildford & King's Lynn

The Publishers' policy is to use paper manufactured from sustainable forests.

Contents

Foreword

Living Corporate Citizenship is in everyone's interest!

The behaviour of corporations has never been more under the spotlight. The issues range from downstream management to the heart of corporate decision-making. There is now a realization that it is difficult for corporations to make socially responsible decisions about their operations in the outlying regions of their empires if the men and women at the top do not have the good society in mind. This means that the honesty and integrity of directors is as much up for discussion as waste packaging and child labour. These corporations are *our* corporations: they are our heart and soul. In them we invest our pensions, our working lives and our custom. When they act they act as both private and public entities.

Much of this book is concerned with the UN Global Compact, a voluntary initiative that requires companies to engage by learning, and then engage again by showing how they have learnt. The Global Compact puts human rights, labour and environmental issues at the heart of the new corporate citizenship – it demands that our largest private economic institutions are complicit with public concerns on social policy. It demands that companies understand that their sphere of interest and influence is not confined to simply rewarding shareholders (or senior executives) financially.

Many incidents in the last few years – from the 1995 Asian banking crisis, through September 11 to the fraud perpetrated at Enron, Xerox, Tyco, WorldCom and other corporations – have proved that the development of new rules of governance, public and private, can only happen within the nexus that is shaped by corporations, the state and communities. In other words, corporate citizenship is for everyone.

Malcolm McIntosh; Ruth Thomas; Deborah Leipziger; Gill Coleman
Bath, England
July 2002

Acknowledgements

Much of the research in this book would not have been possible without the support of Georg Kell, Executive Assistant to the UN Secretary-General and Director of the UN Global Compact Office in New York. He has been tireless in his efforts to promote the UN Global Compact, as have his staff with whom we have worked over the past two years. Our thanks go to Georg and to two Assistant Secretary-Generals, Professors John Ruggie, now at Harvard University, and Michael Doyle, his successor. Our thanks also go to Denise O'Brien, Melissa Powell, Fred Dubee and their colleagues at the UN Development Fund. In the UN agencies it has been an inspirational learning experience working in cross-border relationships with Jacqueline Aloisi de Larderel, Fritz Balkau and Cornis van der Lugt in UNEP, Hans Hofmeiyer and Michael Urminsky in the ILO, Scott Jerbi in the OHCHR and Sirkka Korpela and Casper Sonesson from UNDP.

Our next set of acknowledgements and thanks go to our colleagues at the University of Warwick. In particular we would like to thank Dr Bela Arora and Dr Jan Aart Scholte in the Department of Politics and International Security and Professor David C. Wilson in the Business School. Much of this material has been discussed with students and executives in classrooms at Warwick, Bath, Bristol, INSEAD, the Judge Institute at Cambridge University and other universities, and our thanks go to those enlightened programme managers who have supported development and research in corporate citizenship. In particular we would like to thank Professors John Benington and Jean Hartley at the Warwick Institute for Governance and Public Management.

At the University of Bath, where Malcolm McIntosh, Ruth Thomas and Gill Coleman have strong links, Professors Geof Wood, Anil Markandya, Peter Reason, Judi Marshall and Dr Adrian Winnett have understood the nature of engagement with serious research in a fast-changing political environment.

Individual chapters owe their development to the Norwegian Ministry of Foreign Affairs, Vicki Harris from the UK's Department for International Development and Hugh Salveson from the UK Foreign Office, and all those people from India, Brazil, South Africa, the US, Canada and the UK who took part in the second Internationalising Corporate Citizenship Conference in Oslo in March 2001. Sir Brian Unwin, Sir Richard Freeman, Martyn Bond and Alexis Krachai from a Federal Trust working group contributed to the debate on the nature of corporate social responsibility. Sir Mark Moody-Stuart, Sir Frederick Crawford, Tony Young, Philip Connelly and Melanie Jones from the British-North America Research Committee contributed to the analysis of corporate citizenship and NGOs. Many others too have played a part in the development of different sections of this book, for which we are very grateful.

The chapters on phase one of the Global Compact have been discussed in many forums but we would particularly like to thank members of the European Business Ethics Network at the annual conference in April 2002 at the University of Bath.

However, without one champion this book would not have got this far. Stephen Partridge at FT Management has, against the odds, pushed this book to publication. Nicola Sharp from the University of Bath made sure that attention was paid to detail.

Finally we would like to thank all those with whom the four of us work and live – partners, children and cats. Some are close at hand and support us when human frailty sets in, others are spread around the planet. Many thanks and much love and peace to you all.

Malcolm McIntosh
Ruth Thomas
Deborah Leipziger
Gill Coleman
Bath, May 2002

Introduction

This book is a sequel to *Corporate Citizenship: Successful Strategies for Responsible Companies* which was published in 1998. It has been inspired through working on corporate citizenship with people and organizations around the world. In particular the focus on the development of the United Nations Global Compact has been central to our appreciation of global–local dilemmas and the issues that arise in the growing relationship between business and public policy making, particularly with the United Nations.

The book is structured in two parts. The first part deals with general issues of corporate citizenship and teases out some of the current ambiguities and uncertainties. The second part focuses on the Global Compact. It is here that we present empirical evidence from our work on the UN Global Compact, with the companies which have engaged with this initiative. We have also worked closely with UN agencies that have been at the heart of the development of the Global Compact – the International Labour Organisation (ILO), the United Nations Environment Programme (UNEP) and the Office of the High Commissioner for Human Rights (OHCHR). A sister publication to this book, which we have also had a part in writing for the Global Compact Office, is a *Primer on the Global Compact* which is available at www.unglobalcompact.org.

Chapter 1 introduces the book and makes links between this book and our last joint book, *Corporate Citizenship: Successful Strategies for Responsible Companies*, and the new material and ideas that have emerged in the intervening period.

Chapter 2 clarifies some of the distinctions between corporate social responsibility and corporate citizenship. In particular it makes the claim that responsible corporate citizenship involves engagement in issues of public policy and it recognizes that companies are both private and public entities.

Chapter 3 argues that in *Corporate Citizenship* we were perhaps wrong to suggest that there is a linear progression to becoming a good corporate citizen. It is clear that some companies can never be good corporate citizens, because of what they do or how they choose to do it. There are other companies which have no interest in the agenda espoused in chapter 2; they do not see that public policy or the UN's Millennium Targets have anything to do with their pursuit of profit. Surely, this chapter states, our corporations are the manifestations of our collective action or inaction to promote or curb the growth of global business organizations. And what sort of institutions and institutional behaviours do we need to humanize global and local economies?

Chapter 4 explores how companies can develop their approach to corporate citizenship, drawing on the lessons from organizational change, particularly that which has been learned from the incorporation of environmental issues into organizational behaviour. One of the greatest management competencies that all organizations now need is the ability to work in partnership with people and organizations with which they may not previously have realized they had common objectives. So, this chapter looks at some of the research and typologies of non-government organizations (NGOs) in an effort to help companies, and others, understand how they might think about these significant global and local actors.

Chapter 5 is concerned with the links between the UN Global Compact and seven other corporate citizenship initiatives. Some will ask whether there is too much emphasis on conformity to one global standard; others, particularly in companies, will welcome moves to forge convergence and linkages between symbiotic initiatives. One corporate executive in a major oil company recently confided that his company had signed up to 200 sets of corporate citizenship principles locally and globally, and another oil company regularly talks about 'codemania'. Since we began this book much has happened and the speed of change is impressive. For example, the UN Global Compact has adopted the Global Reporting Initiative (GRI) and the European Union (EU) has published both a Green Paper and a Communication on a CSR (corporate social responsibility) framework for Europe, which also accepts the GRI as a working model. The Swedish government has promoted a framework based on the OECD (Organisation for Economic Co-operation and Development) Guidelines for Multi-national companies and GRI, and Germany has seen the promotion of a voluntary set of guidelines for corporate behaviour. Meanwhile, events such as the destruction of the Twin Towers of the World Trade Center on September 11 2001, the collapse of the Enron corporation and the scandals involving ABB and Iceland foods have heightened interest in the relationship between regulation, initiative and enterprise. We chose a Global Eight – but there are others which have enormous importance, locally, regionally and globally. This chapter is based on work for the UN Global Compact within the Secretary-General's office.

Chapter 6 is about the UN Global Compact. The story is relatively recent, has developed considerable momentum as the Compact has become known around the world and has galvanized companies and critics into a new dialogue which is at the heart of the pro- and anti-globalization lobbies. What the Global Compact argues is that the global economy can be humanized; that corporations, working in partnership with public and civil society organizations, can help reach the UN's Millennium Targets. The jury is out and will most likely reconvene in the courtroom to ask for guidance. What is it we are supposed to be looking at? How might we spot change? How might we be able to accredit that change to one thing or another?

Chapter 7 is drawn from the UN Global Primer, also available at www.unglobalcompact.org. It is a brief guide not only to the Global Compact but also to the sources of information that can be utilized by those seeking to understand the origins of the Nine Principles and to look for further supporting evidence of the development of these new global governance structures. In this respect this chapter has involved significant cross-boundary work with the ILO, UNEP, OHCHR and the Global Compact Office. This chapter includes some of the more developed contributions from companies and analyzes the quality of their engagement in the first phase of development. Thirty-three company submissions from 31 companies are analyzed for content, coverage and linkages. This sample suggests that companies are in general not learning from experience in other change programmes, and they are not engaging in the transformational programmes that are necessary if corporate behaviour en masse is to enable the delivery of the Millennium Targets.

Chapter 8 reviews the conclusions from this book and suggests that there are divergent ways of looking at corporate citizenship. In particular it suggests that unless we look at more fundamental human values and reform our economic and multilateral institutions, engagement with the corporate citizenship initiatives profiled in this book, including the Global Compact, will not succeed.

CHAPTER 1

Living
corporate citizenship

In 1998 Malcolm McIntosh, Deborah Leipziger, Gill Coleman and Keith Jones got together to write an introduction for managers to the topic of corporate citizenship. The book was subtitled *'Successful strategies for responsible companies'*, flagging up a connection between business success and some of the ideas emerging under the broad heading of corporate citizenship. The aim was to provide some sort of reference book to a new area of company engagement: an explanation of the terminology, examples of who was doing what, a guide to where to find practical help and further information. The book ended with some thoughts as to possible future scenarios, for societies rather than for companies, and some suggestions as to the management imperatives that could be derived from corporate citizenship.

In the four years that have elapsed since then there has been an astonishing rise in the amount of activity and interest in corporate citizenship. In returning to write on this topic, three of the original authors, accompanied by Ruth Thomas, have decided to focus on action and practice, on what 'living' corporate citizenship might involve. It seems that the key questions posed in this arena are no longer how to make the business case or whether there is a possibility of 'doing well by doing good'. The front-running corporate citizens, even if they are still a minority within the business community, have largely answered these questions by demonstrating how this might be done. Instead it is time to ask what can be learned from what is currently happening and how we make sense of the developments that are taking place. Above all, the question we ask ourselves, as people whose working lives are spent surrounded by those talking the language of corporate citizenship, is *'what difference is this activity making to business outcomes and to social outcomes?'* Might corporate citizenship really be seen as a new, more humanistic way of conducting business, bringing together a concern with wealth creation and a concern for the wider social good? Or is it simply a new way of *talking* about how business is conducted, a surface gloss beneath which neither business priorities nor impacts are changing?

It is possible to see a number of important developments in the field of corporate citizenship during this relatively short period, which we will mention here and develop further in the chapters that follow. These are voluntary codes and auditable standards, social partnerships, business and poverty, war and conflict, and the UN Global Compact.

Voluntary codes and auditable standards

The first of these is the emergence of voluntary codes of conduct and auditable standards as currently the leading mechanisms for the practice of corporate citizenship. As Chapter 5 will explore, codes of conduct offer such an attractive proposition in containing and making concrete a wide and sometimes conflicting set of 'stakeholder' demands that there has been an explosion of initiatives, and of organizations willing to specify them and audit against them. Setting agreed minimum standards on issues such as the treatment of workers and suppliers gives companies the possibility of specifying required behaviour, being able to check whether that requirement is met, and being able to measure progress from one year to the next. Potentially this enables business risk to be managed and the global 'playing field', which permits very different working conditions and business practices in different parts of the world, to be levelled.

Just at the moment, however, there is confusion as to where this is leading. The proponents of the various standards and codes suggest they are a business-like way to achieve a significant shift in companies'

■ ■ ■ ■ ■ ■ ■ ■ ■ ■ ■ ■ ■

**Setting agreed minimum standards
on issues such as the treatment of workers
and suppliers gives companies the possibility
of specifying required behaviour**

■ ■ ■ ■ ■ ■ ■ ■ ■ ■ ■ ■ ■

attention to the behaviour carried out in their name or under their contracts, with real, positive results for the millions of vulnerable people around the world dependent on their employment for survival. But other interest groups maintain they are simply a means by which inappropriate costs and expectations are levied on those in supply chains who can least afford it, allowing wealthy brand-holders, for example, to push their risk and the costs of minimizing it onto factory owners in Third World countries. This places suppliers, already competing for short-term contracts, under additional pressure, reduces their profit margins and is ultimately detrimental to the very people the standards and codes are intended to help. Meanwhile, it is clear that this is a burgeoning area of new practice.

Cross-sector social partnerships

A second clear development is the emergence of some surprising cross-sector partnerships, bringing together groups and organizations which only a few years ago did not communicate with each other, let alone work together. Boundaries between the responsibilities of governments, civil society organizations and the private sector are becoming blurred at the edges, even if the wholesale privatization of the democratic function is not yet upon us. So-called 'multi-stakeholder partnership agreements', like the Marine and Forest Stewardship Councils, indicate an innovative organizational response to some difficult, systemic environmental problems requiring many different actors to play their parts. One of the interesting aspects of these partnerships is that they can involve organizations of radically different size and reach, suggesting that campaigns by relatively small but well-organized campaign groups can be sufficiently troublesome to those who are their targets to bring them to the negotiation table.

Experience suggests that one of the reasons these cross-sector partnerships sometimes work is that the players can genuinely learn new things from each other that help address a shared problem and develop degrees of mutuality in taking action.[1] The divergent thinking brought by the different actors' perspectives, although not necessarily comfortable, can contribute to the creativity of the response.[2] Some of the case studies in this book illustrate this well. They also suggest that multinational corporations have to grapple with the twin opposing pulls of centralized consistency and local responsiveness in relation to their social and environmental performance. Standards, as already mentioned, offer the former. But meeting the needs of diverse stakeholders, whose lives and experiences may be far removed from those of the corporate representatives they encounter, both geographically and culturally, requires some form of relationship building. Companies have tended to treat the conduct of their business as a technical challenge, and the discovery that *relationships*, and even 'irrational' *feelings* on the part of some stakeholders, can have a material effect on their success has been in some cases difficult and salutary.[3] Gradually, through such partnerships, and through other forms of stakeholder engagement, awareness is growing that doing business in a multi-local, highly interconnected and politicized environment requires new 'relational' capabilities and skills on the part of the busi-

[1] Bendell, J. (2000) *Terms for Endearment: Business, NGOs and Sustainable Development*, Sheffield: Greenleaf Publishing.

[2] Stacey, R. D. (2001) *Complex Responsive Processes in Organizations: Learning and Knowledge Creation*, London: Routledge.

[3] See, for instance, Fineman, S. (1996) 'Emotional subtexts in corporate greening,' *Organisational Studies*, 17 (2).

ness community.[4] One of the keys to the future conduct of successful business may be a more sophisticated understanding of what 'society' is – a concept that is still very underdeveloped in business boardrooms and classrooms alike – and how more successful interaction with different groups may take place alongside the advanced technical skills which continue to be higher on the agenda.

Business and poverty, war and conflict

Third, attention is now being given to the links between business and poverty, and business and war or armed conflict. At the time of writing, the discussion of the implications of the events of September 11 2001 in the USA is still in its infancy. But the fact that terrorists, in seeking to destabilize the United States both materially and symbolically, targeted not just the Pentagon but also the World Trade Center speaks volumes about the closing of the gap between business and politics in some people's perceptions, if not in actuality. In a global market, companies operating overseas stand to represent their countries and cultures, and are sometimes the only expression of a particular nation state that the residents of a country encounter first hand. When opponents seek to put pressure on a particular national government, it is increasingly likely that business personnel are the chosen means.[5]

The debate about the upsides and downsides of globalization rages on, and few commentators seriously think 'un-globalization' is a realistic possibility. But the terms on which global business continues to func-

---

[4] Fletcher, J. K. (1998) 'Relational practice: a feminist reconstruction of work,' *Journal of Management Inquiry*, 7 (2), 163–86.

[5] In February 2002, for instance, Daniel Pearl, a journalist working for *The Wall Street Journal* was kidnapped in Pakistan by a breakaway Muslim fundamentalist group which wanted his employer to 'make' the US government stop attacking the Taliban in Afghanistan. When the paper's editor said it was not within his power to influence government policy, the journalist was murdered.

tion remain contested, and the strong representations by those who see themselves as losers rather than winners are not likely to cease in the near future. Street protests outside the meeting of the World Trade Organization in Seattle in November 2000 have been followed by targeted actions representing a range of different anti-globalization viewpoints in Gothenburg and Genoa. Business stands inside, rather than outside, this new global political arena. At the meeting of the World Economic Forum in January 2002, for instance, the CEOs of 36 major multinationals signed a statement entitled 'Global Corporate Citizenship: the Leadership Challenge for CEOs and Boards' which says:

> For the first time in history most of the world's population live in democratic societies and market-based economies, with the potential for increased political participation and economic prosperity. There are widespread concerns, however, that this potential is not being met: that many people still face high levels of inequality, insecurity and uncertainty as well as new sources of conflict, environmental decline and lack of opportunity. World events since September 11 have reinforced the interconnected nature of these global challenges ... leaders from all countries, sectors and levels of society need to work together to address these challenges by supporting sustainable development and ensuring that the benefits of globalization are shared more widely.[6]

As yet, the exact nature of connections between growing global trade and increasing polarization of wealth in the world is not clear: economists[7] and political scientists[8] offer different explanations. But it is

[6] Joint statement of a task force of World Economic Forum CEOs, developed in partnership with the Prince of Wales International Business Leaders Forum.
[7] Henderson, David (2001) *Misguided Virtue: False Notions of Corporate Social Responsibility*, New Zealand Business Round Table.
[8] Scholte, Jan Aart (2000) *Globalization: a Critical Introduction*, London, New York: Palgrave.

■ ■ ■ ■ ■ ■ ■ ■ ■ ■ ■ ■ ■

**The debate about the upsides and
downsides of globalization rages on,
and few commentators seriously think
'un-globalization' is a realistic possibility**

■ ■ ■ ■ ■ ■ ■ ■ ■ ■ ■ ■ ■

clear that market mechanisms alone are not delivering the benefits of
'development' even-handedly around the world, and the dynamics that
result affect businesses just as they affect citizens, through unpredictable
business environments, unstable political regimes and volatile currencies.

The UN Global Compact

Fourth, we have seen corporate citizenship taken to a new level by the
establishment of the United Nations Global Compact, through which
the UN Secretary-General seeks to align businesses to help strengthen
'capitalism with a human face'. This was a controversial move, strongly
criticized by some NGOs for enabling big businesses to engage in 'blue-
washing', using the moral authority of the United Nations to hide their
unsavoury practices, and implying the privatization and commercializa-
tion of the UN mission. For others it has represented a new pragmatism
on behalf of a creaking UN system, a recognition of where both financial resource and organizational resource lie in the *realpolitik* of the 21st
century. The Global Compact, whether it succeeds in its ambitious mission or not, has raised further the stakes in the corporate citizenship
field, explicitly linking the conduct of business to the realization of the
world's development goals. Again, the connection between the realization of healthy and prosperous *societies* and the production of private
wealth through business is being made, pointing towards wider responsibilities for businesses. This remains a proposition accepted by only a
minority of the business community. In a stout call for businesses to
reject such exhortation, Kapstein urges:

Although some executives might argue that they can do little to shape the business environment, they still have a responsibility to their shareholders and to society to bring the self-declared ethicists to heel when necessary instead of caving in to their demands.[9]

It is also the case that corporate citizenship is becoming an increasingly sophisticated industry. It has become a significant area of business consultancy, with many of the major companies now providing reputation assurance services, social and environmental auditing, and strategic advice, as well as numerous niche consultancies working on communication strategies, branding issues and product development from a corporate citizenship 'angle'. Evidently there is some sort of bandwagon on which to jump, even if the nature of the vehicle is still contested and the standard of the ensuing practice highly variable.

Early in 2002 the UK news media became very interested in the fact that Peter Melchett, the former Director of Greenpeace UK, who two years previously had been prosecuted and then cleared of criminal charges after leading the destruction of a field of genetically modified crops by a Greenpeace direct action squad, had just accepted a consultancy post with a leading international public relations agency, albeit only for six days a year, he later revealed. His new employer was renowned – or notorious, depending on your standpoint – for advising some of the companies which were formerly his opponents. He argued that, if he was seriously committed to bringing about change in company behaviour, this was a sensible way for him to put his considerable experience to work. His critics saw him as selling out on his principles, taking money from the very companies which Greenpeace cite as profiting from unsustainable and environmentally destructive practices. This incident was deemed of sufficient public interest to

---

[9] Kapstein, Ethan B. (2001) 'The corporate ethics crusade,' *Foreign Affairs*, 119, September/October.

■ ■ ■ ■ ■ ■ ■ ■ ■ ■ ■ ■

It has become clear that there is money to be made from socially responsible and environmentally sustainable business, not just through engaging in PR gloss but through business innovation and creativity

■ ■ ■ ■ ■ ■ ■ ■ ■ ■ ■ ■

make the BBC national news in the UK. The vignette nicely illustrates some of the continuing dilemmas of living corporate citizenship, spanning boundaries between pro- and anti-business groups, resting largely on untried practices and untested coalitions, and beset with suspicions about possible profit motives underlying people's actions.

Yet it has become clear that there *is* money to be made from socially responsible and environmentally sustainable business, not just through engaging in PR gloss but through business innovation and creativity. The business visionaries around us have spotted that potential: they range from Hawken, Lovins and Lovins's call for 'natural capitalism'[10] to Fussler's discussion of green innovation,[11] to calls for 'corporate soul'[12] and utilizing 'natural advantage'.[13] At the same time, no-one is seriously saying that a full-blown company commitment to transparency, accountability and stakeholder dialogue is a cost-free exercise. But it may be that we are only just beginning to comprehend the scale of the potential for new business conducted in new ways, moving beyond the relatively simplistic win-win according

[10] Hawken, Paul, Lovins, Amory and Lovins, Hunter (1999) *Natural Capitalism: the next industrial revolution*, London: Earthscan.
[11] Fussler, Claude (1996) *Driving Eco-Innovation*, London: FT Pitman.
[12] Barrett, R. (1998) *Liberating the Corporate Soul*, Boston: Butterworth-Heinemann.
[13] Heeks, A. (2000) *The Natural Advantage: Renewing Yourself*, London: Nicholas Brealey Publishing.

to existing 'bottom lines' to new approaches to the task of wealth creation. This, at least, is the fear of some of the anti-CSR commentators.[14]

So, as we explore the notion of *Living Corporate Citizenship* in the pages that follow, we hope to unpack some of these developments through the emergent practices of companies and their diverse partners. In so doing, we intend to raise paradoxes and dilemmas, as well as highlighting innovative practice and useful lessons. It may be that, as a reader, you would wish for easier signposts as to what you might be doing than we are able to give you. Rather, we are hoping to share with you some of what has been learned and discovered as people in many different parts of the world attempt to take ideas and exhortations about corporate citizenship into day-to-day actions. Some of these actions fall far short of achieving their intentions, some look promising. They add together to create a continuing lively debate and many unanswered questions as to where this is leading.

[14] Henderson, David, *op cit*.

CHAPTER 2

Refining the debate: corporate social responsibility and corporate citizenship

T
he debate about corporate social responsibility is centuries
old, but it developed significantly in the last half of the twentieth century. There are five drivers of this re-emphasis:

- the globalization of markets;

- the establishment of the knowledge economy;

- the ubiquity of global communications technology;

- the coalescence of power, and therefore responsibility, in the
  hands of a relatively small number of international and global
  corporations;

- the need for new social partnerships between corporations,
  states and civil society seeking solutions to local and global
  problems.

The drive to make companies more accountable is hastened when-
ever an example of deception towards investors, governments and
other stakeholders comes to light. The growing dissatisfaction of an
increasingly share-owning society towards secretive, badly managed
companies has also increased calls for greater accountability, stricter
guidelines on corporate governance and company law reform. Coupled to this has been 'the death of deference' and subsequent 'stakeholder empowerment' which have forced companies to invest time
and energy in conversations with a wider range of stakeholders in
order to earn their 'licence to operate'.[1]

....

[1] See the RSA's 'Tomorrow's company report' (1995) London: RSA, and McIntosh,
M. (ed.) 'Good business? Case studies in corporate social responsibility' (1993)
School for Advanced Urban Studies, University of Bristol, and *New Consumer*.

There has been considerable discussion concerning a perceived transition from CSR to corporate citizenship.[2] This latter term involves corporations becoming more informed and enlightened members of society and understanding that they are both public and private entities. Whether they like it or not they are created by society and derive their legitimacy from the societies in which they operate. They need to be able to articulate their role, scope and purpose as well as understand their full social and environmental impacts and responsibilities. Corporate citizenship, as a progression from CSR, is therefore seen as a fuller understanding of the role of business in society.

The social-democratic context

In the social-democratic context the issue of territoriality in any discussion of CSR is profound, for while a CSR framework may be applied to a business of any size, it is most readily applied to large-scale enterprises. The irony of the territorial context is that many businesses operate with a global world view. In other words they are *supraterritorial*: they are able to operate outside territorial regulatory constraints. They can choose where and when to pay tax, and they can opt in and out of other regulatory regimes.

It is possible to provide a broad framework for a definition of the social responsibilities of private organisations operating in market economies. It is also possible to provide a definition of social responsibility in a European, US or Japanese context, but they are not necessarily the same. The relationship between business and society varies in

---

[2] See McIntosh, M., Leipziger, D., Jones, K. and Coleman, G. (1998), *Corporate Citizenship: Successful Strategies for Responsible Companies*, London: FT Management, and McIntosh, Malcolm and Andriof, Jorg (eds) (2001) *Perspectives On Corporate Citizenship*, Sheffield: Greenleaf Publishing.

▪ ▪ ▪ ▪ ▪ ▪ ▪ ▪ ▪ ▪ ▪

It is possible to provide a broad framework for a definition of the social responsibilities of private organisations operating in market economies

▪ ▪ ▪ ▪ ▪ ▪ ▪ ▪ ▪ ▪ ▪

divergent capitalisms,[3] and the development of a European CSR framework, for instance, will be applied globally whether that is the intention of the EU Commission or not. Similarly, the development of local CSR frameworks in Germany, the US and Japan has global implications because of the way business operates across territorial boundaries.

Social responsibilities

Some companies, particularly those with a philanthropic tradition, argue that there is a hierarchy of corporate social responsibilities, with the most fundamental being the economic responsibility to stay in business and reward investors, followed by legal, ethical and philanthropic responsibilities.[4] However, this model has been superseded because of:

▪ a recognition of the mutuality of the four areas (economic, legal, ethical and philanthropic responsibilities);

▪ a recognition of a further hierarchy of regulation, codes, voluntary initiatives and stakeholder engagement which together enable a company to maintain its licence to operate; and

▪ a recognition of the corporation as having rights and responsibilities as a responsible citizen.

[3] See Whitley, Richard (1999), *Divergent Capitalisms: The social structuring and change of business systems*, Oxford: Oxford University Press, and Davidson, Ian (1997) 'Jobs and the Rhineland Model,' London: The Federal Trust.
[4] Carroll, A. B. (2001) 'The moral leader: essential for successful corporate citizenship' in McIntosh *et al.*, *op cit.*, 139–50.

The situation is further developed by the large number of agreements, directives, conventions and declarations which apply to corporate behaviour, that notionally have the force of law but which without local enactment and implementation often have little efficacy, except through voluntary corporate compliance. These are sometimes referred to as 'soft law'.

In order to be seen as a responsible corporate citizen all companies must comply with the law. For transnational corporations this is accompanied by observance of international agreements, which often have the force of law, and compliance with company and industry codes. Running through all responsible behaviour are human values, which often form the core content of many company codes of ethics.

The mutuality of corporate social responsibilities

It is possible therefore to list corporate social responsibilities. Codifying in this manner does not imply a hierarchy, although by necessity most incorporated companies – but not all – will see regulatory compliance as a first step.

1 Regulatory compliance

Regulatory compliance covers such issues as incorporation, accounting and reporting practices, workers' rights, consumer safety, health and safety in the workplace, the provision of services, competition, and environmental protection.

2 International directives, conventions and declarations

There are other rules, sometimes referred to as soft law, which demand corporate attention relating to such issues as human rights, labour standards, the environment and international trade. These have the effect of law and they do not require national legislation to take effect. They include the 1948 Universal Declaration on Human Rights.

3 Corporate citizenship initiatives

There are now numerous corporate citizenship initiatives, but there are eight which merit attention where there are varying levels of engagement by a significant proportion of the world's largest corporations:

- OECD Guidelines for Multinational Enterprises
- ILO Conventions on Workplace Practice
- UN Global Compact
- Global Reporting Initiative (GRI)
- Global Sullivan Principles
- ISO standards, including ISO14001S
- AccountAbility 1000S (AA1000S)
- Social Accountability 8000 (SA8000).

These initiatives all draw on international conventions and declarations which have been developed by international institutions with the endorsement of member states.

4 Codes of practice

There may be obligations relating to a company code or an industrial sector code which specify both ethics and operating practices. These may also relate to a company's published statement of values, mission or vision to which it must show compliance in order to gain stakeholder acceptance.

5 Corporate and managerial values

There is a further expression of social responsibility relating to the values that managers might observe. This area is normally known as business ethics, referred to as the role of the individual in the organization. The issues cover integrity, honesty, justice, equality, objectivity or impartiality, loyalty, trust, respect, prudence, tolerance.

Good business practice, in both senses of the word, means that none of the above is necessarily mutually exclusive. Indeed they are mutually reinforcing and supportive.

Case study

European corporate social responsibility

Europe differs from some of the other models of capitalism. The globality of corporate interests and the fact that Europe is the world's largest trading area make this an inescapable reality. Any European CSR definition will set a standard far beyond European territory because supply chains stretch around the world.

Even within the European social contract model there are significant variations across the continent. The European model is largely negotiated and consensus-based and many large European companies operate in other parts of the world where no such natural consensus exists. The challenge is to derive a framework which serves the interests of divergent social norms and the public good, as well as fitting the many corporate models, and which does not impede responsible market activity.

The 2001 Green Paper on 'Promoting a European Framework for Corporate Social Responsibility'[5] talks of a framework for CSR 'based on European values'. These can be defined loosely, post 1945, as democratic participation and social cohesion based on market economies.

CSR is not a concept that applies to corporations alone – it requires transformation across the whole of society. It may initially be presented as a challenge to business, but it is as much a challenge to government and civil society. Government and civil society have to learn how to facilitate change and how to act as partners with business in helping reach societal expectations and delivering public goods. They should expect to be as accountable and transparent as society now expects their partners in business to be.

[5] Brussels COM (2001) 416 final. Commission of the European Communities.

1 There is the desire to reconcile 'social development with improved competitiveness'. This means that there is a belief:
- that a market economy is compatible with a good society;
- that economic co-operation can coexist with social co-operation;
- that competition is compatible with community.

2 The environmental imperative makes sustainable development a strategic objective in European planning.

Coupled to these fundamental values is the European Convention on Human Rights and the 2000 EU Council in Lisbon Declaration on 'building a knowledge society for all'. Marrying social cohesion to an economic model based on knowledge capital requires a re-evaluation of the relationship between business and society.

With these premises in mind it is possible to arrive at a European definition of CSR:

■ CSR starts with compliance by all organizations on all regulations relating to their operations, including reporting, health and safety, environmental management, workplace practice, paying taxes and human rights.

■ Working within the European social model companies must themselves recognize that their responsibilities extend beyond the financial bottom line. This means corporate support for the institutions of both the democratic state and civil society.

■ In a more open network society all organizations are required to take responsibility for aspects of their operations that were previously seen as beyond their scope. This means taking responsibility for the full social and environmental impact of their operations.

■ It is incumbent on all organizations and institutions, whether in government, commerce or civil society, to be accountable for their decisions and the consequences, whether deliberate or accidental. Therefore transparency, accountability and reporting should be at the heart of an EU CSR framework.

▶

■ Finally, the European Union, through the Lisbon Declaration and the Green Paper on CSR, has made it clear that it envisages an EU CSR framework whose criteria for assessment include business's ability to deliver 'the most competitive and dynamic knowledge-based economy in the world, capable of sustainable economic growth with more and better jobs and greater social cohesion'. It would therefore be expected of corporations that their annual reports relate their own efforts to this common cause and explain how they have helped the EU reach these goals.

CHAPTER 3

The boundaries of
corporate citizenship

In our previous book, *Corporate Citizenship: Successful Strategies For Responsible Companies*, we suggested that there is a linear development in corporations becoming good citizens. In other words we said that a company that wished to be thought of as a responsible corporate citizen could follow a linear, and cumulative, progression to become a 'good' company. Yet perhaps some companies can never become good corporate citizens, however much they satisfy all these conditions.

Here are two examples. First, the company that makes anti-personnel landmines. While it may be legally incorporated and profitable, can it ever gain universal social acceptance? Second, can a tobacco company ever shed itself of the responsibility of choice? Is it always the individual's choice and societal permission that enable it to stay in business? By contrast, it is easier for a company that grows bananas, through its product and its practices, to be both profitable and acceptable.

In developing these questions there are a number of other propositions:

■ Corporate citizenship applies to all organizations, and the implication that it applies purely to the private sector is misleading. We might, therefore, recognize that we live in a society of organizations and make the proposition that we rename this field as organizational citizenship.

■ Corporate citizenship has many cultural variants as a result of divergent capitalisms[1] and much of the current debate and literature fails to recognize this reality.

....

[1] See Whitley, Richard (1999) *Divergent Capitalisms: The social structuring and change of business systems*, Oxford: Oxford University Press, and Hampden-Turner, C. and Trompenaars, F. (1993) *The Seven Cultures of Capitalism*, New York: Doubleday.

- The core values and operating practices of many corporations and other organizations are antithetical to the possibility of becoming good corporate citizens serving the common good. They are as selfish, self-centred and non-altruistic as many individuals.

It is also argued that the 'social' in the discourse around corporate social responsibility and corporate citizenship is often misunderstood. All sorts of activities contribute to a good society based on fundamental rights and the delivery of public goods. It is a mixture of for-profit, not-for-profit and not-just-for-profit organizations that create and consume produced, human, natural and social capital. All organizations need to be examined as to what they do, how they do it and what their social and environmental impact is – as well as paying careful attention to their financial viability.

At the beginning of the 21st century this fashionable nomenclature (corporate citizenship) apparently heralds the acceptance by some companies of wider social and environmental responsibilities.[2] The concept of corporate citizenship is not new and, as always, it is contested territory, so it is necessary to clarify its use. First, the legal status of corporations varies from country to country. In some they are constituted as legal persons and in others they are not. Second, however

---

[2] Environmental responsibility is included within social responsibility in this discussion. By 'environmental' we mean the relationship between people and the natural environment, the use of environmental resources and the issues of equity, social justice and futurity that flow from an understanding of environmental sustainability and sustainable development – all of which are social responsibilities. We will, therefore, simply refer to an organization's social responsibilities in discussing corporate citizenship. In accordance with the Gaia hypothesis (see James Lovelock (1995) 'The greening of science' in Wakeford, T. and Walters, M., *Science for the Earth*, London: Wiley), we take it that the natural environment will continue when we have gone and that the way we manage our relationship with the Earth is based on science, mystery and imagination.

■ ■ ■ ■ ■ ■ ■ ■ ■ ■ ■ ■ ■

All sorts of activities contribute to a good society based on fundamental rights and the delivery of public goods.

■ ■ ■ ■ ■ ■ ■ ■ ■ ■ ■ ■ ■

they are legally constituted they are never human beings as you and I know them, with hearts, minds and souls, although strangely some have immortality in a way that humans do not. As Charles Handy has written, they could better be thought of as great and small houses, with the more immortal and useful companies constituting cathedrals or temples.[3] In other words it is important to remember that our organizations are our servants, not our equals or our betters, and that the starting point for society, and for citizenship, is the individual, not the company. In this sense there is a call for corporate leaders to show humility, or as Sandra Waddock has written, for mindfulness and integrity in business decision making.[4]

For many, the term 'corporate citizenship' conveys too much legitimacy for companies and should not be used. For others this terminology is associated with an Anglo-American discourse that has not been accepted or adopted elsewhere. This can perhaps be resolved by simply noting that it is a currently fashionable term, that it does not give companies legitimacy that they have not otherwise earnt, and that it can be misleading. But, it can be argued, its use does herald the development of a new relationship between *some* companies and society.

It is, however, possible to start a conversation with the *people* who run companies, even if the companies themselves, as currently

[3] Handy, Charles (1998) 'The real challenge to business' in McIntosh, M., *Visions of Ethical Business 1,* London: Financial Times Management.
[4] Waddock, Sandra (2001) 'Integrity and mindfulness: foundations of corporate citizenship' in the *Journal of Corporate Citizenship*, Issue 1, Spring, Sheffield: Greenleaf Publishing.

constituted, are bound to report only on their financial profitability. It is this new relationship that is worth exploring and increasingly companies are reporting on their social and environmental performance.

Before proceeding to examine this new breed of corporation we can agree that all companies, indeed all organizations, have social responsibilities which go beyond simply financial viability, and this is as much a day-to-day management reality as a moral imperative. In other words, companies that do not pay attention to their social capital and their use of environmental resources may find it difficult to remain financially viable. This is true whether the company is legally or 'informally' constituted. Archie Carroll, cited earlier, and others have argued for many years that all companies have a hierarchy of responsibilities – economic, legal, ethical and philanthropic.[5] It is now widely accepted that economic, legal and ethical social responsibilities are symbiotic, and that philanthropy, may not serve a social purpose other than to maximize the corporation's reputation. For instance the company that is viable economically through its good use of financial, social and environmental resources may not be good for society. If that company then distributes some of its wealth through philanthropy it does not necessarily make the company socially responsible. For example, as referred to earlier, there are many who would argue that a company that manufactures anti-personnel landmines or cigarettes, even if it has exemplary workplace practices and a significant philanthropic programme, cannot be deemed a good corporate citizen.

In this age of apparent rising transparency and accountability, there are many companies which wish to prove that their activities do no harm, or that if they do cause harm, that this is the responsibility of

[5] Carroll, A.B. (2001) *'The moral leader: essential for successful corporate citizenship'* in McIntosh, M. and Andriof, J. (eds) *Perspectives On Corporate Citizenship*, Sheffield: Greenleaf Publishing.

■ ■ ■ ■ ■ ■ ■ ■ ■ ■ ■ ■

In this age of apparent rising transparency
and accountability, there are many companies which
wish to prove that their activities do no harm, or that
if they do cause harm, that this is the responsibility of
the purchaser, not the company.

■ ■ ■ ■ ■ ■ ■ ■ ■ ■ ■ ■

the purchaser, not the company. First amongst this group are tobacco companies in Europe and North America, second are fast food companies everywhere and third, car manufacturers (in some parts of the world). The wider and more important point is that all companies are increasingly expected to understand and be able to articulate their purpose and values, and to understand their social and economic impact, as distinct from the minimalism of their financial results. One view is that if their activities are unacceptable, they should expect to be sanctioned and regulated. The other view is that some of these companies are so large, powerful and supraterritorial that they appear beyond the realm of this sort of regulation and societal supervision.

So, while the label of corporate citizen can be applied to all companies, we need to then categorize companies that pay more or less attention to their internal and external social responsibilities *and* understand and accept their evolving role, scope and purpose in modern society.

Initiatives in the corporate citizenship movement

The past few years have seen a rush of voluntary initiatives relating to the social and environmental accountability of large organizations, most particularly large private sector companies. Whilst there have been similar rises in the accountability movement in the past 100 years, most notably in the 1960s and 1970s, it is arguable that the current wave of initiatives is for reasons that are new. The debate about

whether or not globalization is a new phenomenon has some validity
– world trade and business having existed for millennia. But most
commentators would agree that exposure to global market conditions
is now a feature of most, if not all, national economies, and that business organizations and their brands dominate a significant proportion
of the world population's daily lives.

The number of companies calling themselves 'corporate citizens'
has increased. Indeed, this integrated, or holistic, view of themselves
has taken the place of various previous descriptions of companies as
'environmentally friendly' or 'socially responsible'. This term has
been accompanied by the establishment of research organizations
with titles like the University of Warwick's Institute for Governance
and Public Management in England, Deakin University's Corporate
Citizenship Research Unit in Australia, and the Catholic University of
Eichstatt's Centre for Corporate Citizenship Research in Germany.
This is not forgetting longstanding institutions such as Boston College
and the Aspen Institute in the USA, the University of Bath and the
New Academy of Business's innovative post-graduate Masters in
Responsibility and Business Practice in the UK, and other centres of
excellence around the world.

So what is to be made of this new direction in the discourse around
the relationship between business and society? How does the use of the
term 'corporate citizenship' differ from previous terms? Does it matter?

Here is how three major corporations – companies that would like
to be thought of as leading *good* corporate citizens – describe themselves. BP talks about corporate 'commitment and engagement in
areas of real difficulty and public controversy where society has problems'.[6] Rio Tinto argues the business case: 'A key idea behind all these

---

[6] Browne, John (2000) 'Large companies cannot afford to disappoint' in McIntosh, M.,
Visions of Ethical Business 3, London: Financial Times Prentice Hall/
PricewaterhouseCoopers/Warwick Business School.

initiatives is that responsible behaviour makes good business sense.'[7] For the Royal Dutch/Shell Group the issue is that 'a responsible business must operate on the basis of core global values'.[8] These examples are from companies that have been stung by fierce criticism of their activities, or *in*activities. They indicate three trends: a commitment to a range of social responsibilities; an integrated view of the company's role in, and impact on, society; and an understanding that the company has a role in society beyond that of just rewarding financial investors.

While some companies in the 19th century saw themselves as arbiters of social sense and pursuers of the common good, in much of the 20th century companies existed to provide goods and services for consumption and to make a good return for their investors, operating, as economist Milton Friedman said, 'within the rules of the game'. Now some companies acknowledge that there are other things they have to do: to uphold their brand status, to earn their licence to operate and to use their power responsibly.

This vision has become reality for just a few companies, *and it is only a few companies in some sectors domiciled in some countries*. For a large number of companies, under the current rules, there is no desire to be good corporate citizens, or to think about being seen at all as corporate citizens, or to do other than make money. It is not part of their strategy, behaviour or motivation. For yet another sort of business there is no desire to be citizens, to be accountable or particularly visible.

Let us not delude ourselves that there is natural linear progression to nirvana and that with a little push and pull all companies could be good corporate citizens. Many of them never could be, or want to be.

---

[7] Wilson, Robert (2000) 'Big business: neither sinner nor saviour' in McIntosh, M., *ibid*.

[8] Moody-Stuart, Mark (2000) 'Putting principles into practice' in McIntosh, M., *ibid*.

■ ■ ■ ■ ■ ■ ■ ■ ■ ■ ■ ■

Let us not delude ourselves that there is
natural linear progression to nirvana and that
with a little push and pull all companies could be
good corporate citizens

■ ■ ■ ■ ■ ■ ■ ■ ■ ■ ■ ■

However keenly some might wish to see all companies become good corporate citizens, this is impossible in current circumstances.

Business for wealth creation

In distinguishing between types of corporation we must also distinguish between types of activity and the creation of wealth – in its different forms. A distinction can be made between market activity (which leads to the creation of profit and private property), enterprise (which can lead to private profit but can also lead to public profit or non-financial wealth creation) and livelihood activity (the caring and sharing of everyday community and family life). All of these activities consume resources and create the wealth of the community. We might also ask: 'Which activities take away from the wealth of the community?' Being aware of this, some sectors of society are asking some companies to explain what it is they do, why they do what they do and how they do what they do. Any manager in any organization should be able to answer these questions.

If we start with the individual living in the community and then look at the organizations that we sanction, new economics tells us that capital can be divided several ways:[9]

---

[9] World Bank (1990) 'World Development Report', New York: Oxford University Press, and Bury, Jeffrey (2001) 'Corporations and Capitals' (2001) *Journal of Corporate Citizenship*, Issue 1, Spring, Sheffield: Greenleaf Publishing.

- *Produced capital.* This is created through manufacturing and the application of technology and investment – financial, social and natural.

- *Human capital.* While there is disputation over the application of the concept of 'capital' to people, human capital is a recognition of people and their state of education, training and health as vital constituents of safe, healthy, stable communities.

- *Natural capital.* There are essentially two forms of natural capital: non-renewable environmental resources and eco-systems.

- *Social capital.* Social capital, while as contentious a categorization as human capital, is distinct from human capital in that it is wealth that is created by trust, love, relationships and networks; in other words the ability to organize creatively and harmoniously and for the common good. In the context of the corporate citizenship initiatives outlined here it means the ability to work across organizational and sectoral boundaries and to work in partnership for the common good as defined in international agreements on human rights, labour standards and environmental protection.

Our organizations demonstrate our ability to manage resources and ourselves communally and in doing so they express power relations and social purpose. All organizations utilize, for better or for worse, all the above forms of capital. The question is: how do our organizations, particularly those in the private sector, increase levels of all types of capital where they choose to operate?

The four categories of corporate citizens

In addition to the idea of minimalist, discretionary, strategic and trans-formational progression advanced in *Corporate Citizenship: Success-*

ful Strategies for Responsible Companies, it is possible to distinguish between four types of *not* mutually exclusive modes of organizational behaviour, or corporate citizenship:[10]

1 *Avoidance.* The 'other' and the informal economy. Many companies operate in legitimate areas but are themselves unincorporated. Companies in 'the other' economy operate in areas such as illegal drugs, arms sales, child prostitution, slavery and immigration. Both categories usually avoid all regulatory and tax regimes. In economies such as India and Brazil, some 80 per cent of the workforce are employed by *un*incorporated 'companies' as part of the informal economy.

2 *Compliance.* The vast majority of legally incorporated companies, many of them small and medium-sized enterprises. In some economies, such as most of Europe and North America, these employ some 80 per cent of the workforce.

3 *Discretionary.* The company that also finds it necessary to argue that it 'does no harm'.

4 *Pro-active.* Those companies that see themselves as pro-active agents of positive social change delivering both private profit and public goods. These companies are aware that the international community, through the United Nations (UN), has set International Development Targets on poverty, health care, education and gender. Authors such as Zadek[11] have referred to these companies as third-generation corporate citizens.

[10] McIntosh, Malcolm (2002) *A Ladder To The Moon: Corporate citizenship in the twenty-first century*, London: Palgrave.
[11] Zadek, S. (2001) *The Civil Corporation: The New Economy of Corporate Citizenship*, London: Earthscan.

None of these groups is exclusive, and indeed companies that fall into category 4 are normally in 2 and 3, but no company can occupy all four categories. However, it is possible for a company to be in category 1 and increase social capital and therefore contribute to public goods. Similarly, all companies in category 2 would see themselves fulfilling societal aims because they are legally constituted: society allows them to trade and therefore sanctions their activities and sees them as contributing to the common good. Controversially, companies in category 4 increasingly recognize that they cannot avoid doing business with category 1. Just ask most banks what they know about all their account holders.

In the fourth category of pro-active companies there are some who see a distinction between companies such as Volvo, which sees itself as delivering public goods while also making a profit for investors, and companies such as The Body Shop, which sees its purpose as serving the public.

Why is this important?

There are two reasons why this is important. First, in the context of corporate citizenship it is important because the debate about business leadership, about business and development, about the role of business in managing conflict or about business operating in conflict areas can be discussed under three headings:

1 *What is happening?* There is a distinction to be made between market activity, enterprise and livelihood.
2 *What is being created?* The creation of wealth can be categorized under the headings of produced, natural, human and social capital.
3 *Who is doing it?* Here we are talking about organizational form and behaviour – legitimate or illegitimate, incorporated or networked, informal or formalized.

Second, it is important because the evidence is that a small cluster of global companies (category 4) is emerging which is searching and arguing for a specific licence to operate. These companies' sense of legitimacy and their desire to be seen to be earning their licence to operate derive from their domicility, their sector and their experiences over the past few decades. What is most important about this group of companies is that perhaps they can push or pull other companies, of all sizes, with them in the pursuit of global public goods so that international development targets can be met.

Many of this cluster, or club, of both transnational corporations and small and medium-sized enterprises were founder-supporters of the UN Secretary-General's Global Compact.[12] This explains, in this early stage of the Compact's life, the attendance of many of the companies at the UN on July 26 2000. Within this cluster there were a significant number of Northern European companies from the extractive industry sector as well as other companies that are having to re-earn their licence to operate, such as Nike Inc, Royal Dutch/Shell Group and Rio Tinto plc.

In addition, most of the companies that are supporters of the Global Compact are also engaged in other corporate citizenship initiatives. Indeed, their support for the Global Compact is preceded by their work on global social investment, community relations, internalizing externalities, social and environmental reporting and recognizing social capital.

Specifically we can examine how this cluster of companies can help build global governance structures that deliver global public goods.

The debate about the role of business in society, local and global, is both ongoing and sometimes savage. Some people and businesses see any discussion about corporate social responsibility and corporate citizenship as a distraction from the real business of business: to pro-

---

[12] www.unglobalcompact.org

■ ■ ■ ■ ■ ■ ■ ■ ■ ■ ■ ■

**The debate about the role of business in society,
local and global, is both ongoing and sometimes savage**

■ ■ ■ ■ ■ ■ ■ ■ ■ ■ ■ ■

duce goods and services that society wants – and therefore make
money. The dialectic of shareholder (or stockholder) value versus
stakeholder value, which occupies much political and academic space,
over-simplifies the issues involved. Business does not operate in a vacuum and it is not separate from society's values. Its leaders share the
rest of humanity's values even if they take rewarding shareholder
investment as their sole responsibility. Is it just that market activity
requires a different set of values or is it that our largest institutions,
namely corporations, now have their own momentum and their
employees are merely servants of the greater good of the company?
On this basis corporate leaders serve the corporation first, themselves
personally second and the common good third. Many would argue
that at present these are 'the (current) rules of the game'. On occasion,
of course, they change the order of priorities and CEOs reward themselves first.

Whilst much market activity is quite obviously designed to be separate from the regulatory and tax regimes but may nonetheless produce public goods, the initiative shown by some companies locally
and globally gives cause for hope that some managers recognize their
social as well as their fiduciary duties. Increasingly corporate managers know that they can and will be held accountable for their decisions, both internally and externally.

CHAPTER 4

Developing
corporate citizenship competence
and working with NGOs

Introduction

One of the most significant changes that we noted in Chapter 1 is the development of cross-sector social partnerships between business, states and civil society organizations, or non-government organizations. This has exercised the minds of managers particularly in business and civil society. The engagement has been a real learning experience, often fraught with danger and ambiguity. Both sides have had to learn to listen and share in a world view which at first they have found difficult to accept. But from these new social partnerships have come some of the most vibrant initiatives. It has been shown that business, trade unions and NGOs can develop codes, standards and initiatives that find common resonance across all sectors because they accept that problems shared and aired can lead to innovative and creative solutions.

For example, the moves that McDonald's has made in its new social reports have come about through a partnership between the company and many pressure groups, led by Environmental Defense.[1] Similarly, the UN Global Compact has engaged business, trade unions and NGOs, as have other initiatives such as the Global Reporting Initiative, AccountAbility 1000S, the Forest and Marine Stewardship Councils and Social Accountability 8000, which are discussed later.

This chapter is an account of the development of the concept of corporate citizenship in relation to the civil society and NGOs. It is a much more in-depth analysis of the issues raised in the previous chapters.

....

[1] www.mcdonalds.com/corporate/social/

Developing corporate citizenship

As researchers and practitioners strive for a shared understanding of corporate citizenship[2] and map out the implications of engagement for business, civil society and governments worldwide, one of the central questions that arises is: 'What should the relationship be between business and society?' As with any field where the concepts and territory remain open to interpretation, definitions and practical frameworks are evolving in tandem. It is perhaps not surprising, then, that companies seeking to engage both intellectually and at an operational level with the citizenship agenda should encounter difficulties. At a time when there are more questions than answers, it is inevitable that progress towards active citizenship, and therefore *good* corporate citizenship, may be hampered by a lack of accord. However, an increasing willingness from business to engage in dialogue and partnerships with a range of civil society groups means that a number of key initiatives have emerged through joint thinking that are leading the way in directly addressing corporate citizenship issues.

Central to the current debate is the evolution of civil society and NGOs and the relation of this sector to the market and the state. For some corporations this has been difficult territory as their relations with some NGOs have been antagonistic, if not extremely hostile. Other corporations see the emergence of civil society organizations in general and INGOs (international NGOs) in the same light as their own international and global development. This corporate group sees sense and strength in engaging with groups which may share *some* values, but which also may have a different message and modus operandi. This chapter links the development of civil society and NGOs to the growing corporate citizenship debate in two parts.

[2] For a recent synopsis of contemporary writing in this area, see Andriof, J. and McIntosh, M. (eds) (2001) *Perspectives on Corporate Citizenship*, Sheffield: Greenleaf Publishing.

This first part of the discussion charts a path through some of the key issues being explored by businesses seeking to engage with the citizenship agenda and with NGOs. The discussion synthesizes current thinking on corporate citizenship. It shows that while attempts to define and conceptualize corporate citizenship vary, they draw on a number of common themes that form the foundations of the debate. Important here is an understanding that the issues involved are challenging and for most organizations will demand learning new skills, unlearning old habits and being prepared to initiate and experience change. For many organizations, engaging in real conversation with NGOs and civil society requires fundamental conceptual and organizational change, in many cases redefining their role, scope and purpose. In this sense, understanding what it might mean to be a corporate citizen redefines not only the relationship between the different sectors of society but also the nature of corporations themselves.

Fundamental to this change is the development of an institutional environment that will support and nurture new initiatives. While an organization can influence and is able to shape elements of its external environment, the key to its survival is the ability to transform the immediate organizational context of daily operations. This is perhaps the most challenging element for any company engaging with citizenship initiatives as it can mean a fundamental reappraisal of the way business is conducted. In particular, it requires that attention be given to the more intangible aspects of company culture, as well as to the core values that shape the way individuals in the business conduct their activities.

Putting into practice or operationalizing citizenship initiatives can demand the development of new organizational competencies. For example, much of the work on citizenship draws its strength and legitimacy from a social partnership approach where businesses work alongside the organizations of the state and civil society groups. For many businesses, some aspects of this form of joint working present

■ ■ ■ ■ ■ ■ ■ ■ ■ ■ ■ ■

Putting into practice or operationalizing
citizenship initiatives can demand the development
of new organizational competencies

■ ■ ■ ■ ■ ■ ■ ■ ■ ■ ■ ■

new territory, for which there are few organizational precedents and little internal management competence. Successful delivery of citizenship goals may therefore necessitate training and skills development beyond those acquired in the course of business activity to date.

With citizenship initiatives growing apace it is not always clear which initiatives are delivering substantive change. Incorporating performance measurement internally to steer change, and reporting performance externally to ensure transparency, also focuses attention on which initiatives are successful in making a difference. The ongoing development of appropriate standards and codes means that companies are subject to a bewildering array of initiatives focused on the measurement of performance. The discussion outlines some basic issues for consideration and a key initiative is highlighted which uses a multiple stakeholder approach (AA1000S) and aims to allow for benchmarking and reporting as well as internal performance improvement.

Corporate citizenship is evolving. While the debate is characterized by change it is also grounded in some sense of shared values and beliefs by those who promote it as a new form of corporate behaviour. It is suggested that institutionalizing and operationalizing corporate citizenship initiatives depends on the development and leverage of appropriate types of organizational capital. This in turn relies on identified organizational characteristics which include collaborative working, learning through partnership and the ability to be receptive to new ideas and change. Performance indicators are an important part of measuring progress and there are some basic principles to assist companies working towards citizenship ideals.

■ ■ ■ ■ ■ ■ ■ ■ ■ ■ ■ ■

As the potential roles of NGOs evolve, so too does the scope of their activities

■ ■ ■ ■ ■ ■ ■ ■ ■ ■ ■ ■

The second part of the chapter focuses on the role and scope of NGOs. To begin, the discussion supplies simple overarching definitions of civil society and NGOs. In doing so, this book acknowledges the range and scope of organizations embraced by this interpretation. It is this inherent, underlying complexity that is explored further in the subsequent discussion. The analysis continues by outlining a series of contextual factors that explain why conversations about business and society are increasingly concerned with NGOs. Particular consideration is given to the rise of civil society, the 'death of deference' and the multifaceted agenda that is globalization. The discussion provides a basic outline of NGOs which indicates their position in relation to other sectors of society. In addition, typologies that have organized and 'mapped' NGOs on the basis of how they choose to interact with business are presented.[3]

The role of NGOs is explored further as the discussion considers a range of possible stances that NGOs can adopt in relation to business. These stances draw on the reported case study experiences of both parties. The evidence suggests that while conflict is still commonplace, there is increasingly room for manoeuvre that is building on an imperative for participatory outcomes. As the potential roles of NGOs evolve, so too does the scope of their activities. Significant is the ability of organizations to harness new technologies for communication and to achieve progressive change through a collective voice. The discussion emphasizes the key role that NGOs are playing in redefining the institutional landscape and the market environment.

[3] Elkington, J. (1997) *Cannibals with Forks: The triple bottom line of 21st century business*, Oxford: Capstone Publishing Ltd.

Perspectives on corporate citizenship

As the power and influence of business has increased and in some cases outstripped that of some nation states, increasingly difficult questions have been posed that ask: 'What, then, is the role and responsibility of business?' It is for this reason, amongst others, that corporate citizenship has been described as one of the 'big issues' of the 21st century.[4] However, what has crystallized from the exploration of business activities in a new global context is an understanding that businesses do have, or can have, a wider 'citizenship' role to play in society.

In their discussion, Andriof and McIntosh suggest that citizenship is not only about legally defined rights and duties, including fiduciary responsibility, but also, crucially, has a political element that concerns active commitment.[5] With commitment come responsibilities, and that commitment stems in turn from a more thorough understanding of rights and responsibilities. These extend beyond the boundaries of the firm to include society and the natural world we share. In a global economy, these responsibilities have global implications and embrace economic, social and environmental dimensions. Engagement with these three elements means that citizenship has become strongly associated with the concept of environmental sustainability.[6] In addition, citizenship has overlapped and in many texts superseded the longer standing discussions that have been captured under the heading 'corporate social responsibility'.[7]

[4] Habish, A. (2001) 'Foreword' in Andriof J. and McIntosh, M., *op cit.*

[5] Andriof J. and McIntosh, M. (2001), *op cit.*

[6] For one of the original discussions on sustainability issues and their implications for business, see Stead W. and Stead J.G. (1996) *Management for a Small Planet: Strategic decision-making and the environment*, London: Sage.

[7] For a critique of the relationship and contrasts between the two concepts, see Wood, D. and Logsdon, J. (2001) 'Theorising business citizenship' in Andriof, J. and McIntosh, M., *op cit.*

This broader conception and interpretation of corporate social responsibility brought by the citizenship debate has meant that corporations have been encouraged, and some would say forced, to extend their horizon of interest beyond the traditional areas of markets and the workplace, to include the community (both proximal and distant) and the natural environment. Significantly, some commentators have also argued strongly that this redefining of the relationship between business and society requires a new, more systemic and holistic approach to the processes of business. This includes new visions and values of mindfulness, integrity, an 'ethic of care', co-operation and understanding.[8] If we reflect on the depth and breadth of this new agenda it is not surprising that citizenship has been variously interpreted. A selected number of author, company and business association perspectives are illustrated in Table 4.1. While definitions can be an important part of scoping the debate, it is arguably more relevant to have a shared appreciation of founding principles and concepts which guide conversations. It is on this basis, for instance, that the UN's Global Compact was launched both as a platform for commitment to universal principles in the areas of human rights, labour standards and the environment and to facilitate progress and change around citizenship issues.[9]

All these selected quotes, from business and commentators alike, share common aspects:

▪ business is of society;

▪ business is in the business of developing society;

▪ business is in partnership with other elements of society;

▪ social responsibility and citizenship, far from being a burden just for the private sector, concerns active citizenship by all actors in society.

[8] Waddock, S. (2002) *Leading Corporate Citizens: Visions, Values, Value Added*, New York: McGraw-Hill.

[9] www.unglobalcompact.org/

TABLE 4.1 ■ Perspectives on corporate citizenship

Author/organization definitions	Corporate interpretations
Corporate citizenship is a continuum that stretches from 'minimal' at one extreme (consisting of compliance with laws governing the operation of the business but nothing else) to a complex relationship of interlocking rights and responsibilities at the other end[10]	Corporate citizenship is about commitment and engagement in areas of real difficulty and public controversy where society has problems and where solutions are not readily apparent – the global natural environment, for instance, or human rights or the use of child labour or the legal and tax framework within which international companies have to operate in many transition societies[11]
Good corporate citizenship . . . can be defined as understanding and managing a company's wider influences on society for the benefit of the company and society as a whole[12]	In Shell, we believe that a responsible business must operate on the basis of core global values. It should listen to society's messages, justify its legitimacy in the eyes of societies and opinion leaders, and regulate itself effectively and openly[13]
Global citizenship is about making sure you have the right relationships in the community and environment in which you operate, while working in partnership with key players for mutual tangible benefit[14]	A key idea behind these initiatives [corporate social responsibility and corporate citizenship] . . . is that responsible behaviour makes good business sense . . . At Rio Tinto we have found that maintaining the trust of local communities is essential for the long-run success of our operations. A sound reputation on ethical issues also helps us to recruit and retain high-calibre employees[15]

[10] McIntosh, M. *et al.* (1998) *op cit.*

[11] Quote from BP in Browne, John, *op cit.*

[12] Marsden, C. and Andriof, J. (1998) 'Towards an understanding of corporate citizenship and how to influence it,' *Citizenship Studies*, 2 (2), 329–52.

[13] Moody-Stuart, M. (2000) 'Putting principles into practice', in McIntosh, M. (ed) *Visions of Ethical Business 3*, Financial Times Prentice Hall/PricewaterhouseCoopers/ Warwick Business School.

[14] Foreign and Commonwealth Office (2001) 'Global Citizenship: Business and Society in a Changing World,' March 2001:2, London.

[15] Quote from Rio Tinto plc in Wilson, Robert, *op cit.*

Author/organization definitions	Corporate interpretations
Good corporate citizens live up to clear, constructive visions and core values. They treat well the entire range of stakeholders who risk capital in, have an interest in, or are linked to the firm through primary and secondary impacts, through developing mutually beneficial operating practices and by working to maximize the sustainability of the natural environment[16]	Cable & Wireless is a global corporate citizen with long traditions . . . Our values give us a framework for our behaviour, both individually and corporately. Through our global community involvement programme, we aim to strengthen the social and economic development of the communities in which we operate[17]
Understanding business as a public culture, not just 'concerned' with values and human rights but more thoughtfully aware of how it shapes the cultural politics (and economics) of those values, is at the heart of our definition of corporate citizenship[18]	Tomorrow's market leaders know that globalization means more than simply doing business as usual on a global scale. To compete successfully, companies must navigate a complex and constantly changing set of economic, environmental and social challenges and stakeholder demands. Long considered business 'externalities', such factors are now integral to corporate operations and directly contribute to brand reputation and financial performance (Business for Social Responsibility, 2002)[19]
Civic responsibility, being a partnership between government, civil society and the private market, necessarily depends on the active collaboration of political leaders, citizens and business people[20]	Corporate social responsibility is the commitment of business to contribute to sustainable economic development working with employees, their families, the local community and society at large to improve their quality of life[21]

[16] Waddock, S., *op cit.*

[17] www.cw.com/community

[18] Birch, D. and Glazebrook, M. (2000) 'Doing business – doing culture: corporate citizenship and community' in Rees, Stuart *et al. Human Rights, Corporate Responsibility*, Sydney: Pluto.

[19] www.brs.org

[20] Barber, B.R. (2001) 'Civil society and strong democracy' in Giddens, A. (ed) *The Global Third Way Debate*, Cambridge: Polity Press.

[21] World Business Council for Sustainable Development (WBCSD) (2002) 'Corporate social responsibility: WBCSD's journey' – www.wbcdsd.org/

Let us remind ourselves of the defining principles of corporate citizenship from Chapter 2:

1 Corporate citizenship involves companies understanding that they are both public and private entities. They are creatures of society and derive their legitimacy from the societies in which they operate. They need to be able to articulate and support their understanding of their role, scope and purpose.

2 Corporate citizenship involves companies understanding their social and environmental impacts and responsibilities alongside their financial responsibilities. These responsibilities include both aspects of regulation, such as financial reporting and health, safety and labour laws, and society's wider licence to operate.

Institutionalizing corporate citizenship

Faced with such a wide-ranging and intrinsically transformational agenda, it is not surprising that firms are asking: 'How should we go about institutionalizing these new values and ideas?' To appreciate the possible routes for change it is useful to reflect on what we understand the processes of institutionalization to be about, and the different levels at which these processes can occur.

Institutional perspectives argue that firms operate within a social framework of norms and values that govern what constitutes appropriate or acceptable behaviour. In this context, choices are constrained not only by economic criteria but also by socially constructed limits, such as norms, habits and customs.[22] Those activities that become accepted in this social context and are not directly reliant on [economic] rewards become 'taken for granted' and endure as the orthodox way of operating or behaving. As long as an activity remains

22 Powell, W.W. and Dimaggio, P.J. (1991) *The New Institutionalism in Organisational Analysis*, Chicago: University of Chicago Press.

■ ■ ■ ■ ■ ■ ■ ■ ■ ■ ■ ■ ■

Institutional perspectives argue that firms operate within a social framework of norms and values that govern what constitutes appropriate or acceptable behaviour

■ ■ ■ ■ ■ ■ ■ ■ ■ ■ ■ ■

legitimate, or it is insulated from change, it will persist or be institutionalized.

The difficulty arises when existing activities and ways of operating no longer conform to, or are appropriate for, society's expectations. Routines and habits are hard to break, even when they no longer serve the company well. To understand the problems of change, it helps to view institutional activity at three levels: the individual, the firm and the inter-firm.

■ At an individual level, we are concerned with managers' norms, habits and conformity to tradition.

■ At the firm level, institutional activity is expressed in corporate culture, shared beliefs, political processes and organizational structures.

■ At the inter-firm level, structure and activity within a particular sector will reflect the pressures of government, society, civil society alliances and industry groups.[23]

The corporate citizenship agenda with its emphasis on human rights, fair workplace practices and consideration of the natural environment is progressively redefining the context within which companies operate. In other words, the socially constructed norms that have influenced the way companies choose to conduct their activities are changing. Increasingly there is a need for company activity to be transparent and accountable to an expanded constituent group. New circumstances require new

[23] Oliver, C. (1997) 'Sustainable competitive advantage: combining institutional and resource-based views,' *Strategic Management Journal*, 18 (9), 697–713.

ways of working, and to embed these ideas and values in a firm means addressing changes at the three levels suggested. Tables 4.2, 4.3 and 4.4 suggest different mechanisms that firms may wish to employ.

TABLE 4.2 ■ Institutionalizing corporate citizenship – individual level

■ Provide training on citizenship issues, tailored to employees' needs in the work and management environment.

■ Use cascade and action learning techniques that allow for shared experience and reflection on learning. Examples include cascade training for environmental management at the former Rover Group and employee involvement in training needs analysis at BASF.[24]

■ Develop recruitment procedures to build and enhance in-house knowledge and competence of citizenship concerns.

■ Expand performance targets, rewards and incentives beyond traditional [economic] markers of achievement.[25]

TABLE 4.3 ■ Institutionalizing corporate citizenship – firm level

■ Encourage empowerment of the individual through participatory decision making.

■ Generate a clear vision for the company with well-articulated underlying values. Invite comments and communicate responses to encourage commitment and loyalty. See, for example, Shell's 1998 report 'Profit and principles – does there have to be a choice?'[26]

■ Share information across organizational levels to create trust and remove hierarchical barriers.

■ Use teams, and work across functions, to share ideas and stimulate creativity. For example, Herman Miller's (the German furniture manufacturer) use of ephemeral teams to address specific environmental issues.[27]

[24] North, K. and Daig, S. (1996) 'Environmental training in British and German companies' in Wehrmeyer, W. (ed) *Greening People: Human Resources and Environmental Management*, Sheffield: Greenleaf Publishing.

[25] Milliman, J. and Clair, J. (1996) 'Best environmental HRM practices in the US' in Wehrmeyer, W., *ibid*.

[26] www.shell.com

[27] Azzarello, J. (1993) 'Long-time environmental leadership pays off in many ways at Herman Miller,' *Total Quality Environmental Management*, Winter, 187–91.

TABLE 4.4 ■ Institutionalizing corporate citizenship – inter-firm level

■ Engage with industry associations to debate the issues and develop appropriate codes and standards.

■ Participate in business forums that raise awareness, educate and provide training in the area of corporate citizenship. Established examples include the Prince of Wales International Business Leaders Forum (IBLF) in the UK and the World Business Council for Sustainable Development (WBCSD).[28]

■ Contribute to cross-sector citizenship initiatives that involve civil society groups and government. For example, the Ethical Trading Initiative (ETI) in the UK (see page 57).[29]

■ Work along the supply chain with contractors and suppliers to develop and change practices. See, for example, Levi Strauss and Co.'s Global Sourcing Guidelines.[30]

In essence what the institutionalization of corporate citizenship ideals requires is an organizational climate that promotes and encourages *learning*. This includes recognizing and addressing factors that can *inhibit* learning, such as management loyalty to outdated traditions and vested interests in the status quo. This is a complex and challenging agenda, but for citizenship initiatives to be successfully supported and managed in an organization requires the development of this *institutional capital*. Without appropriate institutional capital, citizenship initiatives fail or are delivered in a half-hearted manner. In many organizations, even those that would claim to be proactive on social issues, corporate citizenship remains a life-boat activity, essentially external to their main operations.

Operationalizing corporate citizenship

It has been suggested that engaging with the corporate citizenship agenda requires the development of a contextual environment, where

[28] www.pwblf.org/; www.wbcsd.ch
[29] www.ethicaltrade.org/
[30] Levi Strauss and Co. (1996) Global Sourcing and Operating Guidelines.

the organizational culture and structure is supportive of learning and change. However, this condition alone is not sufficient to ensure that citizenship initiatives are delivered. Realizing new visions and values, through various schemes and initiatives, can require new and/or adapted organizational competencies. Specifically, the cross-boundary nature of citizenship suggests the need for organizational capability in a range of areas that includes:

- good governance
- political and social awareness
- responsible supply chain management
- stakeholder management
- human rights
- business ethics
- pollution prevention
- product stewardship and clean technology.[31]

How, then, do organizations develop these and other appropriate capabilities? Crucial here is an understanding that key capabilities are realized through the cumulative growth of skills and resources. For example, as indicated in the introduction, the ability to work in partnership with a range of organizations is a key resource for organizations looking to make positive moves forward in this field. It is the development of these partnership skills that will, over time, be realized as a 'stakeholder management' competency. The relationship between key resources and the development of citizenship competencies is illustrated in Figure 4.1.

The figure suggests that much of the learning necessary for the development of citizenship capabilities occurs at the level of the firm

---

[31] Thomas, A.R. (2001) 'How does environmental capability develop in a firm?: A case analysis combining resource-based and institutional perspectives,' University of Bath: unpublished PhD thesis.

FIGURE 4.1 ■ Citizenship capabilities – a summary framework

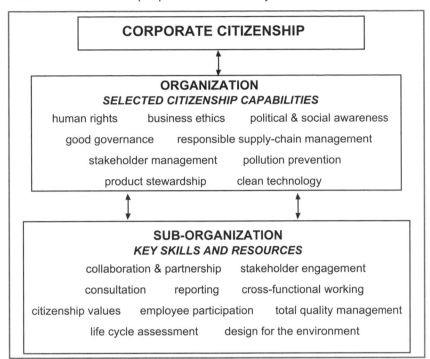

(This is a simplified representation that excludes a range of 'moderating factors' that may influence the development of skills and resources.)[32]

and the individual. Therefore, while capabilities may be acquired, for example, through mergers and acquisitions, the most enduring foundations are built by development from within. In order to do this, firms need to engage with initiatives that promote learning and focus on identified skills development.

The growing prominence of citizenship concerns means that the range of available initiatives focusing at operational and managerial levels has expanded considerably in recent years. In the following boxes a number of initiatives are considered. Some are established and others are emerging as the corporate citizenship agenda matures. In each instance,

---

[32] For a discussion of the influence of moderating factors on environmental capability development, see Thomas, A.R., *ibid*.

they are highlighted as useful examples because they address a range of issues that corporations need to consider when working towards the operationalization of citizenship issues. These issues include:

- training needs and organizational change, both structural and cultural;
- compatibility with existing organization systems and other [citizenship] initiatives;
- performance improvement;
- standards, certification and reporting.

The following boxes are three examples of voluntary corporate citizenship initiatives on environment management, social auditing and ethical trade.

ISO 14001

ISO 14001 is one of a range of voluntary industry standards produced by the International Organisation for Standardisation, launched in 1996. The 14000 series, to which ISO 14001 belongs, provides a framework for the private sector and others looking to manage their *environmental issues*. The standard focuses on organizational processes, not necessarily their products or environmental impacts. Specifically, the standard describes how a firm might manage and control its organizational system so that it measures, controls and continually improves the environmental aspects of its operations.

AA1000S[33]

AA1000S was launched in 1999 by the Institute of Social and Ethical Accountability (AccountAbility). The Institute is a not-for-profit professional membership organization, built through a coalition of businesses, non-government organizations, business schools and service providers. The focus of AA1000S

---

[33] www.AccountAbility.org.uk

and its forthcoming revision is on the social dimensions of an organization's accountability. The standard comprises both the *principles* of a quality standard and a set of *process* standards that cover five stages:

■ planning
■ accounting
■ auditing and reporting
■ embedding
■ stakeholder engagement.

The Ethical Trading Initiative (ETI)[34]

In common with each initiative discussed above, the UK's ETI focuses on a particular area of corporate citizenship – managing an organization's *supply chain* in a socially and ethically responsible manner. The ETI was launched in 1998 with the aim of bringing together different sectors of society and harnessing their collective strengths to bring improvements to the lives of poor working people around the world. In order to do this, the ETI encourages the endorsement and adoption of a series of base codes, drawn from International Labour Organisation conventions. Specifically, the ETI seeks to encourage a *shared approach* to the sourcing of goods and services that leads to a raised standard of living for workers around the globe. Unlike the initiatives considered above, the ETI does not involve the adoption of a management system. However, engagement with the ETI does require a series of *management steps* that includes:

■ the establishment of commitment and a clear policy;
■ training, communication and the allocation of responsibility;
■ monitoring, auditing and planning for improvement; and
■ engagement with a range of identified stakeholders.

[34] www.ethicaltrade.org

Companies that commit to working with the ETI co-operate with at least one pilot scheme that may target certain products or suppliers or focus on a particular country (for example, clothing manufacture in China or banana production in Costa Rica). This pilot work provides the opportunity to develop improved practice and to test methods for monitoring and verification. This work is reviewed, with progress reported on an annual basis.

This commitment to public reporting communicates a transparency and accountability in the way supply operations are conducted. For companies operating a global supply chain, involvement with the ETI provides an opportunity to develop approaches that take into account the views and perspectives of key stakeholders. This inclusivity has become increasingly important in an era when gaining and maintaining public trust and confidence is dependent on establishing a track record of openness.[35] For companies looking to build key skills around ethical supply, initiatives such as the ETI provide experience, methods and tools within a supportive framework. It is this type of engagement that will facilitate a more effective operationalization of ethical sourcing in the future.

In this section, it is suggested that the operationalization of corporate citizenship depends on developing a range of identified skills and resources that forms the foundation of citizenship competencies. In order to do this, companies may need to progressively engage with the growing range of citizenship initiatives. The discussion has highlighted several prominent initiatives on the basis that they include guidance on the internal management of change, involve working with partners, and in some cases encourage organizational learning as an intrinsic part of the development process. There are, however, no simple solutions and an important issue for companies stepping into the citizenship arena is the need to investigate and determine which initiatives will be most suitable for their organization in the medium and longer term.

[35] See Chapter 4 in Zadek, S., *op cit.*

Developing performance indicators

Measuring and monitoring performance, and developing indicators of performance, is not a new activity for business. Performance management has long been a key part of company operations and has typically been tied to financial measures of cost, revenues and profit. The rationale for these activities has therefore been linked to core familiar, business principles. The issues embraced by corporate citizenship are, however, less easily framed and do not necessarily link well or directly to financial metrics. As such, the reasons 'why' companies should be looking towards developing indicators in the area of corporate citizenship are broader than those associated with economic criteria. Factors include:

▪ a recognition that company systems may benefit from the re-evaluation brought by engaging with corporate citizenship issues. New targets and measures can stimulate the search for better ways of managing and working, both structurally and culturally;

▪ informing and engaging all stakeholders, particularly those who are either involved or interested in the activities and outputs of the company;

▪ meeting and where possible raising the ceiling of standards in the areas of citizenship, be they voluntary or regulatory;

▪ communicating on a wider scale the impacts and contributions of the company to sustainability on local and global scales.

The requirement to develop performance indicators has occupied those focused on the environmental elements of citizenship for a significant period.[36] Indeed, frameworks for measuring environmental performance are amongst the most established and have benefited from the

---

[36] See, for example, Young, W. (1996) 'Measuring environmental performance' in Welford, R. (ed) *Corporate Environmental Management: Systems and Strategies*, London: Earthscan.

standardization of environmental management practice around ISO 14001 (see page 56).[37] The pervasive sense that these non-financial aims and outcomes will 'count' only when they are effectively measured has led to environmental performance being evaluated through a combination of quantitative and qualitative measures. However, the need to legitimize these measures continues to see the 'twinning' of environmental and social practice with financial metrics and benefits to 'core' business activity.[38] A key example is the Dow Jones Sustainability Index (DJSI), which has attempted to show that companies screened by their social and environmental performance perform as well as the equivalent unscreened portfolio indexes.[39]

While this need to prove the link between engaging in environmental and socially responsible practice and improved financial performance is unlikely to diminish, the key debate in the development of indicators has more progressively shifted to ask questions about the deeper 'value' implications of this form of communication. Therefore, in this discussion, the relevance of indicators arguably lies less in their financial worth and more in whether the information they communicate is understood and of use to those receiving it.

From this perspective the development of indicators is not only about the intrinsic ability of the company to collect and produce data but more importantly it is about dialogue with interested stakeholders. As such, it is suggested that indicators will emerge through a *process* rather than being based on a set of norms. Basic principles and issues that a company might want to consider when developing indicators, include:

[37] Early discussions on this subject include James, P. (1994) 'Business environmental performance measurement,' *Business Strategy and the Environment*, 3 (2) 59–67. Wolfe, A. and Howes, H.A. (1993) 'Measuring environmental performance; theory and practice at Ontario Hydro,' *Total Quality Environmental Management*, Summer, 355–366.

[38] See Chapter 14, in Zadek, S., *op cit.*

[39] Available via www.dowjones.com

■ ■ ■ ■ ■ ■ ■ ■ ■ ■ ■ ■

From this perspective the development of
indicators is not only about the intrinsic ability of the company
to collect and produce data but more importantly
it is about dialogue with interested stakeholders

■ ■ ■ ■ ■ ■ ■ ■ ■ ■ ■ ■

■ *Internally:*
- identifying key areas of company activity and output and determining meaningful measures;
- ensuring that the measures are appropriate and understandable for those acting on them;
- involving employees with indicator development, to encourage commitment;
- ensuring that indicators are consistent with policy objectives.

■ *Externally:*
- inviting the involvement of key stakeholders with indicator development from the outset;
- using stakeholder participatory techniques to grow transparency and accountability;
- listening to feedback and criticisms;
- being prepared to 'trial' and review indicators that do not 'work'.

Developing indicators therefore involves working on the basis of clearly articulated policy and value objectives (see Table 4.3) in partnership with stakeholder organizations. Crucially though, this process cannot occur in a vacuum and companies need to be cognizant of the growing range of standards being promulgated in industry sectors both nationally and internationally. One initiative that is working to unite the vast range of approaches by developing a standardized approach to measurement and reporting is the Global Reporting Initiative (summarized below).

The Global Reporting Initiative (GRI)[40]

The Global Reporting Initiative was conceived in 1997 by the Boston-based Coalition for Environmentally Responsible Economies (CERES) in collaboration with the Tellus Institute. Since then the GRI has evolved into a set of reporting criteria on all aspects of a company's performance. The initial draft standard was 'field tested' in 1999 by over 20 companies and released in June 2000. The next revision was published in 2002.

These are some basic issues for consideration in the development of performance indicators for citizenship. While companies may wish to draw on existing experiences of performance measurement, there needs to be a recognition that indicators for citizenship break the cast of traditional, financially oriented measures. Developing indicators therefore involves new approaches, working with stakeholders internally and externally. As such, indicator development is evolutionary and companies embarking on this process, or seeking to consolidate their work in this area, can benefit from the frameworks being constructed by multi-stakeholder groups.

Non-governmental organizations

It is not clear whether the common use of the term NGO is complemented by a shared understanding. Rather, it appears that conversations about or relating to NGOs are often formed on the basis of individual constructions that are associated with high-profile or distinctive organizations.[41] As such, any debate that involves NGOs may be tempered by divergent interpretations.

---

[40] www.globalreporting.org/

[41] Lunt, A. (2001) 'Rethinking corporate social responsibility: an exploration of ethics, morality and social legitimacy in the mining industry,' University of Bath: unpublished PhD Thesis.

NGOs themselves, and their associated literature, have a long and rich history rooted in development studies and social history.[42] In recent years this has been complemented by a growing interest in the activities of both new and existing NGOs, which has been expressed in a range of disciplines including sociology, economics, law, management and the environmental sciences.[43] This chapter seeks to bring some clarity to our understanding of NGOs by selecting, where appropriate, contributions from those aspects of the field which best explain the changes we are witnessing in this area. In particular, the focus here is on the increasing level of interaction between NGOs and businesses.[44]

Definitions of NGOs

Free civil societies embrace NGOs as representing organic diversity, innovation and creativity, just as they see trade or labour organizations as important representative bodies for collective workers. It is difficult to generalize about the huge diversity of organizations,[44] but it is useful to consider just what this diversity may include. This allows subsequent conversations about NGOs to take account of this diversity

[42] The literature that considers NGOs in the context of relief, aid and development is extensive and is not considered further in this discussion. See, for example, Edwards, M. and Hulme, D. (1995) *Non-Governmental Organisations*, London: Earthscan.

[43] DeSimmone, L.D. and Popoff, F. (1997) *Eco-Efficiency: The Business Link to Sustainable Development*, Massachusetts: The MIT Press. Welford, R. (1997) *Hijacking Environmentalism: Corporate Responses to Sustainable Development*, London: Earthscan.

[44] Bendell, J., *op cit.*

[45] It has been argued that while most constituents use the term NGO in a way that is compatible with UN practice, exclusions (for example, criminals, guerrillas, NGOs that operate in more than one country) mean that the only comprehensive term is 'transnational actor' (Willets, P. (1998) 'Political globalisation and the impact of NGOs upon transnational companies' in Mitchell, J. (ed) *Companies in a World Of Conflict*, London: Royal Institute for International Affairs and Earthscan).

rather than treating NGOs as a homogenous group, which is how they are frequently referred to in the media and elsewhere.

NGOs may be local groups, such as resident associations or church choirs, comprised of a handful of people who work together through mutual interest and towards common goals, on a small scale. Other groups, for example Amnesty International, may have a regional, national or, in this case, international presence, working with thousands of people and networks around the globe. NGOs may be driven by or inspired by differing values, religious beliefs or political persuasions. So, for example, the US-based Human Rights Watch and the Catholic Institute for International Relations in London both have a remit that relates to protecting and promoting human rights. The latter, however, signals through its title, its particular religious affiliation and spiritual leaning.[46] An NGO can also have values and missions which are antithetical to the participatory democratic state; they may have political aspirations or violence as their modus operandi. The media tends to see civil society activism as represented by NGOs such as Amnesty International, Greenpeace International, the Institute for Social & Ethical AccountAbility or Save The Children. However, there are other civil society organizations, or NGOs, which we might not be so happy to legitimize, such as the National Rifle Association, the Klu Klux Klan, Al Qaeda or the Animal Liberation Front. Of course, between these two extremes are myriad church groups, local children's play groups, golf clubs and horticulture societies. Attention has tended to focus on NGOs seeking publicity and not the milieu of silent, organic civil society activities and organizations that are part of the social fabric of all human life on the planet.

While ideologies vary, so too may the NGOs' focus or outlook. Some organizations choose to centre their attention on environmental issues, others on development or poverty alleviation. Names such as the World

---

[46] Human Rights Watch, www.hrw.org; Catholic Institute for International Relations, Unit 3, Canonbury Yard, 190a New North Road, London, N1 7BJ.

■ ■ ■ ■ ■ ■ ■ ■ ■ ■ ■ ■ ■

While ideologies vary, so too may the NGOs' focus or outlook.

■ ■ ■ ■ ■ ■ ■ ■ ■ ■ ■ ■ ■

Wide Fund for Nature, Oxfam, Action Aid and the Whale and Dolphin Conservation Society have all become synonymous with work in specific, recognizable areas.[47] Therefore, the work of NGOs may be undertaken around single issues or across a range of related fields in areas such as community or environmentally sustainable development.

With this scope of activity it is inevitable that organizations will vary in how they conduct their affairs. Some organizations will be identifiable by their academic, research-oriented perspective, for example, the International Institute for Environment and Development.[48] These research activities may involve the development of standards and codes for benchmarking as well as the provision of independent information for professional and public consumption (see, for example, CERES, the Coalition for Environmentally Responsible Economies).[49] In contrast, others will choose to adopt an outspoken or coercive stance through the expression of opinion, frequently using the popular media as a medium (see, for example, Corporate Watch or Greenpeace).[50] What is notable is how these differing styles and methods of engagement contribute to the profile, public recognition and perceived credibility of the various groups and the issues.

Crucial is a recognition that this 'public face' can also mask a huge variety of organizational structures. Many NGOs with a media presence

---

[47] www.wwf.org; www.actionaid.org/; www.oxfam.org/; www.wdcs.org/

[48] www.oneworld.org/iied

[49] www.ceres.org/

[50] www.corporatewatch.org.uk; a US-based organization also exists which uses the same name and works in a similar area.

may actually operate using a handful of individuals working on an informal, voluntary basis. Some NGOs draw funds from public and/or private sources, while others are founded on a substantial membership base. For instance, Greenpeace International has 1.2 million members worldwide, as does Amnesty International, and Europe's largest single interest group, the Royal Society for the Protection of Birds (RSPB), has 1.1 million members in the UK.[51] This means that their accountability and governance structures span the entrepreneurial–institutional spectrum, with an increasing number demonstrating the resources and organization of professional organizations.

NGOs are therefore a diverse and heterogeneous group of organizations whose numbers have grown significantly in the past decade. Figures which describe this situation fully have yet to be produced with any accuracy, but the following statistics provide an indication of NGO growth.

- The Union of International Associations, which gathers global statistics on NGOs, in 1999 estimated that there were more than 50,000 international or transnational NGOs (INGOs).[52]

- Of these groups well over 1,000 have consultative status with the UN Economic and Social Council.[53]

- In England and Wales there were more than 186,248 registered 'non-governmental' charities at the end of 1998.[54]

The issues discussed in this section are summarized in Figure 4.2.

---

[51] rspb.org.uk

[52] www.uia.org/. See also Bendell, J. (2000) 'Introduction: working with stakeholder pressure for sustainable development' in Bendell, J., *op cit.*

[53] Willets, P. (1998) 'Political globalisation and the impact of NGOs upon transnational companies' in Mitchell, J. (ed) *op cit.* For NGOs to be considered for consultative status by the UN they must be non-profit making, non-violent, non-criminal and not directed against a particular government. International federations of parties and groups showing a general international concern within the human rights area are accepted. ECOSOC (UN Economic and Social Council) Resolution 1996/31/25 July 1996.

[54] Bendell, J., *op cit.*

FIGURE 4.2 ■ NGO characteristics

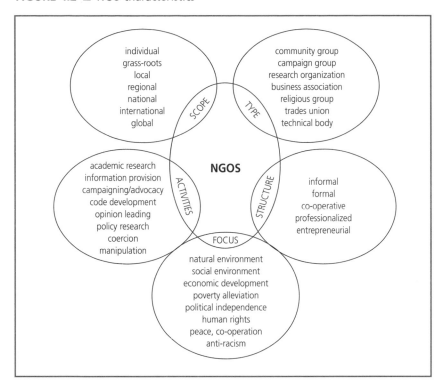

Providing context

In order to understand why NGOs have expanded so significantly over the past decade it is important to be aware of several linked trends: the rise of, and changing definition of, civil society; the 'death of deference';[55] stakeholder empowerment;[56] and the emergence of globalization.

---

55 See www.tomorrowscompany.com

56 McIntosh, M. (ed.) (1993) Introduction: *Good Business? Case Studies in Corporate Social Responsibility*, Centre for Social Management, School for Advanced Urban Studies, University of Bristol.

The term civil society has been used to describe those activities that fall outside the state (political) and business (economic) spheres.[57] A leading US commentator, Sandra Waddock, describes civil society as composed of '. . . organizations and associations that constitute community . . . and that its [civil society's] fundamental purpose is to construct relationships between social institutions and people that give meaning to the terms civility and community'.[58] A British commentator, John Keane, says: 'Civil society describes and envisages a complex and dynamic ensemble of legally protected non-governmental institutions that tend to be non-violent, self-organizing, self-reflexive, and permanently in tension with each other and with the state institutions that frame and constrict their activities.'[59]

Since the bombing of the Twin Towers in New York on September 11 2001 many would question whether this latter description now holds. Terrorist and liberation groups have many of the characteristics listed above, but many are certainly *not* non-violent. Just as we need to decide which businesses enable the realization of the common good, so too it is necessary to decide which NGOs are antithetical to the notion of civility and community.

The overarching focus of NGOs towards building social capital[60] and pursuing values of relationship places them firmly in the civil society sphere (see Figure 4.3). The rise of civil society has been ascribed to a growing disillusionment with public sector institutions

---

[57] Gramsci, A. (1992) *Prison Notebooks: Volume 1*, New York: Columbia University Press.

[58] Waddock, S., *op cit*.

[59] Keane, J. (1998) *Civil Society: Old Images, New Visions*, Cambridge: Polity Press.

[60] Putnam refers to social capital as the 'features of social organisation such as networks, norms and social trust that facilitate co-ordination and co-operation for mutual benefit'. Putnam, R. (1995) 'Bowling alone: America's declining social capital,' *Journal of Democracy*, 6 (1), 67.

▪ ▪ ▪ ▪ ▪ ▪ ▪ ▪ ▪ ▪ ▪ ▪ ▪

The rise of civil society has been ascribed to a growing disillusionment with public sector institutions and established systems of governance

▪ ▪ ▪ ▪ ▪ ▪ ▪ ▪ ▪ ▪ ▪ ▪ ▪

and established systems of governance.[61] People have become alienated from these institutions, established to serve them, and have sought to build new forms of association that better reflect their values, aspirations and goals. NGOs have emerged as result of the frustrations brought by existing institutional structures and have thrived by progressively influencing both public policy and, increasingly, the market agenda.

FIGURE 4.3 ▪ The three spheres of human civilization

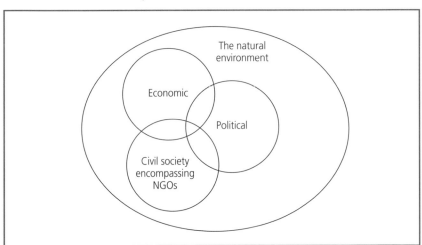

Source: adapted from Waddock (2002) and others[62]
(In this representation the spheres are balanced and underpinned by a healthy natural environment.)

----

[61] Ford, L. (1999) 'Social movements and the globalisation of environmental governance,' *IDS Bulletin*, Vol 20 (3), 68–74.

[62] Waddock, S., *op. cit.*

Part of this rise has been attributed to the decline of trust and respect for both public institutions and private organizations.[63] In the UK, for example, this lack of trust was characterized by the public response to the BSE (bovine spongiform encephalopathy) crisis. As stories of inaccurate government briefings and systematic illegal practices in the meat industry emerged, increasingly answers were sought, not from the scientists and government officials but from organizations such as the Soil Association.[64] This public cynicism has also been reflected in attitudes towards business, where increasingly the extent to which large profits are viewed as contributing to the public good has been questioned.[65] While these changes have required both governments and businesses to review the way they conduct their affairs and communicate with constituents, they have also driven the growth of those NGOs that stepped in to fill (in this example) the information void.

A third key factor explaining the expansion of the NGO sector has been the emergence and realization of the forces of globalization. The term globalization has become much like 'sustainability' in that its meaning and use is the subject of intense discussion and disagreement. Both terms share the difficulties of understanding the issues and links between economic, social and environmental dimensions. There are, however, some basic realities that characterize the globalization process.[66] These factors include the expansion of information tech-

[63] See, for instance, www.tomorrowscompany.com

[64] The Soil Association is a UK-based membership charity which has been campaigning since 1946 for organic food, farming and sustainable forestry. www.soilassociation.org. The changing nature of this 'trust' relationship is analyzed by Zadek (*op cit.*) who outlines the growing significance of NGOs as trust receptacles for the general public.

[65] MORI, Market Opinion Research International (1999) 'British public increasingly cynical about business,' Polls Archive February 22.

[66] For further discussion of this point, see Edwards, M., Hulme, D. and Wallace, T. (1999) 'NGOs in a global future: marrying local delivery to world-wide leverage,' *Public Administration and Development* 19, 117–36.

nology and electronic communication; mobility brought by declining transport costs; the importance of mobile assets such as finance and knowledge; deregulation and the changing role of the nation state; and the liberalization of markets.[67] While globalization may bring benefits, it has also been credited with reinforcing the inequality that arises from a world of unequal producers and consumers, where the triumvirate of North America, Europe and Japan become wealthy in contrast to poorer nations. The rise of NGOs in this context reflects a belief that civil society can act as a countervailing force to some of the negative aspects and inequity brought by the market and the perceived declining authority of states. In particular, NGOs have engaged with some of the cultural elements of globalization and have looked towards generating non-exploitative relationships. In essence, therefore, globalization may also be considered to be producing a global civil society.[68]

Mapping NGOs

The previous discussion has provided an overview of the range of organizations that fit into the category of NGO and the diversity of characteristics they display. An appreciation of these differences is important because it goes some way towards dispelling the picture of NGOs (frequently presented in the popular media) as always being campaigning, direct-action entities driven by hard-line, predominantly left-wing constituents. In reality, NGOs represent the full spread of views and values embraced by civil society, from local to global, and therefore businesses seeking to understand these organizations need to look more closely at each group's individual motivations and goals.

[67] For a discussion of some of the factors outlined, see Newell, P. (2000) 'Globalisation and the new politics of sustainable development' in Bendell, J., *op cit.*
[68] See Willets, P. (1998) 'Political globalization and the impact of NGOs upon transnational companies' in Mitchell, J. *op cit.*

One of the few attempts to 'map' NGOs in this way was undertaken by the consultancy SustainAbility, which conducted a project for BP in 1996.[69] The aim of this work was to help the company to understand and evaluate NGOs in terms of potential partnerships. The resulting typology categorized NGOs along two dimensions. First, organizations were considered by the extent to which they sought to 'integrate the role of businesses and interest groups' in order to achieve [environmental] goals. Second, NGOs were categorized on the basis of whether they discriminated against companies within an industry 'with respect to their real or perceived environmental commitment and performance'. The results used marine species to characterize the differing behaviours of various NGOS, as shown in Table 4.5.

The typology is useful for companies as it takes a more detailed look at NGOs from a behavioural perspective and considers the way they operate and how they might respond in different situations. This is strategically valuable information for companies considering closer connections to NGOs. The work could, however, be criticized for its corporate-centric approach, as well as for producing groupings that simplify the situation and do not necessarily reflect the full scope of NGOs operating today.[70] It is, however, a more rigorous and analytic approach than continues to be displayed in the media. For example, a 2001 article in the *Financial Times*, reporting on the anti-globalization debate, described NGOs as either *'fluffies'* or *'spikies'* which arguably contributes to the stereotypical perspectives of NGOs that more intelligent analyses have sought to dispel.[71]

---

[69] For further information on the source for this section, see Elkington, J. and Fennel, S. (2000) 'Partners for sustainability' in Bendell, J. *op cit.*

[70] Note that SustainAbility has subsequently supplemented this analysis with a typology of companies which considers organizations on the basis of their openness and solution-oriented behaviour.

[71] Beattie, A. (2001) 'Plan for globalisation debate finds antagonists poles apart,' *Financial Times*, 21 August.

TABLE 4.5 ■ NGO typology

NGO Characteristics	Polarizer: • Business unfriendly • Avoids alliances with companies • Prefers confrontation to collaboration	Integrator: • Business friendly • Seeks productive relationships with companies • Prefers collaboration to confrontation
Discriminator: • Scrutinizes company performance • Takes relative environmental progress into account in target and partner selection	Orca • Intelligent and strategic • Can adapt behaviour but prefers to use fear • Appears fierce • Associates with its own kind	Dolphin • Intelligent and creative • Adapts behaviour but strategic in approach • Can fend off sharks • Can be loner or intensely social
Non-discriminator: • Ignores company performance • Tends to view all companies as fair game	Shark • Relatively low intelligence • Tactical but undiscriminating in terms of targets • Associates with own kind • Swims and attacks in packs	Sea lion • Moderate intelligence • Tactical and friendly • Menu item for sharks and orcas • Safety in numbers, stays in shallow waters

Source: SustainAbility 2000.

A more progressive mapping of NGOs recognizes these differing levels of engagement but makes explicit the growing scenario that sees NGOs marrying confrontational approaches with 'business-friendly' tactics simultaneously. Zadek (2001) considers three potentially overlapping stances that, his analysis indicates, are increasingly intertwined – see Figure 4.4.

Future classifications need to consider the characteristics considered in section two – type, structure, focus, activities and scope – as well as the behavioural aspects contained in these business-NGO typologies.

FIGURE 4.4 ■ NGO approaches to changing the world

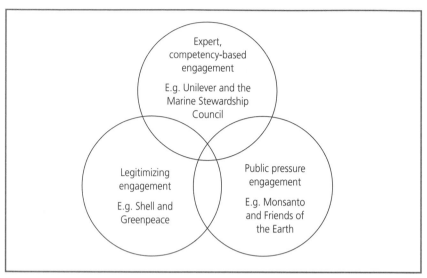

Source: adapted from Zadek (2001).
Many NGOs adopt a fluid position and may move between or occupy more than one position at any one time.

The role of NGOs

Our consideration of changing context, and illustration of the heterogeneous nature of NGOs, points to a variety of roles that these organizations may adopt. As indicated above, on a macro scale, NGOs are increasingly playing a key role in forming and developing the response of civil society to the changes brought by globalization. Currently these roles may include constructive engagement, embracing globalization as a social revolution or more radically looking to de-link activity from the world economy and work towards a more self-reliant local civil society. Within this broader framework it is possible to envisage a number of roles that NGOs may perform, particularly when engaging with business. Figure 4.5 suggests a continuum of company-NGO relationships.

At one extreme we see the most *challenging*, hostile relationships, in which companies and NGOs come into conflict. This position,

FIGURE 4.5 ■ Company/NGO relationships

Source: adapted from Elkington and Fennel, 2000

which produces the stereotype of NGOs most frequently presented in the popular media, sees the NGO adopting a confrontational stance. This role is characterized by high-profile campaigning against companies, often on a 'single issue' basis. The use of the Internet to bombard company sites with email communications so that they will 'crash' or to co-ordinate campaigns (as occurred during the NGO opposition to the Multilateral Agreement on Investment) are increasingly common tactics.[72] While this role is one of the most difficult and potentially most damaging for companies to deal with, it has arguably forced decision makers to recognize NGOs and reassess their relationship with these organizations. The interactions between Shell and

[72] Bray, J. (2000) 'Web Wars: NGOs, companies and governments in an Internet-connected world' in Bendell, J. *op cit.*

■ ■ ■ ■ ■ ■ ■ ■ ■ ■ ■ ■

One response to the role of NGO as 'challenger'
has been for companies to pre-empt negative press
through media campaigns of their own

■ ■ ■ ■ ■ ■ ■ ■ ■ ■ ■ ■

Greenpeace following the Brent Spar incident illustrate this point.[73] One response to the role of NGO as 'challenger' has been for companies to pre-empt negative press through media campaigns of their own. Monsanto's 1998 UK advertising campaign in support of genetically modified organisms (GMOs) saw the company *'sparring'* with NGOs and inviting responses.[74] However, the continued wariness of Europeans (the world's largest consumer group) towards GMOs, and the rush for organic produce, suggests that these communications were treated with some scepticism.

A more progressive but 'arm's-length' relationship has seen both NGOs and companies adopting a mutual *support* role. In these instances companies may choose to support select NGOs or projects through financial aid and gifts in kind such as secondments. Patagonia Inc, for example, allows paid leave of absence for employees to work with environmental non-profit organizations.[75] This enables NGOs to benefit from the commercial expertise of employees while at the same time providing an opportunity to educate company workers about NGOs and their practices from the inside.

[73] See Neal, A. (1997) 'Organisational learning in contested environments: lessons from Brent Spa,' *Business Strategy and the Environment*, 6, 93–103.

[74] See Elkington, J. and Fennel, S. (2000) 'Partners for sustainability' in Bendell, J., *op cit.*

[75] Zint, M. and Frederick, R. (2001) 'Marketing and advertising a 'deep green' company: the case of Patagonia Inc,' *Journal of Corporate Citizenship*, 1, 93–113.

A key role that NGOs are increasingly playing on a global basis is in the development, administration and promotion of standards, codes and certifications. These initiatives embrace a range of citizenship principles and include issues such as human rights, labour standards and the environment. Representative examples include the development of the Ethical Trading Initiative in the UK, profiled earlier, which was launched in order to develop best, ethical practice along company supply chains. Commitment to and ongoing involvement with the initiative means that member companies will benefit from *product endorsement*. Similarly, some NGOs have sought to develop standards that bring together existing but fragmented codes of conduct. SA8000, which was launched by the Council on Economic Priorities Accreditation Agency in 1997 (now known as Social Accountability International), explicitly addresses workers' rights and includes a requirement for external monitoring. The position of the Council on Economic Priorities (CEP) as a 'bridging NGO', able to embrace other social auditing initiatives, gave it an important convening role.[76] These examples illustrate clearly how NGOs are taking a leading role in formulating standards that impact and have direct relevance to the commercial activities of companies. By working with NGOs on these initiatives, companies are stimulated to promote change throughout their operations which, with ongoing commitment, can bring benefits that include *company endorsement and endorsement of the NGO*.

The role of the NGO as *facilitator* comes more sharply into focus where both companies and NGOs make a positive choice to engage formally in communication and agenda setting. This may occur for individual projects or extend into *strategic dialogue* in relation to core business issues. The UK-based utilities company Wessex Water, which until 2002 was part of Enron, worked closely with Jonathon Porritt from the leading NGO 'Forum for the Future' during the

---

[76] For a discussion of the development of SA8000 see McIntosh, M. *et al.*, *op cit*.

development of new company headquarters. This *project dialogue* contributed to the successful completion of an award-winning building that incorporates fundamental principles of sustainable development.[77] In February 2002 the company's headquarters in Bath was named 'global building of the year' by the Royal Institute of Chartered Surveyors.

It was noted previously that Shell has experienced a number of conflict situations with NGOs (in relation to the disposal of Brent Spar and operations in Nigeria). These critical incidents brought into focus ongoing difficulties and convinced senior-level employees that the company needed to engage more openly with its stakeholders.[78] A series of high-level negotiations with a range of leading NGOs ensued, illustrating the emerging role of NGOs as contributors to strategic, long-term change in organizations.

This progression towards more participatory working, that aims to share the critical issues and challenges facing organizations, is beginning to lead to long-term *joint ventures* between NGOs and companies. A leading project in this area is the Global Reporting Initiative, which was profiled earlier. This uses a multi-stakeholder approach involving business and the NGO community to 'develop, promote and disseminate an accepted framework for voluntary reporting of the economic, environmental and social performance of an organization'.

In this section we have outlined a range of possible roles adopted by NGOs that the authors have documented in their studies of NGO-business relationships. The spectrum remains broad and there is no necessary progression or evolution towards a participatory stance. Important, however, is the recognition that the primary concerns of NGOs 'do not automatically make them hostile to companies'.[79] In

---

[77] www.wessexwater.co.uk; www.forumforthefuture.org.uk/

[78] For a detailed discussion of Shell's experience see Elkington, J., *op cit.*

[79] Willets, P., *op cit.*

■ ■ ■ ■ ■ ■ ■ ■ ■ ■ ■ ■

This progression towards more participatory working,
that aims to share the critical issues and challenges
facing organizations, is beginning to lead to long-term
joint ventures between NGOs and companies

■ ■ ■ ■ ■ ■ ■ ■ ■ ■ ■ ■

fact, as noted previously, NGOs are increasingly combining a number of roles that can see them working with other like-minded NGOs as well as business and government. As such, companies need to be increasingly aware that NGOs can and do adopt different stances dependent on their particular experiences and goals.

The scope of NGOs

We have indicated how NGOs have become an established part of the business landscape. In particular, there is now a rich discussion and much analysis of the challenges and opportunities brought by the various levels of interaction between businesses and NGOs. This volume of research gives an important indication of the growing reach of NGOs.

Perhaps the most important reflection of this scope has been the emergence of NGOs as the 'civil regulators' and trend-setters of the 21st century. The role of NGOs in terms of filling the gaps left by apparently shrinking states, and shaping the rules and norms of business behaviour, means that they have become increasingly influential. Whilst their remit to exert this influence is not without its critics and challengers, it has generated a momentum and agenda that few can ignore.[80] This influence is expressed in a number of ways.

....

[80] For a discussion of and references to NGO accountability, see Chapter 7 in Zadek, S., *op cit.*

First, the scope of INGOs may be expressed quite literally through their global reach. This global presence has been achieved in part by making use of the rapid spread of communications technologies. NGOs have been particularly quick to recognize the potential of the Internet for alerting the world's media to causes or issues, regardless of location. Very few companies, particularly those which are visible either through their activities or branding, can expect to operate in a sub-standard manner undetected.[81] This means that no corner of the planet is invisible or sheltered from external scrutiny.

New technologies have also facilitated far greater public access to information than at any time in history. This allows like-minded NGOs, driven by a committed workforce, to build extensive knowledge databases and to share this expertise more efficiently. Specifically, this enables small, local NGOs to draw on the networks and resources of larger organizations. In this way, local concerns, whether they be the plight of an indigenous group displaced by mining activity or glaciers retreating as a result of climate change, can be brought to the attention of a global audience.[82] The 'think global, act local' dictum that emerged from early debate around the sustainable development agenda could now, in this age of instant communications, work both ways. This ability to act collectively on a worldwide scale has been employed in both campaign (Seattle, Prague) and partnership (ethical trade) initiatives. In this communications arena, NGOs have created new territories and successfully dominated old positions that were previously occupied by public and private institutions. Public recognition and trust (as observed below) of NGOs is at an all-time

---

[81] For case studies that draw on leading company archive material, see McIntosh, M. and Thomas, R. (2000) *Global Companies in the Twentieth Century: Selected Archival Histories*, London: Routledge.

[82] Bray, J., *op cit.*

high.[83] Indeed, conversely Unilever now describes itself as a 'multi-local multinational company'.[84]

NGOs, as noted above, are a key constituent of the civil society sphere and have increasingly sought to pursue their aims through a range of partnership approaches with organizations that include commercial corporations. It is the nature and detail of these partnerships that has opened the scope of NGOs onto another level.

More often than not, leading NGOs are now invited to forums where they share a platform with key business decision makers. This opportunity for dialogue and consultation means that NGOs have progressed from commentator to participant. By building bridges between businesses and NGO activity, the opportunity for NGOs to access companies and to act as educators and trainers in their field of expertise is extended. This is significant because it points to the sharing of competencies and cultures, which brings benefits for both parties. Companies gain access to the networks and relationships developed by NGOs. For NGOs it brings the opportunity to influence key areas of company operations and strategy as well as, in the more progressive cases, developing the more intangible facets of organizational values and culture.

Examples of business-NGO partnerships, which have been well documented, show that this is neither an easy nor a comfortable place to be for either partner.[85] However, they do illustrate how the scope of NGOs has progressed in such a way that their role and influence in these partnerships has become an important facet of the new 'civil governance'.[86] In other words, the scope of NGOs is moving beyond

[83] As reported in a recent survey by the global public relations company Edelman, www.edelman.com

[84] www.unilever.com

[85] Classic examples include the development of the Marine Stewardship Council by the World Wildlife Fund for Nature, in collaboration with Unilever.

[86] See Chapter 8 in Zadek, S., op cit.

■ ■ ■ ■ ■ ■ ■ ■ ■ ■ ■ ■

*More often than not, leading NGOs are now
invited to forums where they share a platform
with key business decision makers*

■ ■ ■ ■ ■ ■ ■ ■ ■ ■ ■ ■

'conferring legitimacy' to working with companies seeking to demon-strate improved or changing business practices.

This has been a necessarily selective cut through some of the key issues concerning businesses engaging with the citizenship agenda. Work on citizenship is in a state of flux and businesses are witnessing changing boundaries and a redefinition of their position in society. Where the only constancy is change, those companies that remain sta-tic or resist entering the debate will experience difficulties in all spheres of their business. To understand how a company might best interpret citizenship will require entering into dialogue with a range of groups and participating in initiatives that facilitate learning and encourage new thinking.

It is suggested that to successfully embed citizenship into the fabric of the company will require change at three key levels: the individual, the firm and the inter-firm. The challenge revolves around redefining the culture and, in some cases, the structural and operational elements of the company. A number of practical approaches may be employed in the development of this institutional capital.

Firms develop their competitive abilities and distinctive strengths on the basis of core competencies developed over time. It has been argued that successful corporate citizenship will also depend on the development of key competence in a number of new areas. We have highlighted three initiatives that can assist companies in the develop-ment of the skills and resources that form the foundation of this citi-zenship competency development.

Transparency and accountability are key tenets of the citizenship movement and companies working in this area need to be able to communicate their progress satisfactorily. In recent years citizenship has become 'crowded' by new codes and standards, all aimed at measuring and reporting progress. Unsurprisingly, the resulting confusion and competition between the different codes has stalled rather than expedited substantive change. This discussion has suggested that indicator development is best achieved by reflecting on why companies should report and by using basic guiding principles. In addition, one significant initiative has been highlighted that is seeking to unify the disparate work in this area and provide clear guidelines for business.

To understand NGOs more fully, they need to be considered in relation to a number of criteria: type, structure, focus, tactics and scope. While it is possible to distinguish sub-groups, this has tended to result in media stereotyping. Generalizing about NGOs is, therefore, best avoided in favour of a more informed analysis based on an individual assessment of the group or organization concerned.

In a context of changing political structures and fast evolving market activity, NGOs have risen as significant leading institutions, educating and publicizing the key issues as they relate to social, environmental and economic development. This movement has a momentum and a credibility that, while not without its critics, is leading the debate about new conceptual and institutional frameworks in a global society.

For business it is essential to consider how NGOs choose to pursue their aims in relation to corporate activity. Importantly, though, there is no definitive blueprint for the form of engagement that may occur. Rather, what we see is a situation of 'shifting sands' as these multifarious organizations move to redefine and re-evaluate their position in line with changing circumstances. For businesses, this suggests that relationships, of any nature, cannot be taken for granted and need to be continually reassessed.

■ ■ ■ ■ ■ ■ ■ ■ ■ ■ ■ ■

For business it is essential to consider how NGOs choose to pursue their aims in relation to corporate activity. Importantly, though, there is no definitive blueprint for the form of engagement that may occur

■ ■ ■ ■ ■ ■ ■ ■ ■ ■ ■ ■

An awareness of the ability of established and emerging NGO groups to make sophisticated use of communications technologies is important in order to understand the growing influence of NGOs. This is particularly the case when much of the available material is transmitted in a raw, unregulated form. While the scope of NGOs may be considered in this literal sense, it has been suggested that the true scope of NGOs may be realized through the organizational development and reciprocal learning that should occur as a result of partnering activity. It is here, at these points of creative exchange, where old ideas are challenged and new ideas are introduced and debated, that the scope of NGOs to contribute to 'change practice' will be most effectively realized.

A future framework

Corporate citizenship will make sense only within a political framework that recognizes three features of a civilized and healthy society:

1 the strengths of the regulated free market;

2 the authority of the participatory and inclusive state;

3 the vitality of a free civil society.

A new understanding, locally and globally, of the relationship between these three sectors is needed. In order to change we must learn new ways and unlearn old habits. Unlearning can be more difficult than learning. Reflection and reflexivity[87] are key strategies.

---

[86] See, for instance, Soros, G. (1998) *The Crisis of Global Capitalism*, New York: Little, Brown.

CHAPTER 5

Linkages, convergence
and change

This chapter considers the linkages and convergence between eight voluntary global corporate citizenship initiatives: the UN Global Compact, the Global Reporting Initiative, OECD Guidelines for Multinational Enterprises, ILO Conventions, the ISO 14000 Series, the Global Sullivan Principles, AccountAbility 1000S and Social Accountability 8000.

This highlights the rapid development of numerous frameworks, standards, codes and management systems involving corporate citizenship initiatives in the past few years. These initiatives all share one principle: that it is possible to reconcile a market economy with a good society, and that economic competition can coexist with social co-operation. The jury is out on whether, or how, this could be possible, but the 'Global Eight' profiled here are testimony to the wealth of activity and energy being devoted to what the UN Secretary-General has described as 'giving a human face to the global economy' – by corporations, labour organizations, non-government organizations, government and international institutions.

In recent decades there has been a wide range of initiatives within business, governments and civil society concerned with 'corporate citizenship' and 'corporate social responsibility'. In particular, since 1995 a number of standards and codes of conduct have emerged, intended to guide company practice. As innovation in this area continues, the need emerges for an understanding of the ways in which these various codes overlap, interlink and complement each other. This might have the effect of strengthening moves towards more informed and beneficial social practice on the part of profit-led enterprise and other organizations.

This chapter maps some of the global initiatives and the convergence and linkages between them. Further, it explores the lessons that can be learned from the totality of these developments and the areas in which there appears to be a lack of attention, suggesting the need for further research. Some individual companies find themselves struggling to work with dozens of standards simultaneously. Clarification of this area is needed, with the expectation that this will assist all parties involved in the formulation of their strategic responses.

In the shifting social and political geography of the 21st century, companies focusing on their relationship with society are looking for guidance. New codes of conduct and management standards offer some guide for companies on how to proceed. But ultimately, codes and other current initiatives are useful only if they bring about change in corporate behaviour and practice. Codes may be able to help companies create social value, for themselves and for the societies of which they are a part, if they are successful in creating opportunities for learning and the development of new kinds of relationships with stakeholders.

All of the recent corporate citizenship initiatives have sought to marry the delivery of social improvements and public goods with increased company performance and private goods. There are indications that in many cases, but not all, such a linkage is possible. Many in the business community remain to be convinced and see engagement in the corporate citizenship debate as an unnecessary burden on their delivery of stockholder or shareholder earnings. But it is important to mention this debate in the context of this report because the 'Global Eight' quoted here, and in particular the UN Global Compact, have legitimacy only if they can be seen to be delivering global public goods[1] while working with private market activity.

One high-profile example of the new expectations being placed on business is the UN Global Compact. In January 1999, the UN Secre-

---

[1] For an excellent discussion of the concept of 'public goods' see Kaul, I. (ed.) (1999) *Global Public Goods*, Oxford: Oxford University Press. By public goods is normally meant intangibles such as the rule of law, social justice, peace, education, freedom and development.

■ ■ ■ ■ ■ ■ ■ ■ ■ ■ ■ ■

*In the shifting social and political geography of the
21st century, companies focusing on their
relationship with society are looking for guidance*

■ ■ ■ ■ ■ ■ ■ ■ ■ ■ ■ ■

tary-General challenged the business community to support a compact with society based on human rights, labour standards and environmental principles. The speech he gave at the World Economic
Forum at Davos in January 1999 signalled a significant development
in the field of corporate citizenship.[2] According to the Secretary-General, the Global Compact is an attempt to give a 'human face' to the
globalization process. Since the speech was made, hundreds of companies have indicated their support for it. These commitments are
being followed with written submissions from companies on how they
are enacting the Compact. This chapter draws on the work of companies involved in the Global Compact, to illustrate changing corporate citizenship practice. In the words of UN Secretary-General Kofi
Annan:

> . . . let's choose to unite the powers of markets with the
> authority of universal ideals. Let us choose to reconcile the
> creative forces of private entrepreneurship with the needs of
> the disadvantaged and the requirements of the future
> generations.[3]

---

[2] See the Global Compact website for the full speech, www.unglobalcompact.org

[3] Quoted in speech by Jacqueline Aloisi de Larderel, Director, UNEP Division of
Technology, Industry, and Economics, 'UNEP and the Global Compact', presentation
at OECD Roundtable on Global Instruments for Corporate Responsibility, Paris,
June 19 2001.

Corporate citizenship and the Global Eight

The existence of the Global Compact and other major initiatives (see 'The Global Eight', below) indicates dynamic development within the area of activity that has come to be known as corporate citizenship. Some of these developments are taking companies into entirely new areas of activity and giving rise to operational and procedural innovation. Some companies, such as BP and ABB, are redefining the nature of their business, from product-oriented to service-oriented. Others are trying to address abuses they committed in the past. BASF, for example, is seeking to come to terms with the forced labour it employed in the Second World War and the implications for how to conduct business now. Unilever explores the lessons of a partnership to promote sustainable fisheries. Statoil and its major Norwegian Trade Union have established an agreement on a range of human rights and environmental concerns, defining a common vision and agenda.

Codes of conduct

The five years prior to writing has seen a proliferation of codes of conduct relating to aspects of corporate citizenship – to such an extent that some observers refer to 'code mania'. According to the OECD, in 2000 there were 246 codes of conduct.[4]

In addition, competition is emerging between different corporate social responsibility and sustainable development (SD) standards, giving rise to considerable confusion on the part of those who need to decide which codes and standards to adopt for their own operations. The buying director of a Scandinavian retail chain revealed in 2001 that one of his key suppliers had 60 audits in one year – variously for

[4] OECD, *Codes of Conduct – An Expanded Review of their Contents*, OECD Working Party of the Trade Committee, TD/TC/WP (99) 56/Final, Paris, 2000.

▪ ▫ ▫ ▪ ▪ ▫ ▪ ▪ ▪ ▪ ▪ ▪

Codes of conduct represent a formalized and uniform way of dealing with a range of complex issues – that is both their strength and their weakness

▪ ▫ ▫ ▪ ▪ ▪ ▪ ▪ ▪ ▪ ▪ ▪

quality, environment and social concerns, not to mention financial auditing. In addition, choosing to implement a code involves a substantial investment of resource and effort on the part of any organization. Not knowing which codes will prove to be widely adopted in the future makes it very difficult for companies to commit themselves. It may not be as clear-cut as the battle between video standards Betamax and VHS (which occurred in the 1960s), but companies fear there could similarly be long-term costs to backing the wrong player at this early stage.

The result of this 'code mania' has been a certain level of inertia, while companies hang back to see what will happen, and a good deal of wasted time, as effort is duplicated across codes. Some companies have responded by deciding to write their own codes, which has led to a degree of 'cherry picking', leaving out key (usually difficult) dimensions. This is a charge levelled by some commentators at the Global Sullivan Principles which lack the explicit references to all the core ILO labour standards which are contained in the UN Global Compact.

The many new corporate citizenship initiatives, of which the Global Compact is one of the most prominent, pose both *risks* and *opportunities*. They are also potential challenges to 'business as usual'.

Codes of conduct represent a formalized and uniform way of dealing with a range of complex issues – that is both their strength and their weakness.

At their best, codes and standards offer an opportunity to companies and individuals within them to think differently and to act in new ways. They ask companies to give attention to new questions and to prioritize issues that have hitherto been the concern of others. They also provide opportunities for businesses to collaborate with their suppliers and their critics in new ways, and to innovate in response to these challenges.

Information and communication technologies have had the effect of interconnecting the people of the world. In this context, the case for internationally recognized standards becomes more compelling. The uniformity created by international standards facilitates comparisons between suppliers, products and customers, and enables judgements of quality to be made. In addition, codes seek to transfer best practice without the constant need for each player in the system to create new processes and procedures: there is no need to 're-invent the wheel'.

But such limitations are not always a good thing. Some companies suggest that the very process of consultation and defining values associated with creating a code of conduct is crucial in creating the commitment to changed behaviour. Most, however, adopt an existing code irrespective of its compatibility with their own way of doing things and even their other business systems. Companies with very well-known and respected brands tend to reject off-the-shelf codes, arguing that the brand should speak for itself and serve as a guarantee of good quality procedures on all fronts, including social policies.

In addition, one of the biggest limitations of international standards is that they do not reflect local culture and practice, a point which will be developed further later.

Finally, there is a risk that codes and standards facilitate the translation of corporate citizenship into 'business as usual', that they will simply be absorbed within business processes in ways which do not bring about significant changes in behaviour and priorities. In some cases, this is already happening. It is common to hear that companies must 'be *seen* to care about social issues'. To some companies, corporate citizenship is a marketing question, involving image and symbol rather than the delivery of broader social benefit.

Different types of codes

One way of understanding the plethora of codes is to categorize them by their point of origin. The groups of constituents that originated and developed the standards and principles determine its priorities, influence, longevity and power. Jenkins (2001) divides them into the following groups:

- company codes
- trade association codes
- multi-stakeholder codes
- model code
- inter-governmental codes[5]

These can be viewed as a continuum, with company codes of conduct being the most embedded within a company, and the inter-governmental codes having the greatest legitimacy, credibility and recognition at the global level:

Company -- Trade association -- multi-stakeholder -- Inter-governmental

Company codes are unilateral statements by companies. While it is usually very beneficial for companies to define a set of values and communicate them internally, company codes may omit many key issues. As a study by an ILO analyst[6] and research carried out by the Centre for Responsible Business suggest, companies often exclude the most difficult issues, such as wages, collective bargaining and freedom

[5] Jenkins, Rhys (2001) 'Corporate codes of conduct: self-regulation in a global economy, technology, business and society programme, Paper Number 2, April, United Nations Research Institute for Social Development.

[6] For more information, see Sajhau, J.P. (1997) 'Business ethics in the textile, clothing and footwear industries: codes of conduct', Sectoral Activities Programme Working Paper SAP, 2.60/WP.110, ILO, Geneva. See also Ferguson, C. A. (1998) 'Review of UK company codes of conduct', DFID, Social Development Division, London.

of association. In addition, company codes are rarely followed up with external monitoring. Examples of company codes are:

- Shell Statement of General Business Principles[7]
- Philips General Business Principles[8]
- Levi Strauss & Co.'s Business Partner Terms of Agreement.[9]

Trade Association codes are adopted by trade bodies within a sector and/or within a geographic area. The ability to represent an industry provides these codes with greater leverage and public awareness than individual company codes. However, these are often very diluted, as they must conform to and reflect a wide range of interests, establishing a lowest common denominator. Examples are:

- International Chamber of Commerce's Business Charter for Sustainable Development[10]
- British Toy and Hobby Association[11]
- Bangladesh Garments Manufacturers and Exporters Association[12]
- Kenya Flower Council Code.[13]

Model codes are a statement of best practice or benchmarks. These codes tend to serve as good reference points rather than practical guidelines. The following codes are among the most well known:

[7] www.shelloman.com/st_generalbusiness.htm

[8] www.investory.philips.com/ethics/GenBusPrincl.html

[9] www.levistrauss.com/responsibility/conduct/guidelines.htm

[10] www.un.org/esa/sustdev/viaprofiles/Icc_Busines_Charter.html

[11] www.btha.co.uk/codeofconduct.html

[12] www.bgmea.com/social.htm

[13] www.kenyaflowers.co.ke/

- ICFTU Code of Conduct covering Labour Practices[14]
- Principles for Global Corporate Responsibility.[15]

Multi-stakeholder codes are developed by a range of stakeholders, which can include civil society, companies, trade unions and, in some cases, governments. They include:

- AccountAbility 1000 (AA 1000)[16]
- GoodCorporation.com (UK)[17]
- Project Sigma (UK)[18]
- Ethical Trading Initiative (UK)[19]
- Apparel Industry Partnership (USA)[20]
- Social Accountability 8000 (SA 8000).[21]

Inter-governmental codes are negotiated within multilateral organizations. Signatories are governments rather than companies. The most significant are:

- The Universal Declaration of Human Rights[22]
- International Labour Organization (ILO) Conventions[23]
- Guidelines on Multinationals (OECD)[24]
- European Union Code of Conduct (EU).[25]

---

[14] www.itcilo.it/english/actrav/telearn/global/ilo/guide/icftuco.htm

[15] www.web.net/~tccr/benchmarks/

[16] www.accountability.org.uk/

[17] www.goodcorporation.com

[18] www.projectsigma.com/

[19] www.ethicaltrade.org/

[20] www.dol.gov/dol/esa/public/nosweat/partnership/report.htm

[21] www.cepaa.org/

[22] www.unchr.ch/udhr/

[23] www.ilo.org/public/english/standards/norm/whatare/fundam/

[24] www.oecd.org/EN/home/0,,EN-home-93-no-no-no,FF.html

[25] www.fas.org/asmp.campaigns/cde/eucode.html

Developing themes for the future

Despite the multiplicity of codes, it is clear that there are several gaps to be considered:

1 *Social and environmental issues are splintered.* Until now, codes have generally dealt with social *or* environmental issues. This is beginning to change as some environmental initiatives add social criteria. For instance, the OECD Guidelines for Multinational Enterprises, discussed in more detail below, are among the most comprehensive of voluntary initiatives, and the Global Compact integrates both social and environmental issues.

2 *Numerous issues are being ignored altogether.* For example, indigenous rights, corruption, governance, the rights of homeworkers and animal welfare receive limited mention in voluntary codes of conduct. By contrast, some issues are referenced many times. This may be an indication of the immaturity of the development of the codes.

3 *There is a lack of definition and consensus on several major terms.* For example, the 'precautionary principle'[26] and 'spheres of influence of a company' are both terms that are used but without a clear definition that is universally accepted.

4 *Some initiatives are more voluntary than others.* While these codes are voluntary, i.e. not required by law, brand capital investor and consumer pressure is so high in some industries that it may drive companies to adopt voluntary measures. It is not the case that they are necessarily adopted proactively by the company concerned. For companies with limited public and particularly NGO visibility, however, such codes are less relevant.

---

[26] The precautionary principle was enshrined in the1992 Rio Conference on the Environment and Development.

5 *Companies vary dramatically in their levels of commitment and management systems.* Some companies appear to be adopting management systems to embed codes into practice, while others are simply supporting a code, without clear implementation strategies.

6 *Increased accountability brought about by codes of conduct can bring benefits to the company.* Among the benefits to companies are enhanced reputation and social capital, decreased risk, lower legal bills, enhanced employee morale, easier access to capital, and new customers. If the various corporate citizenship initiatives are to gain legitimacy, society will also have to be seen to be benefiting through enhanced social development and greater access to information.

7 *There are often unintended consequences.* While voluntary initiatives aim to improve social conditions, there may be unintended consequences that, in practice, create adverse social conditions. For example, efforts to curtail child labour have in some case led to children being fired and resorting to begging or prostitution. Likewise some efforts to promote codes of conduct have also had adverse impacts on homeworkers, who subsequently need to work in a factory setting, as factories are easier to monitor than homes. Commuting and childcare costs have added to the burden of these workers.

The OECD inventory of codes of conduct concludes that there is movement towards a 'consensus on global norms for business conduct.'[27] How this consensus is developing is considered in more detail in the next section.

[27] OECD *Codes of Conduct, op cit.*

The Global Eight

Among the myriad corporate citizenship initiatives around the world in recent years, eight have attained a high degree of recognition and a significant following. These are voluntary initiatives with a global constituency that can also be defined as multi-sectoral, in that they can be applied in a wide range of industries. They have all evolved through social partnerships involving some elements of business, governments, labour organizations and non-government organizations. They are explored here in further detail because of their usage and take-up, their reference to the Global Compact submissions and their multi-stakeholder approach to corporate citizenship issues. This is an indicative rather than an exhaustive list of global initiatives. It is also exclusive and there may be others that merit consideration, but we felt at this stage that the focus should be on these eight voluntary initiatives. Those included are voluntary and do not address issues of regulation, even though many derive some of their legitimacy by reference to international conventions and regulation. In this respect, they exemplify innovative organizational responses to the current socio-political business environment.

Each initiative is described below and compared with the others. Many of the initiatives have a common starting point: either conventions of the ILO and/or the UN Declaration on the Rights of the Child and/or the Universal Declaration on Human Rights. Most of the 'Global Eight' reflect a northern perspective; this is balanced only partially by the inclusion of ILO conventions, which are developed in a multilateral setting. While there are standards developed in the south, they tend to be national and/or regional in application.

The Global Eight are:

- The UN Global Compact
- ILO Conventions
- The OECD Guidelines for Multinational Enterprises

■ ■ ■ ■ ■ ■ ■ ■ ■ ■ ■ ■

Among the myriad corporate citizenship initiatives around the world in recent years, eight have attained a high degree of recognition and a significant following

■ ■ ■ ■ ■ ■ ■ ■ ■ ■ ■ ■

- ■ ISO 14000 Series
- ■ The Global Reporting Initiative
- ■ The Global Sullivan Principles
- ■ Social Accountability 8000
- ■ AccountAbility 1000.

Principles and standards

The Global Eight may be divided into principles and standards. Principles are a set of overarching values that underpin behaviour and so by their very nature are non-specific in behavioural terms. Standards, on the other hand, are specific and advocate a set of benchmarks to be attained. There are several different types: process, performance, foundation and certification.

- ■ Process standards define the procedures a company should put in place, such as how to conduct stakeholder dialogue, how to communicate with stakeholders or how to develop management systems.
- ■ Performance standards define what a company should do or not do, such as pay a living wage or prevent discrimination.
- ■ Foundation standards seek to lay the foundation for a new field, describing what constitutes best practice in an emerging area.
- ■ Certification standards establish a system under which certificates of compliance are awarded to companies that comply and have passed an independent (third-party) audit.

It is possible for standards to have several of these characteristics:

- principles (Global Compact and Global Sullivan Principles)
- standards (GRI, OECD Guidelines, SA 8000, AA 1000S, ILO Conventions)
- foundation (ILO Conventions, AA 1000S)
- process (SA 8000, AA 1000S, ISO 14000S)
- performance (SA 8000, OECD Guidelines, ILO Conventions)
- certification (SA 8000 and ISO 14000 Series).

ILO Conventions on Core Labour Standards

The International Labour Organisation is the oldest UN agency and unique in one respect from other international organizations: its decision-making is tri-partite, with representation from governments, labour organizations, and employers' organizations. Its tri-partite nature enhances the credibility of the ILO and therefore its conventions, but makes decision making a lengthy and at times difficult process. One of the weaknesses of the ILO Conventions is lack of implementation and enforcement, even by governments that have formally ratified them as part of their national law.

The ILO has defined core labour standards, which include:

- freedom of association (Convention 87)[28]
- Right to collective bargaining (Convention 98)[29]
- prohibition on forced labour (Convention 29 and 105)[30]
- minimum wage (Convention 138)[31]

---

[28] www.unhchr.ch/html/menu3/b/j_ilo87.htm
[29] www.unhchr.ch/html/menu3/b/j_ilo98.htm
[30] www.unhchr.ch/html/menu3/b/j_ilo25.htm
www.unhchr.ch/html/menu3/b/j_ilo105.htm
[31] www.unhchr.ch/html/menu3/b/d_ilo138.htm

- freedom from discrimination (Convention 111)[32]
- right to equal pay for equal work (Convention 110).[33]

In addition, there is a wide range of ILO Conventions covering health and safety, employment of disabled people, child labour and homeworking which are also significant. The logic behind the core labour standards is that, if properly implemented, they will prevent a wide range of problems such as those associated with child labour and health and safety.

In 1998, the ILO issued the Declaration on Fundamental Principles and Rights at Work. The Declaration seeks to address the challenges of globalization and promote the consideration of the social side of business. The Declaration is not binding.

OECD Guidelines for Multinational Enterprises[34]

The Organisation for Economic Co-operation and Development is a club of 30 member countries in which governments 'discuss, develop, and perfect economic and social policy'.[35] Thirty-four governments have signed up to the Guidelines, giving them a critical mass and notionally global application.[36] The Guidelines are more comprehensive than any other of the Global Eight, covering competition, financing, taxa-

---

[32] www.unhchr.ch/html/menu3/b/d_ilo111.htm

[33] www.unhchr.ch/html/menu3/b/d_ilo110.htm

[34] The OECD Guidelines are part of the OECD Declaration on International Investment and Multinational Enterprises.

[35] www.oecd.org/about/general/index/htm

[36] The OECD countries include Australia, Austria, Belgium, Canada, Czech Republic, Denmark, Finland, France, Germany, Greece, Hungary, Iceland, Ireland, Italy, Japan, Korea, Luxembourg, Mexico, The Netherlands, New Zealand, Norway, Poland, Portugal, Slovak Republic, Spain, Sweden, Switzerland, Turkey, UK and US. In addition, Argentina, Brazil and Chile have signed onto the Guidelines but are not OECD members.

■ ■ ■ ■ ■ ■ ■ ■ ■ ■ ■ ■

For their time, the OECD Guidelines could be considered a foundation standard, which certainly impacted the codes that followed

■ ■ ■ ■ ■ ■ ■ ■ ■ ■ ■ ■

tion, employment, as well as industrial relations and environment, science and technology. Like the ILO Conventions, the OECD Guidelines are for governments to promote among the private sector. Since their revision in 2000, the OECD Guidelines now include all of the core labour Conventions of the ILO.

The OECD Guidelines were established in 1976, earlier than most other codes in the Global Eight. For their time, the OECD Guidelines could be considered a foundation standard, which certainly impacted the codes that followed. In 2000, the Guidelines were revised to focus on sustainable development. They use local practice rather than internationally agreed standards as a norm. For example, they encourage companies to observe the right to unionize and adopt terms and conditions of work which are '*not less favourable than those observed by comparable employers in the host country*'. Hence, if workers' rights are not upheld in an OECD country, the company seeking to adopt the Guidelines would not necessarily need to bring practice up to internationally accepted standards, as more recent codes would recommend.

Like the Global Compact, the OECD Guidelines seek to promote development by fostering local capacity, enhancing development through training and other forms of human capital expansion. The question the OECD Guidelines seek to address is: How can multinational enterprises operate in harmony with local practice?

According to the ILO:

The basic approach to the Guidelines is that internationally agreed guidelines can help to prevent misunderstandings and build an atmosphere of confidence and predictability between business, labour and governments.[37]

The Guidelines seek to reinforce and complement other voluntary initiatives:

... by providing a common frame of reference and by providing an institutional home for international efforts to encourage progress in these fields.[38]

Moreover:

As the only multilaterally endorsed comprehensive code of conduct, the Guidelines have an important role to play .. The Guidelines' institutions could be used to strengthen and encourage the emergence of consensus and to contribute to the accumulation and dissemination of expertise.[39]

These Guidelines are unique among the Global Eight in that they have national contact points in each OECD country who promote the Guidelines, respond to inquiries and arrange for discussions in the event of problems.

The strength of the OECD Guidelines is the comprehensive nature of the approach. However, like the ILO Conventions, they are for *governments* to commit to – making it more difficult sometimes to hold *companies* directly accountable. Another difficulty is that they compare company behaviour to local norms rather than to ILO or other internationally accepted norms.

---

[37] www.itcilo.it/english/actrav/telelearn/global/ilo/guide/oecd.htm

[38] OECD Guidelines for Multinational Enterprises Frequently Asked Questions, OECD Online. Question 3. Available at www.oecd.org/daf/investment/guidelines/faq.htm

[39] OECD, 'Private initiatives for corporate responsibility: an analysis', p. 5.

ISO 14000 series

The International Standards Organisation has developed an extensive range of standards. Among those that are directly related to corporate citizenship are those that refer to quality, health and safety and the environment through the ISO 9000 and ISO 14000 Series. These standards are used at several hundred thousand facilities around the world. Of all of the Global Eight initiatives, ISO standards have attained the greatest dissemination and adoption by companies.

ISO 14001

ISO 14001 is one of a range of voluntary industry standards, launched in 1996. The 14000 Series, to which ISO 14001 belongs, provides a framework for the private sector and others looking to manage their *environmental issues*. The standard focuses on organizational processes, not necessarily their products or environmental impacts. Specifically, the standard describes how a firm might manage and control its organizational system so that it measures, controls and continually improves the environmental aspects of its operations. ISO 14001 embraces five key elements:

- an environmental policy
- an assessment of environmental aspects
- an assessment of legal and voluntary obligations
- a management system
- a series of periodic internal audits and reports to top management.

The development of the standard, and its use when compared with other initiatives in the field (see, for example, the Eco-management and Audit Scheme, EMAS) has been the subject of extended debate.[40]

---

[40] See Krut, R. and Gleckman, H. (1998) *ISO 14001: A missed opportunity for sustainable global industrial development*, London: Earthscan.

However, for the purposes of this discussion the focus is on those aspects of this initiative that may contribute to the development of key resources underlying citizenship capabilities. The development of policy requires that senior management cultivate an understanding of the nature and scale of the environmental aspects associated with their companies' activities. This stage of awareness development and commitment to change around environmental issues has arguably been the first rung on the ladder for many companies now working on broader citizenship issues.

The central part of engaging with ISO 14001 is the development of the management system itself. This includes establishing procedures, documentation and operational control of the system. Crucial here is the 'human' element of the system. That is, developing an awareness and understanding of the issues amongst the workforce through targeted training and the allocation of responsibility. It is this part of the system development (in terms of building an understanding around the issues as well as the technical and managerial knowledge of how to tackle environmental concerns) that forms the core building blocks for capabilities such as pollution prevention.

While environmental management may be considered only one part of the citizenship agenda, it has for many organizations acted as the catalyst for change. A significant contribution has come from initiatives such as ISO 14001 because this tool has provided a framework to allow organizations to systematically address the issues. In particular, a focus on management and *process* has allowed companies the opportunity to develop an internal 'competency to deliver' in anticipation of future legislative change and stakeholder demands.

The question posed by ISO 14001 is: How can my company implement a system to manage environmental impacts and improve environmental performance?

One of the problems with ISO 14001 is that it is easier for large companies to adopt than small and medium-sized companies. However, in some regions this is being addressed, as government subsidies

■ ■ ■ ■ ■ ■ ■ ■ ■ ■ ■ ■

*While environmental management may be
considered only one part of the citizenship agenda,
it has for many organizations acted as the catalyst for change*

■ ■ ■ ■ ■ ■ ■ ■ ■ ■ ■ ■

are available to combat this inequality. While quite costly to implement, studies have shown that adopting ISO 14001 is an investment that generates savings, despite the significant costs of implementation which run, on average, from $25,000 to $128,000.[41]

The greatest strength of ISO is its development of management systems and areas such as training, which allows the standards to be embedded within the company. The greatest weakness is the exclusion of performance standards. It is possible that a company with an ISO 14001 certificate has excellent management systems in place while maintaining deplorable environmental conditions.

The Global Reporting Initiative

The Global Reporting Initiative[42] was conceived in 1997 by the Boston-based Coalition for Environmentally Responsible Economies (CERES) in collaboration with the Tellus Institute. Over the past five years the GRI has evolved into a set of reporting criteria on all aspects of a company's performance. The initial draft standard was 'field tested' in 1999 by over 20 companies and released in June 2000. A revision was published in 2002.[43]

---

[41] 'The ISO 14001 Information Guide', (1999), quoted in *OECD, Private Initiatives for Corporate Responsibility*, p. 20.

[42] www.globalreporting.org/

[43] www.globalreporting.org/

In common with other corporate citizenship initiatives, this development has taken place through a new social partnership between non-state actors that include businesses, NGOs and accountancy organizations. The GRI has been adopted by the UN Environment Programme (with funding from the UN Development Fund) and is to become established as an independent organization. The GRI is built on a simple premise. By providing a broadly agreed mechanism, reached through negotiation between the partners in the process, to measure environmental and social performance, the GRI aims to assist investors, governments, companies and the wider public to understand more clearly the progress being made towards sustainability. The use of a common framework is seen as a way to improve related analysis and decision making. For example, the Guidelines suggest the following (summarized) approach for reporting on energy:

- a measurement (in joules) of total energy usage;
- a broad indication of the types (e.g. primary sources) and uses of that energy;
- initiatives taken towards renewable energy sources and energy efficiency.

The Guidelines provide assistance on the format and content of reports, as well as information on how to normalize and verify data. In addition, work is being undertaken by accountants to adapt traditional principles to this new form of accounting. As noted above, it is increasingly being recognized that conventional financial measures do not capture the intangible assets being considered by this broader based-measurement of company performance.

It is inevitable that some companies will experience difficulties applying the guidelines and some stakeholder groups will be critical that the performance measures are not sufficiently detailed and challenging of company activity. However, for companies looking to develop a consistent approach that will be robust amongst the range of external benchmarking work being undertaken by NGOs and investors (for example, FTSE4Good), the GRI provides a clear path through a densely populated field.[44]

The GRI has an ambitious mission: 'To elevate sustainability reporting to a level equivalent to financial reporting through the development of a generally accepted reporting framework.'[45] The GRI Guidelines address economic, environmental and social reporting. Although in the long term the GRI Sustainability Reporting Guidelines are intended to be applicable to all types of organizations, the GRI's initial development work has focused on reporting by business organizations.

In March 1999, the GRI released the Sustainability Reporting Guidelines as an exposure draft for public comment and testing through the spring of 2000. Twenty-one companies from around the world pilot tested these guidelines and hundreds of stakeholders from around the world provided substantive comment. In June 2000, the GRI launched the Sustainability Reporting Guidelines which have been adopted by more than 100 companies worldwide.

The GRI has strong backing from companies and NGOs around the world and is convening a multi-stakeholder group to look into verification issues in general. The GRI encourages companies to set targets and then to report on whether or not those targets were met. If the company has not met its targets, it should give reasons. In this way, stakeholders have parameters to which they can hold the company accountable. The GRI also encourages organizations to engage with stakeholders and to select organization-specific performance indicators most relevant both to the reporting organization and to its

---

[44] FTSE4Good is a set of four tradeable indices for the UK, Europe, the United States and the world. The index screens companies against a range of indicators that are focused on the areas of environment, human rights and stakeholder relations – www.ftse4good.com

■ ■ ■ ■ ■ ■ ■ ■ ■ ■ ■ ■

The GRI has strong backing from companies and NGOs around the world and is convening a multi-stakeholder group to look into verification issues in general

■ ■ ■ ■ ■ ■ ■ ■ ■ ■ ■ ■

key stakeholders. The questions that the GRI asks include: How can a company communicate to its stakeholders? On what issues should a company report?

The GRI is valuable as it serves as an 'internal tool for evaluating the consistency between corporate sustainability policy and strategy on the one hand, and actual performance on the other'.[46]

In 2002 the GRI was adopted by the UN and the UN Global Compact, as well as being cited in the EU white paper on a European CSR Framework. From a social partnership based in a local NGO has come a global standard with support from business, states and civil society.

The Global Sullivan Principles

The Global Sullivan Principles (GSP) are intended to promote corporate social responsibility. Companies (and cities) sign up to the principles and then report annually on their progress. The Global Sullivan Principles were preceded by the Sullivan Principles on South Africa which were significant in helping to support moves by South Africans to dismantle *apartheid*.[47] Like the Global Compact, the

[45] www.global_reporting.org, comparison between GRI and Global Compact, 14 June 2001.

[46] Sustainability Reporting Guidelines, GRI (99), p. 5.

[47] According to Nelson Mandela, *apartheid* means 'apartness' and represents the codification in one oppressive system of all laws and regulations that kept Africans in an inferior position to whites for centuries. Mandela, Nelson (1994) *Long Walk to Freedom: The Autobiography of Nelson Mandela* London: Little Brown & Co.

Global Sullivan Principles are a set of principles rather than auditable standards with management systems. The Global Sullivan Principles do not include the right to freedom of association, a core labour standard, and as such do not have the full support of labour organizations. The majority of companies signing on to the GSP are American.

The question that the Global Sullivan Principles asks is the same as that posed by the Global Compact: what are the principles that define responsible corporate behaviour?

Both the Global Compact and the Global Sullivan Principles require signatory companies to provide an annual update on progress made in implementing the principles. Like the Global Compact, cities as well as companies are implementing GSP. Among the US city signatories to the GSP are Atlanta, Cambridge, Charleston, Columbus, Detroit, Houston, Los Angeles, Milwaukee, Philadelphia, and Wilmington. As this list suggests, the Global Sullivan Principles are considered a US initiative and the majority of the signatory companies originate in the US.

The greatest strength of the GSP is the reputation of the initiative's founder, Reverend Sullivan, developed through the success of the Sullivan Principles for South Africa. Some people believe his death in 2001 has left the future of the initiative unclear.

Social Accountability 8000

SA 8000 is a standard for companies seeking to make the workplace more humane. Unlike other codes, SA 8000 is a global code that can be implemented in any country and in any sector. SA 8000, is the first auditable standard on working conditions. The New York-based Social Accountability International (formerly known as the Council on Economic Priorities Accreditation Agency) developed SA 8000 with the support of non-governmental organizations, trade unions and companies. The majority of the companies adopting SA 8000 are in the retail sector or manufacture clothing, toys, and shoes. Interest is greatest in the sectors where there are well-known brands which need protecting and is growing among the agricultural and electronics sectors. Companies adopting SA 8000 have a combined annual revenue of $106 billion. SA 8000 certificates have been issued in 14 countries to over 80 companies.

SA 8000 draws on the Conventions of the International Labour Organization and other UN documents as well as the management systems of the ISO. By using the ILO conventions as a point of departure, SA 8000 provides the necessary definitions and management systems to develop an auditable system, which can be checked by qualified auditors. Social Accountability International accredits certification firms and NGOs to audit and certify companies.

The question that SA 8000 asks is: how can I ensure that my company and/or supply chain are respecting workers' rights?

One of the strengths of SA 8000 is that it is auditable. It also has management systems to embed the standard into the company culture. Like ISO standards, it is easier for large companies to adopt SA 8000 than small and medium-sized companies.

AccountAbility 1000S

AA 1000S[48] was launched in 1999 by the Institute of Social and Ethical Accountability (AccountAbility). The Institute is a not-for-profit professional membership organization, built through a coalition of businesses, non-government organizations, business schools and service providers. The focus of AA 1000S and its forthcoming revision is on the social dimensions of an organization's accountability. The standard comprises both the *principles* of a quality standard and a set of *process* standards that cover five stages:

----

[48] www.AccountAbility.org.uk

- planning

- accounting

- auditing and reporting

- embedding

- stakeholder engagement.

The evolution of AA 1000S has been stimulated by a recognition that organizations need guidance both to develop social and ethical practice and, crucially, to construct more progressive relationships with an expanded range of stakeholders. AA 1000S makes reference to, and builds on, previous quality-inspired initiatives such as ISO 9001 and ISO 14001. This means that the systems developed and lessons learned from previous management initiatives remain *relevant and applicable* to the new challenges brought by social concerns. However, the innovation brought by AA 1000S comes from the initiative's explicit support for *organizational learning* alongside performance improvement. If we reflect on the expressed need for the development of appropriate resources and skills for corporate citizenship, it is clear that a system which focuses expressly on creating conditions for learning and professional development will contribute directly to these aims. Engaging with AA 1000S will see a focus on effective methods for communication with stakeholders, as well as an opportunity to learn from this engagement. As a result, participant organizations will gain expertise in operationalizing initiatives whose success depends, for example, on partnerships with civil society groups.

AA 1000 is a foundation and process standard and, as such, it seeks to define what constitutes best practice in social auditing, accounting and reporting, with particular reference to understanding and communicating with stakeholders.

AA 1000 provides a framework for companies by suggesting a set of steps they can take to become more socially responsible over time. Companies are urged to:

▨ ▨ ▨ ▨ ▨ ▨ ▨ ▨ ▨ ▨ ▨ ▨

*Engaging with AA 1000S will see a focus on
effective methods for communication with stakeholders,
as well as an opportunity to learn from this engagement*

▨ ▨ ▨ ▨ ▨ ▨ ▨ ▨ ▨ ▨ ▨ ▨

▪ commit to social and ethical accounting, auditing and
reporting (SEAAR);

▪ identify stakeholders;

▪ define and review values;

▪ identify issues in consultation with stakeholders;

▪ set the scope of SEAAR activities;

▪ identify indicators.

The standard requires that social, ethical accounting, auditing and
reporting should seek to be inclusive, complete, material and regular.
Other key principles include quality assurance, accessibility, compara-
bility, reliability, relevance and 'understandability' of information.

Among the strengths of AA 1000 is that it can be used by any type
of organization, in any country, in any sector. Its methodology translates across borders. Some companies and NGOs have criticized the
standard for being too complex, an issue which has been addressed in
the last revision.

The Global Compact

The Global Compact (described at length in Chapter 6) is an initiative
of UN Secretary-General Kofi Annan, which includes nine basic principles on environment, labour and human rights. The Compact is seen
as a major milestone since for the first time a substantive global institution, and the only global political body, has articulated a position on
corporate social responsibility. By contrast most other initiatives are
seen as 'sectoral', having originated from think-tanks or consortia of

trade unions and NGOs. The Global Compact has the potential to bring credibility and legitimacy to corporate citizenship, and perhaps eventually to develop a global governance structure to manage CSR issues. According to one of its key architects, John Ruggie, 'the hope and expectation is that through the power of dialogue, transparency, advocacy and competition, good practices will help drive out bad ones'.[49]

Early in 2002 the Compact had support from more than 1,000 companies. Six cities had also agreed to join. Member companies are required to file reports which will be posted on the Global Compact website as a reservoir of good practice and a shared learning resource.

The Global Compact is a set of 'nested networks'[50] which are expanding. These include:

1   the five United Nations offices directly involved in the Global Compact, the Office of the Secretary-General, the ILO, the UN Environmental Programme (UNEP), the UN Development Programme (UNDP) and the Office of the UN High Commissioner on Human Rights (OHCHR);

2   the UN, companies, the International Confederation of Free Trade Unions (ICFTU – an international association of national and sectoral labour federations), global NGOs and business associations, including the International Chamber of Commerce, the International Organisation of Employers and the World Business Council for Sustainable Development, and several universities;

---

[49] Ruggie, John Gerard (2001) 'The theory and practice of learning networks: corporate social responsibility and the Global Compact,' paper presented at the 4th Annual Warwick Corporate Citizenship Unit Conference, Corporate Citizenship: International Initiatives on Corporate Citizenship, Warwick Business School, University of Warwick, July 9–10, p. 6.

[50] *Ibid.*, p. 7.

3 regional, national and sectoral initiatives in Brazil, India, Scandinavia, the Philippines and other countries.

The nine principles of the Global Compact are drawn from the Universal Declaration of Human Rights, the ILO's Fundamental Principles on Rights at Work, and the Rio Principles on Environment and Development.

In order to comply with the Compact, companies must make three commitments:

- 'to advocate the Compact and its nine principles in mission statements, annual reports and similar public venues, on the premise that their doing so will raise the level of attention paid to, and the responsibility for, these concerns within firms;

- to post on the GC website at least once a year concrete steps they have taken to act on any or all of the nine principles, discussing both positive and negative lessons learned – and triggering, thereby, a structured dialogue among the various participants about what deserves to be labelled as good practice;

- to join with the UN in partnership projects of benefit to developing countries, particularly the least developed, which the forces of globalization have largely marginalized.'[51]

The questions that the Global Compact poses are: What are the principles that define responsible corporate behaviour? How can corporate citizenship promote development? How can the United Nations and governments begin to create mechanisms to address the governance of a globalized world? What constitutes best practice in corporate citizenship?

Given its UN background, the Global Compact must reflect a wide range of interests and nations and hence is far less specific than standards

....

[51] *Ibid.*, p. 5.

such as SA 8000 and AA 1000, which are developed by experts from NGOs, the private sector and labour organizations. The non-specificity of the Compact, and its relatively fluid and organic nature, represent both its possible strength and its possible weakness. It is intended to develop dynamically, forming alliances as needed, as the activities associated with it develop. It has also provided a convening platform for regional dialogue on shared values among business, government and civil society organizations. Critics point to its lack of accountability structure, an absence of mechanisms to hold companies to live up to the commitments they make.

Connecting the codes

As companies begin to work with the codes, new ways of combining them are emerging, which seek to combine their strengths and weaknesses to provide balanced coverage. Table 5.1 outlines the Global Eight.

Global Compact and GRI

The Global Reporting Initiative was adopted by both the UN and the Global Compact in early 2002. There is an obvious symbiosis between the GRI and the Compact, and while the former does not provide a monitoring tool for the latter it does give companies a guide as to how they might approach engagement with the Compact in their annual submissions.

The GRI was convened not only by the CERES but also by the UNEP. In fact, the United Nations Foundation has been the primary sponsor of GRI activities thus far. The United Nations Foundation grant was awarded to fund the transition activities of the GRI until a permanent, independent GRI could be created by 2002.

Although the UNEP contributes its expertise and activities to the Global Compact, it continues to define and improve corporate environmental, social and economic indicators as part of the multi-stakeholder Global Reporting Initiative.

The ISO–SA 8000 Nexus

SA 8000 is designed to integrate with the ISO series. SA 8000 resembles the ISO series in that both require management systems that aim at continuous improvement. Both systems are based on a similar methodology for auditors and for accreditation bodies. However, there are several differences between them. First, unlike ISO standards, SA 8000 has performance provisions; management systems alone are not enough to ensure conformance with SA 8000. Second, ISO standards are initially developed at the national level and then harmonized by the International Standards Organisation in Geneva, while SA 8000 was developed as a global standard from the beginning. Third, interviews with workers play a more significant role in an SA 8000 audit than in ISO audits, given the focus of the standard on workers' rights.

Companies are beginning to combine audits for SA 8000 with ISO 9000 and/or ISO 14001 audits. For example, Otto Versand, the world's largest mail order company, combines, and Dole, one of the world's major soft fruit companies, has plans to do so. The advantages of combined audits are numerous: they save time and money, and rather than preparing for multiple audits, companies need prepare for only one. 'Combined and integrated audits will eventually lead to dovetailed or integrated management systems, thereby streamlining these processes.'[52]

AA 1000–GRI

AA 1000 and GRI constitute two pieces of the same puzzle, with GRI specifying format and indicators for reporting and AA 1000 addressing stakeholder consultation, as well as reporting.[53]

---

[52] Leipziger, Deborah (2001) 'SA 8000: The Definitive Guide to the New Social Standard', *Financial Times*, May, p. 130.

[53] The GRI's website, www.globalreporting.org/, has a comprehensive chart which compares many of the Global Eight standards to GRI, showing the high degree of complementarity of the standard.

TABLE 5.1 ■ Map of Global Eight

	Type of initiative	Description	Issues covered	Date	Origins	Signatories	Key countries	CSR issues NOT covered	Distinguishing feature	Funding sources	Positive elements	Negative elements
ILO Conventions	Conventions	Foundation	Forced and bonded labour Freedom of association Right to collective bargaining Equal remuneration/ equal work Workers' representatives Minimum age Health and safety Disabled persons Homework	1919 (onwards)	ILO	Governments	International	Environment Animal welfare Corruption	Tri-partite	Governments	Tri-partite nature of ILO gives legitimacy and credibility	Ratification by governments does not necessarily include enforcement
OECD Guidelines	Guidelines	Foundation	Environment Employment Disclosure/privacy Competition Financing Taxation Science/technology Product quality/safety Corporate governance Marketing/advertising	2000 (revised) 1976	OECD Multilateral	34 governments	OECD countries International	Animal welfare Indigenous people Wages/benefits	Comprehensive National contact points	OECD	Breadth of issues	
ISO 14001	Standard	Process	Environment Management systems	1996	ISO International	20,000+	International	Social issues	Simplicity	Fees	Well known	Comparison with local rather than international norms
Global Reporting Initiative	Standard	Process	Reporting procedures Corporate governance Philanthropy/advertising	2000 (revised) 1997	CERES (US)	55 companies	Europe/US		Performance indicators	Grants	Good governance, transparency	Easier for large companies to achieve

	Type	Category	Content	Year	Founder	Adoption	Geography	Environment	Auditability	Foundation	Accreditation framework	Ability of auditors to address social issues inadequate southern representation Easier for large companies to achieve
SA 8000	Standard	Performance Process Auditable Foundation	Child labour Forced labour Discrimination Compensation Working hours Management systems Health and safety Freedom of association Collective bargaining Disciplinary procedures	1997	Council on Economic Priorities (US)	80+ certifications	US, Europe, Asia, Latin America	Environment Indigenous people Animal welfare Corporate governance Corruption		Foundation US Government Royalties/fees	Accreditation framework Potential for integrating with ISO	Ability of auditors to address social issues inadequate southern representation Easier for large companies to achieve
AA 1000	Standard	Process	Social, ethical accounting Auditing and reporting Identifying stakeholders, issues and indicators Defining, reviewing values	2001 (revised) 1999	ISEA (UK)	Widespread influence rather than adoption	Europe, Australasia	No performance criteria	Methodology for stakeholder engagement and reporting	Membership grants	Methodology	Complexity makes it inaccessible to some
Global Sullivan Principles	Rev. Sullivan	Performance	Human rights Environment Ethics Fair competition	1999	Rev. Sullivan (US)	177 companies (5.01) business/public sector/religious organizations	US	Freedom of association/ Collective bargaining Indigenous peoples Animal welfare Corruption Corporate governance	Rev. Sullivan's reputation Path breaking nature in South Africa		Rev. Sullivan	Rev. Sullivan passed away Uncertainty Lack of trade union support
Global Compact	Principles	Performance	Human rights Freedom of association Forced/child labour Environment	1999	United Nations	300+ companies and cities	Europe, Brazil, India	Animal welfare Corruption Corporate governance Indigenous peoples	UN's moral authority	Governments UK, Norway, Switzerland, Sweden, Netherlands, Germany	UN moral authority	'Talk shop' No monitoring

	Implementation requirements	Conflict resolution/appeals mechanism
ILO Conventions	Governments ratify conventions which become legally binding	ILO representatives located in many countries but only provide training and promotion of ILO
OECD Guidelines	Respect law	Contact points in each OECD country
ISO 14001	Guidelines No complete implementation requirements	
Global Reporting Initiative	Certification	
SA 8000	Certification	Yes Right of appeal is given to all interested parties
AA 1000		Not intended for use in this way
Global Sullivan Principles	Annual update Implement policies, procedures Training, reporting	No
Global Compact	Letter from CEO Annual submission relating to implementation Participation in issues	No

Signatories and endorsements by companies to global initiatives

Table 5.1 lists the companies participating in the Global Compact, companies using the Global Reporting Initiative and endorsing the Global Sullivan Principles and SA 8000. AA 1000 does not track the list of companies using its model. Signatories to ISO 14001 are extensive.

Several trends can be noted from the table. First, there are very few companies that have signed more than one of the four initiatives. Shell, British Airways, BT, Avon, Kesko and Ford are among the companies that have publicly supported two initiatives. Second, the presence of particular sectors is notable. Oil companies, airlines and airports and alcohol manufacturers are well represented, whereas banks, investment firms and public relations firms are not. Third, there are very few competitors appearing on the same list. Fourth, it would appear that 'the new economy' companies are not signing onto these initiatives. The majority of those which have done so are large multinational enterprises, based primarily in Western Europe and the US.

Initiatives that integrate

Although there is a noticeable lack of integration between social and environmental concerns in the recent codes and standards, there are some initiatives which are seeking to synthesize corporate citizenship approaches by building on and co-ordinating between multi-stake-holder projects.

One good example is the International Social and Environmental Accreditation and Labelling Alliance (ISEAL).[54] ISEAL is seeking to increase co-ordination among accreditation and labelling organizations in the social and environmental fields by developing common systems and protocols. Members of ISEAL include:

- Social Accountability International
- The Forestry Stewardship Council
- The Marine Stewardship Council
- The Fair Trade Labelling Organization
- Conservation Agriculture Network
- International Federation of Organic Movements
- International Organic Accreditation System.

ISEAL brings together three different accreditation systems – organic, fair trade and SA 8000 – to distil similar audit methodologies. ISEAL is researching the overlap of standards and developing a framework for increasing compatibility. Joint training programmes are another priority. Members are committed to using ISO Guide 60.

---

[54] www.isealalliance.org

Rather than creating a single standard, the goal of this process is to learn and share experiences and develop common procedures and protocols, which will strengthen each of the participating initiatives.

Areas for future development

Taken overall, the Global Eight constitute innovative practice in corporate citizenship. There are, however, a number of issues which are not being addressed and where policy development will be needed in the near future if these initiatives are to flourish with the support of companies, governments and NGOs.

1 *Conflict resolution mechanisms.* It is necessary to develop common or parallel systems among the corporate citizenship initiatives to avoid spurious appeals and complaints.

2 *Relationship to local, regional, and national law.* This relationship is, at present, unclear and is likely to be tested in courts around the world in coming years.

3 *Creating local context, building bridges to local organizations.* Many global standards will require 'localization'. The Global Compact is creating national and regional compacts in Brazil and Scandinavia in order to make connections at the more local level. The OECD Guidelines have national contact points. It is necessary to bring the national and regional voices into the global debate.

4 *Addressing issues that are ignored by the Global Eight.* As Table 5.1 demonstrates, there is a wide range of issues that are excluded from the Global Eight, such as animal welfare, indigenous rights and corruption.

5 *Bias in favour of large companies.* In many cases, it is easier for large companies to adopt corporate citizenship initiatives than for small and medium-sized companies. Finding ways to advance the issues without imposing prohibitive cost and

other resource barriers on the participation of the majority of the world's businesses will be crucial.

6   *Compensation for the 'losers' in social development.* Corporate citizenship is often portrayed as a win-win proposition. But initiating change in the social impacts of business activity will inevitably create losers as well as beneficiaries. For example, in trying to create safer and more humane workplaces, Reebok has decreased its reliance on homeworkers. This makes it harder for women with children by adding commuting and childcare to their already heavy burden. Such measures will require imagination, partnership with local organizations, resources, and co-ordination.

Conclusion

This chapter has looked at some of the linkages between various voluntary initiatives within the sphere of corporate citizenship. These developments should not be viewed in isolation but as together constituting significant social innovation. Some leading multinational corporations are committing themselves to a number of codes and standards. Understanding how these initiatives inter-relate is necessary for developing clear and consistent strategy – for companies, governments and non-government organizations. The Global Compact signifies a new turn in corporate citizenship, deriving legitimacy through the moral authority of the UN Secretary-General and sharpening the demands on the business community to widen its perspectives and broaden the reach of its considerable power.

CHAPTER 6

What is the UN Global Compact?

T his chapter describes the background to the UN Global Compact and the Nine Principles. It includes some brief case studies or examples from business engagement.

Why a Global Compact?

Since the 1990s the world has witnessed substantial changes in patterns of trade, development and the use of natural resources. A great deal of this change has been driven by the developing forces of globalization. The world has become increasingly interconnected and interdependent as communications technologies have shortened distance and promoted knowledge-based capital. There has been a substantial increase in international trade and foreign direct investment brought by liberalized markets. As a result, globalization has brought unparalleled opportunities for existing, new and emerging economies.

However, as the United Nations Secretary-General Kofi Annan indicated in his 1999 speech to the World Economic Forum, at Davos in Switzerland, globalization has also become characterized by elements of fragility.

- While some economies develop, others have become marginalized, resulting in an uneven distribution of wealth and opportunity both within and between countries.

- The capacity of the state to fulfil its 'traditional' role has altered, creating a 'void' in governance which has seen economic systems protected by rules and regulations while social issues, human rights and environmental protection have not been supported by equivalent robust frameworks.

- The degradation of natural resources, upon which all the peoples of the planet depend, has continued to occur at unsustainable levels.

■ ■ ■ ■ ■ ■ ■ ■ ■ ■ ■ ■ ■

To realize the opportunities and challenges of the globalization process there is a clear need to address the unequal distribution of benefits, imbalances in rule making and the unsustainable use of natural resources

■ ■ ■ ■ ■ ■ ■ ■ ■ ■ ■ ■ ■

To realize the opportunities and challenges of the globalization process there is a clear need to address the unequal distribution of benefits, imbalances in rule making and the unsustainable use of natural resources. In looking for solutions to these issues a common thread has emerged. If the growing backlash against the negative aspects of globalization is to be slowed and reversed, there needs to be a 'reconnect' between the rapidly expanding global markets and societal preferences with their core values. The size and scope of international business means that those companies whose turnovers are often greater than the gross domestic product of many countries have a significant and substantial role to play alongside small and medium-sized enterprises.

In particular, there is an imperative for organizations of all types and sizes around the world to re-examine existing frameworks and to consider how new models of success that embrace relationship management, resource efficiency and responsiveness to systems and service needs might be employed. Governments need to be supported by the collective capacity that comes from this wider organizational engagement.

While the case for change is evolving, some key issues are emerging as firm influences in this progression towards new models of business.

■ *Shareholders and investors* are increasingly considering the social and environmental performance of companies alongside financial returns.

▪ Evidence that social and environmental risks can bring substantial financial costs is leading to a more inclusive approach to *risk management*.

▪ *Reputation*, and the values and aspirations captured by brand, increasingly require that companies are transparent in their activities and can demonstrate a commitment to good practice across human rights, labour and environmental issues.

Developing these new models will crucially involve governments, civil society and labour organizations engaging alongside the private sector through partnerships. Establishing effective networks that draw on the different strengths and capabilities of these key participants lies at the heart of the Global Compact. The cross-boundary nature of globalization means that few existing organizations are appropriately placed to provide a forum for change. However, the UN can offer both a unique range of core competencies and an unmatched global authority that is built on the basis of its own founding values and mission.

▪ The UN is the only truly global, inter-governmental organization with a comprehensive mandate that embraces development and humanitarian issues.

▪ With 30 agencies and over 50,000 employees the UN offers an unrivalled network of global, regional and national actors whose expertise can be used to leverage vision and change. In particular, the International Labour Organisation, the United Nations Environment Programme and the Office of the High Commissioner for Human Rights offer extensive technical expertise and information to organizations seeking to address the human rights, labour and environmental aspects of their business.

▪ The UN has numerous communication vehicles and is able to impart key messages in all the world's major languages.

▪ The UN has convening power at the highest levels and provides an unparalleled platform for dialogue and issues exchange.

■ The UN has a moral authority underscored by the personal commitment and involvement of the Secretary-General Kofi Annan in this agenda.

If globalization is to be made to work for all the world's people, there needs to be multilateral co-operation, openness and transparency amongst all the participants across the three areas embraced by the nine principles of the Global Compact: human rights, labour standards and the environment.

The Global Compact: origins

The Global Compact was initiated by a speech made by the United Nations Secretary-General Kofi Annan at the World Economic Forum in Davos, Switzerland, on January 31 1999. In his address, the Secretary-General challenged world business leaders to 'embrace and enact', both in their individual corporate practices and by supporting appropriate public policies, nine universally agreed values and principles in the areas of human rights, labour standards and the environment.

However, the foundations for the Global Compact, and the challenge from the UN to world business leaders, can be traced to the beginning of Kofi Annan's tenure at the UN. Shortly after taking office the Secretary-General signalled a shift in the UN's approach to business, outlined in an earlier speech at the Davos Forum. He indicated that the UN had recognized the need to build partnerships with government, business and NGOs. In doing so, the Secretary-General explicitly invited businesses to become involved in the UN's mandate to reduce poverty and promote sustainable development. This call for change was also reflected internally, through a programme of cultural reform that would enable the UN to work more effectively with business. This redefinition of the UN's relationship with business combined with emerging social, political and economic trends to form the foundations for the 1999 Davos speech.

■ ■ ■ ■ ■ ■ ■ ■ ■ ■ ■ ■

This call for change was also reflected internally, through a programme of cultural reform that would enable the UN to work more effectively with business.

■ ■ ■ ■ ■ ■ ■ ■ ■ ■ ■ ■

This speech was a 'call to action'. It challenged business leaders to tackle some of the imbalances brought by the forces of globalization by giving a 'human face to the global market'. Kofi Annan argued that businesses could use their economic power and leverage their authority to uphold human rights and ensure responsible work practices within their spheres of influence. Further, businesses should strive to operate to the highest standards, even in countries where the law was lacking and seek where possible to influence public policy to raise standards in the areas of labour and the environment.

The address was also important in positioning the UN as a contributor to solutions. Specifically, three UN agencies – the OHCHR, the ILO and the UNEP – were offered to assist and provide resources for businesses prepared to engage with the challenges presented.

The Secretary-General's speech was well received and generated an enthusiastic response from those companies and ministers present, who sought to collaborate with the UN. This commitment to change provided the momentum to take the Global Compact from an aspirational statement towards a real initiative built on a credible and practical framework for action. The Global Compact now has extensive support from multinational, small and medium-sized enterprises around the world; key environmental, social and development organizations; business associations; labour organizations and national employer associations; and academic and public policy institutions.

The Global Compact: objectives

The Global Compact is a call to business of all sizes, in all countries around the world, to help build the social and environmental frameworks that will support the continuation of open and free markets, whilst ensuring that people everywhere gain the opportunity to share the benefits that can come from a global economy.

The strategic goal of the Global Compact is to encourage the alignment of corporate policies and practices with universally agreed and internationally applicable values and goals. The initiative is an opportunity for companies, governments, United Nations agencies, civil society groups and labour organizations to work collectively by forging new partnerships and building on existing connections. These core values of the Global Compact have been distilled into nine key principles in the areas of human rights, labour standards and the environment. They are:

■ *Human rights.*
   1   Businesses should support and respect the protection of internationally proclaimed human rights within their sphere of influence; and
   2   make sure that they are not complicit in human rights abuses.

■ *Labour standards.*
   3   Businesses should uphold the freedom of association and the effective recognition of the right to collective bargaining;
   4   the elimination of all forms of forced and compulsory labour;
   5   the effective abolition of child labour; and
   6   eliminate discrimination in respect of employment and occupation.

■ *Environment.*
   7   Businesses should support a precautionary approach to environmental challenges;

8 undertake initiatives to promote greater environmental responsibility; and

9 encourage the development and diffusion of environmentally friendly technologies.

The objective of the Global Compact is to serve as an issue network and as an organizing framework for those organizations seeking to manage global growth in a responsible manner. This is a challenging agenda and will involve exploring uncharted territory and developing creative solutions to problems as they arise. As such, the Global Compact is a flexible tool that offers the opportunity for companies of all sizes to engage with new partners at a pace and a level that reflects their own capacity.

To achieve these objectives the Global Compact has explicitly adopted a learning model for stimulating conversation and inducing change. This involves establishing a network of participants from a range of groups, who can bring contrasting competencies and perspectives to a shared vision and sense of purpose. The use of a learning and network approach is recognized as conferring both strengths and weaknesses, and these are issues with which participants will need to engage.

The Global Compact *IS*
- a voluntary initiative;
- a framework to promote good corporate citizenship through committed and creative leadership.

The Global Compact *IS NOT*
- a prescriptive instrument or code of conduct linked to external monitoring;
- a regulatory instrument;
- a 'safe haven' for companies.

The Global Compact seeks to be both inclusive and accessible to a wide range of organizations. To participate, organizations are required to take the following steps:

1 The company chief executive officer must send a letter to the Secretary-General expressing support for the Global Compact.

2 Issue a clear statement of support for the Global Compact and its nine principles and publicly advocate the Compact. This may be achieved by:

   • informing employees, shareholders, customers and suppliers;

   • integrating the Global Compact and its nine principles into corporate development and training programmes;

   • incorporating the Global Compact principles into the company's mission statement;

   • including the Global Compact commitments and progress in the company's annual report, and other publicly available documents;

   • issuing press releases and company statements that make the commitment public.

3 Provide, on an annual basis, a clear, concrete example of the progress made and lessons learned in implementing the principles. Selected examples will be developed further as case studies using academic support.

Letters should be addressed to Kofi Annan, Secretary-General, United Nations, New York, NY, 10017.

The development of the initiative is supported by an Advisory Council, which met for the first time on January 8 2002. The Council is composed of 17 senior business executives, international labour leaders and heads of civil society organizations from across the world, all acting in their individual capacities. This group, which will convene on a twice yearly basis, is working to assist the Secretary-General in forwarding the aims of the Global Compact and in considering issues such as the standards of participation and protection of the initiative's integrity.

Summary

This section has outlined the rationale underpinning the development and establishment of the Global Compact. As the forces of globalization have advanced, the creation of imbalances and inequity has become more pronounced. In a move to combat the fragility brought by changing markets and governance structures, the UN has sought to utilize its convening power and channel the strengths of private enterprise and civil society toward sustainable development and good citizenship.

The Secretary-General's original call to businesses has now developed into a framework that comprises an open learning network, designed to stimulate debate and encourage action in line with the nine principles that address human rights, labour standards and the environment.

Principles and practice

Human rights

Principle One

Businesses should support and respect the protection of internationally proclaimed human rights within their sphere of influence.

Principle Two

Businesses should make sure they are not complicit in human rights abuses.

The origin of the human rights principles

Human rights are universal and belong to everyone equally. The origin of Principles One and Two is in the 1948 Universal Declaration of Human Rights (UDHR). The aim of this Declaration was to set basic minimum international standards for the protection of the rights and freedoms of the individual. The fundamental nature of these provisions means that they are now widely regarded as forming a foundation of international law. In particular, the principles of the UDHR are considered to be international customary law and do not require signature or ratification by the state to be recognized as a legal standard.

The UDHR is a keystone document and has been translated into over 3,000 languages and dialects, and while some principles may not be directly applicable to business, consistency with the declaration is important.

What does the Universal Declaration say?

Equality

The Declaration begins by laying down its basic premise that 'all human beings are born free and equal in dignity and rights'. It goes on to give content to its understanding of equality by prohibiting any distinction in the enjoyment of human rights on such grounds as race, colour, sex, language, religion, political or other opinion, national or social origin, property, birth or other status.

Life and security

The rights to life, liberty and security and the right to be free from slavery, servitude, torture or cruel, inhuman or degrading treatment or punishment further develop the notion of personal dignity and security. The rights of the individual to a just national legal system are also set out. The right to recognition as a person before the law, to equal protection of the law, to a judicial remedy before a court for human rights violations, to be free from arbitrary arrest, to a fair trial before an independent court, to the presumption of innocence and not to be subjected to retroactive penal laws are all set out in the Declaration.

Personal freedom

Rights protecting a person's privacy in matters relating to family, home, correspondence, reputation and honour and freedom of move-

■ ■ ■ ■ ■ ■ ■ ■ ■ ■ ■ ■

*Freedom of thought, conscience and religion and
freedom of opinion and expression are set out along
with the right of peaceful assembly and association and
the right to take part in government*

■ ■ ■ ■ ■ ■ ■ ■ ■ ■ ■ ■

ment are all part of the Universal Declaration. The right to seek asylum, to a nationality, to marry and found a family and the right to own property are also proclaimed by the Declaration. Freedom of thought, conscience and religion and freedom of opinion and expression are set out along with the right of peaceful assembly and association and the right to take part in government.

Economic, social and cultural freedoms

Touching other aspects of the daily lives of people, the Declaration proclaims the right to social security and to the economic, social and cultural right indispensable to human dignity and the free development of each individual's personality. These rights are to be realized through national efforts and international co-operation in accordance with conditions in each state.

The right to work is set out, and to equal pay for equal work and to just and favourable remuneration ensuring for the worker and the worker's family an existence worthy of human dignity (which can be supplemented if necessary by other means of social protection). The Declaration also recognizes the right to form and join trade unions, the right to rest and leisure, reasonable limitations on working hours and periodic holidays with pay. The right to a standard of living adequate for health and well being, including food, clothing, housing, medical care, and to social services and security, if necessary, are also proclaimed, as are the rights to education and to participate in the cultural life of the community, and to the protection of the moral and material interests resulting from any scientific, literary or artistic production.

Global Compact Principles One and Two call on business to develop an awareness of human rights and to work within their sphere of influence to uphold these universal values, on the basis that responsibility falls to every individual in society.

Engaging

Human rights: Principle One

Businesses should support and respect the protection of internationally proclaimed human rights.

Understanding the principle

Human rights are an entitlement or legal claim that everyone has by virtue of being human. These rights are based on universal norms and are applicable to every society.

Taking action

- Develop an understanding of the issues by making reference to the UDHR and international covenants.
- Ensure that existing national laws for the protection of human rights are observed and respected.
- Identify that the business may face issues related to industry and culture that will guide the focus and depth required.
- Develop policy using the available guidelines, internal participation, input from relevant external groups and company experience to date.
- Implement policy – as an ongoing and progressive challenge, being prepared for adaptation.

Suggested strategies for implementation

- Carry out 'human rights impact assessments', especially where new operations, facilities or investments are planned.

■ Provide staff training and education according to location/culture, business process.

■ Establish a core team dealing with human rights issues.

■ Engage in dialogue, collaboration and partnership with governmental and non-governmental groups.

■ Work up and down the supply chain using training, auditing and contractual agreements.

■ Use existing management systems and cycles if and where appropriate.

■ Audit, review and revise policy and implementation strategies in the light of experience work towards external verification, disclosure and reporting of activities and progress.

Case study

SAP in Nigeria

For the full company submission go to: www.unglobalcompact.org/un/gc/unweb/nsf/content/sap.htm

Building on an employee initiative designed to overcome issues of corrupt business practices in Africa, SAP is working towards the development of a code that is appropriate for its businesses worldwide. SAP has strong internal visions and values that seek to support fair business practices. The company is working to develop these issues more formally so that they may be incorporated into policy and practice worldwide.

One key example of how the company is developing its stance on human rights is through SAP Nigeria's support of the Convention on Business Integrity (CBI). The CBI is a declaration against corrupt business practices and stands for ethical conduct, competence, transparency, accountability and a commitment for the company and its partners to do what is right, just and fair.

Developed initially by an employee in the company's Nigeria office as a response to practical problems experienced in the course of business, the

▶

initiative seeks to promote fair business practices and encourages partners and customers to play an active role. The code, which has been developed with the support of advisers from Transparency International and INTEGRITY Nigeria, is not a legal document. Rather, it is a moral contract between consenting parties. Periodic compliance checks and stakeholder transparency seek to guard against substandard practice.

SAP is seeking to drive the project forward and to support the independence of the CBI secretariat. If successful, the project may be expanded to other countries where business activities are affected by corruption.

Fact file

- SAP is the world's largest inter-enterprise software company and the third largest independent software supplier.
- SAP is a recognized leader in providing collaborative e-business solutions for all types of industries and markets.
- The company was founded in 1972 and employs over 27,800 people in 50 countries worldwide.
- Transparency International is an international movement devoted exclusively to curbing corruption. It is a centre of expertise seeking to empower civil society.

Contacts:

- www.sap.com/
- www.transparency.org/

Case study

Voluntary Principles on Security and Human Rights

Governments

- US government
- UK government

Companies
- BP
- Chevron
- Conoco
- Freeport McMoran
- Rio Tinto
- Shell
- Texaco

NGOs
- Amnesty International
- Business for Social Responsibility
- Council on Economic Priorities
- Fund for Peace
- Human Rights Watch
- International Alert
- International Federation of Chemical, Energy, Mine, and General Workers' Unions
- Lawyers Committee for Human Rights
- The Prince of Wales International Business Leaders Forum

The Voluntary Principles constitute an important beginning. They are significant because, as a model, the Voluntary Principles can be used by other sectors and in other issue areas. The model used involves a dialogue convened by governments to facilitate an exchange between NGOs and companies.

The Voluntary Principles address the issue of security forces, including:

1   the criteria companies need to consider in assessing the risk to human rights in forming security agreements;
2   the relationship between a company's security and state security, such as army or police;
3   the relationship between the company's security force and private armies.

By narrowing the debate to include only security arrangements, the negotiations bypassed more difficult areas of debate which could have polarized the process.

The role of governments as convenors is an emerging trend in some areas of corporate citizenship. The US and UK governments, for example, are concerned with the reputation of their companies abroad. Another key concern in the security of their citizens abroad.[1] According to Bennett Freeman, one of the architects of the Voluntary Principles: 'One key to success was the willingness of the two governments to use their convening authority and diplomatic capacity not only to facilitate the dialogue between companies and NGOs but to draft and announce a standard that would advance the interests of the companies, NGOs and governments alike.'[2]

Like all ground-breaking agreements, the Principles have been criticized. One of the criticisms is that the Principles are voluntary – a similar criticism is made of the Global Compact, the OECD Principles and SA 8000. There is widespread agreement that the companies would not have been able to commit to binding principles for fear of litigation. A second criticism levelled at the Principles is the absence of other key governments affected by these issues, especially governments in the South. After all, the governments of Ecuador, Colombia and Nigeria are but a few of those that have a significant interest at stake. The US and UK governments opted to broker an agreement and then work with other governments to gain their approval. The goal of the initiative was to reach an agreement within one year, which would have been difficult with more governments involved.

As in the case of oil and human rights, complicity is also being debated around the mining of diamonds. Global attention is focused on the 'conflict' or 'blood' diamonds from Angola, Sierra Leone, Guinea and Congo

---

[1] For an excellent overview of US interests in promoting human rights and corporate social responsibility, see the speech given by Bennett Freeman, 'Corporate responsibility and human rights', at www.globaldimensions.net/articles/cr/freeman.html

[2] *Ibid.*, p.6.

that are used to purchase arms. Conflict diamonds fund weapons, prolong conflict and lead to human rights abuses in poverty-stricken countries. A key theme is the role of NGOs in bringing the issue to the forefront and the power of alliances in bringing about a solution deemed impossible.

Human rights: Principle Two

Businesses should make sure they are not complicit in human rights abuses.

Understanding the principle

Understanding complicity and avoiding complicity in human rights violations is a challenge for business. Importantly, business needs to recognize that the notion of complicity in this context can take a number of forms.

- *Direct complicity* – occurs when a company knowingly assists a state in violating human rights. For example, assistance of forced relocation of peoples in circumstances related to business activity.

- *Beneficial complicity* – suggests that a company benefits directly from human rights abuses committed by someone else. For example, violations committed by security forces, such as the suppression of peaceful protest against business activities or the use of repressive measures while guarding company facilities, are often cited in this context.

- *Silent complicity* – describes the way human rights advocates see the failure by a company to raise systematic or continuous human rights violations with the appropriate authorities. For example, inaction or acceptance by companies of systematic discrimination in employment law against particular groups on the grounds of ethnicity or gender could bring accusations of silent complicity.

Taking action

- Human rights issues are applicable in all countries of operation without exception, but companies need to be especially vigilant in countries where the state infrastructure is less developed and key legislation that protects human rights is lacking.

Suggested actions for business

- Respect existing international guidelines and standards for the use of force (UN basic Principles on the use of Force and Firearms by Law Enforcement Officials and the UN Code of Conduct for Law Enforcement Officials).

- If financial or material support is provided to security forces, establish clear safeguards to ensure that these are not then used to violate human rights; and make clear in any agreements with security forces that they will not condone any violation of international human rights laws. All such agreements should be made public and transparent.

- Privately and publicly condemn systematic and continuous human rights abuses.

Case study

BT

For the full company submission go to: www.unglobalcompact.org/un/gc/unweb/ns/content/bt.htm

As part of a corporate-wide 'Commitment to Society' and ethical business practice, BT has developed a supply chain initiative that promotes universal standards of human rights to direct suppliers and aims to advance these standards throughout the supply chain.

BT has recognized through its Statement of Business Practice 'The Way We Work' that the company can have a global impact. As such the company has acknowledged the need to manage activities in a socially responsible manner. This commitment has resulted in an extensive human rights programme that is managed by a number of departments and units throughout the business. One key project has been the establishment of 'Sourcing with Human Dignity', a supply chain initiative.

Sourcing with Human Dignity promotes universal standards, in particular the United Nations Universal Declaration of Human Rights and the International Labour Organisation Conventions on labour standards. By working collaboratively with suppliers, BT is seeking to identify areas of risk and work towards the improvement of practices and standards so that any identified human rights abuses are eradicated.

Existing suppliers and new tenders are required to read and sign an agreement or clause that commits them to working towards principles which include public reporting, awareness raising and training, monitoring and independent verification, and continuous improvement. As part of this programme BT has committed to reporting publicly the number and proportion of suppliers signing an agreement, as well as the number of suppliers which have contractually agreed to work towards the standard. The company also aimed to hold at least two forums with suppliers and other network members by March 31 2002.

Fact file
- British Telecom (BT) is a wholly owned subsidiary of BT Group Plc.
- Principal BT activities are local, long-distance and international telecommunications services, Internet services and IT solutions.
- BT is focused on services in the UK and Western Europe, but has operations worldwide.
- The Dow Jones Sustainability World Index rates BT as the leading telecommunications company in the world.

▶

Contacts

- www.bt.com/
- www.groupbt.com/betterworld/
- www.un.org/overview/rights.html – full text of the Universal Declaration for Human Rights
- www.ilo.org/ – gateway to the International Labour Organisation resource sites.

Labour

Principle Three

Businesses should uphold the freedom of association and the effective recognition of the right to collective bargaining.

Principle Four

Businesses should uphold the elimination of all forms of forced and compulsory labour.

Principle Five

Businesses should uphold the effective abolition of child labour.

Principle Six

Businesses should eliminate discrimination in respect of employment and occupation.

The origin of the labour standard principles

The four labour principles of the Global Compact draw on the International Labour Organisation's Declaration on Fundamental Principles and Rights at Work, which was adopted at the 86th International Labour Conference in 1998.

The Declaration identifies four categories of principles and rights that emanate from the fundamental values inherent in the ILO consti-

> ■ ■ ■ ■ ■ ■ ■ ■ ■ ■ ■ ■ ■
>
> *Significantly, the Declaration underlines an obligation for member countries to respect the fundamental principles involved, even if they have not ratified the relevant Conventions*
>
> ■ ■ ■ ■ ■ ■ ■ ■ ■ ■ ■ ■

tution. These principles and rights are also the subject of ILO Conventions, which are treaties that member states may ratify, thus accepting to be legally bound by them. Significantly, the Declaration underlines an obligation for member countries to respect the fundamental principles involved, even if they have not ratified the relevant Conventions.

The ILO was established in 1919 and became part of the UN system in 1945. The organization has a unique (tri-partite) structure composed of governments, employers and workers. A large range of additional and related instruments also provide useful starting points in the area of labour standards. Key amongst these are:

■ the Universal Declaration on Human Rights (UDHR)
■ the International Covenant on Economic, Social and Cultural Rights (ICESCR)
■ the International Covenant on Civil and Political Rights (ICCPR)
■ the UN Convention on the Rights of the Child.

Principles Three, Four, Five and Six deal with fundamental principles in the workplace. The challenge for business is to take these universally accepted values and apply them at the company level.

Engaging

Labour standards: Principle Three

Businesses should uphold the freedom of association and the effective recognition of the right to collective bargaining.

Understanding the principle

Freedom of association means that all workers and employers have a right to form and join groups with the aim of promoting and defending their interests at work. This is a basic human right and is the basis of democratic representation and governance. Association will include activities of rule formation, administration and the election of representatives. Bargaining collectively on working conditions is an important facet of the relationship between workers and their employers or organizations. The freedom to associate involves employers, unions and workers' representatives freely discussing issues at work in order to reach agreements that are jointly acceptable. These freedoms also allow for industrial action to be taken by workers (and organizations) in defence of their economic and social interests.

Taking action

- Adhere to all relevant local and national regulation.
- Adopt policies that allow workers to freely choose whether or not they wish to associate, be represented by trade unions and bargain collectively, without fear of reprisal or intimidation.
- Ensure that employment terms and career progression are not influenced by union membership.

Suggested actions for employers

- The provision of education and training for management and employees is vital for an understanding of rights and responsibilities. This is particularly the case in countries where legal protection may be insufficient.
- The provision of facilities for workers to meet and carry out the union activities of discussion, information exchange, representative election and fee collection.

Collective bargaining is a useful mechanism to determine remuneration and conditions of work. Management–worker dialogue can also be used to achieve more productive and mutually rewarding outcomes when considering issues such as health and safety, redundancy procedures and discipline and grievance concerns.

Case study

Statoil

For the full company submission go to: www.unblobalcompact.org/ un/gc/unweb/insf/content/statoil.htm

Statoil has developed a groundbreaking agreement with an international employee organization that contributes to company aims of creating low levels of conflict, informed management decisions, job satisfaction and employee retention.

The company has an approach to labour relations that builds on Norwegian traditions of dialogue and co-operation between employers and workers. The company recognizes that the extent to which labour rights are respected can vary from one country to another. To meet the challenges of upholding labour standards universally Statoil entered into an agreement with the International Federation of Chemical, Energy, Mine and General Workers Union (ICEM) in 1998, which was renewed in March 2001. This is the oil sector's first ever globally applicable agreement on industrial relations.

Working with ICEM assists Statoil in developing an approach to labour relations that respects the integrity of employees and their intrinsic human rights. The agreement specifically embraces freedom of association and collective bargaining, which the company aims to promote through joint training and awareness-raising events with ICEM.

The company believes that labour relations are best managed in accordance with local conditions, with employees responding most effectively to those closest to the issues. Implementation is therefore devolved to specific business units and countries. For example, the company has been involved in projects such as the training of trade union representatives at its operations in Azerbaijan. In addition, Statoil suggests that the agree-

▶

---

ment provides an excellent approach to risk management as it allows a greater insight into the causes of labour disputes and facilitates collaborative means for conflict resolution.

Fact file

- Statoil is a leading gas supplier in Europe, with operations in 23 countries worldwide.
- Statoil is the biggest producer of North Sea crude oils and the world's third largest trader of crude.
- The International Federation of Chemical, Energy, Mine and General Workers Union is an industry-based world labour federation dedicated to practical solidarity.
- The ICEM represents 399 industrial trade unions in 108 countries.

Contacts

- www.statoil.com
- www.ICEM.org/

Labour standards: Principle Four

Businesses should uphold the elimination of all forms of forced and compulsory labour.

Understanding the principle

Forced labour is all work or service which is extracted from any person under the menace of any penalty and for which the said person has not offered themselves voluntarily.

Forced and compulsory labour can take a number of forms:

- bonded labour where a person works to pay off a debt;
- indentured labour where workers are unable to leave their job

without employer permission (for example, through the removal of identity papers);

■ work imposed as a punishment for the expression of views in opposition to established political, economic or social systems;

■ child labour in abusive conditions (see also Principle Five).

Taking action

■ Determine whether forced labour is a problem in the business.

■ Forced labour can occur worldwide, in both developed and developing countries.

■ If forced labour is identified these people should be removed, with the support of facilities and services that enable them to make adequate alternatives.

Suggested actions for business

■ Develop and make available to all employees employment contracts stating the terms and conditions of service, the voluntary nature of employment, the freedom to leave (including the appropriate procedures) and any penalties that may be associated with a departure or cessation of work.

■ Develop additional training for staff, working towards the development of systems that allow for the review and revision of practice where necessary.

■ Investigate the opportunities to work outside company facilities and co-operate with other business, up and down the supply chain.

■ Use industry forums to develop solutions for workers removed from forced labour, for example, through micro-credit schemes.

Case study

BASF

For the full company submission go to: www.unglobalcompact.org/un/gc/unweb/msf/content/basf01.htm

In collaboration with 15 other major German companies, BASF has founded an initiative that explicitly recognizes and takes responsibility for the use of forced labour and human rights abuses that occurred in the company's past.

BASF has committed to the protection of human rights and to upholding labour standards by incorporating these issues into the new company values and principles, issued in 2000. The company observes the standards set out in the International Labour Organisation's June 1998 'Declaration on Fundamental Principles and Rights at Work'. With over 90,000 employees around the world, BASF has developed a comprehensive employee programme that includes issues such as flexible working, personal development, occupational health and safety, co-operation with unions, anti-discrimination and equal opportunity.

However, BASF recognizes that for a period of the company's recent history these employee rights were not respected. During the Second World War BASF was merged with other industries which forced millions of people to work for the German war effort. A significant period of the company's development was therefore marked by substandard labour practices. In reconciliation for this mistreatment, BASF and a group of 15 companies have founded 'Remembrance, Responsibility and the Future'. This initiative will contribute towards a Federal German Foundation fund of €5 billion so that recompense may be made to former forced labourers under the Nazis. Exploring the company's history and reporting on these past experiences demonstrates an accountability and reinforces the commitment for contemporary activities to provide fair and just working conditions.

Fact file

▪ BASF is one of the world's leading transnational chemical companies with sales in excess of $34 billion in 2000.

▪ The company produces a range of products that include high-value chemicals, plastics, colourants and pigments, automotive and industrial coatings, agricultural products and fine chemicals.

▪ The ILO works for the promotion of social justice and internationally recognized human and labour rights.

Contacts

▪ www.basf.com

▪ www.basf.de/forced_laborers

▪ www.ilo.org/

Labour standards: Principle Five

Businesses should uphold the effective abolition of child labour.

Understanding the principle

Child labour is frequently hidden and can be difficult to detect. Children may work long hours for low wages which prevents them from receiving an education and can be harmful to their health and long-term well being. Standards have been developed which set out the minimum employable age in both developed and developing countries – increasingly, 15 years is considered the minimum age for employment, with the worst forms of labour prohibited for those under the age of 18. These include hazardous activity, slavery, debt bondage, child prostitution, child involvement in illegal activity and forced recruitment in armed conflict.

Taking action

- Develop an awareness and understanding of the causes and consequences of child labour. This means identifying the issues and crucially determining whether or not child labour is a problem in the business. (Companies sourcing in specific industry sectors with geographically distant supply chains need to be particularly vigilant.)

- Discovering whether child labour is being used can be difficult (for example, where documents or records are absent) and companies may consider using local non-government organizations, development organizations or UN agencies to assist in this process.

- If identified, children need to be removed from the workplace and provided with viable alternatives. Companies need to be aware that without support children may be forced into worse circumstances, such as prostitution, and that in some instances where children are the sole providers of income, immediate removal from work may exacerbate rather than relieve hardship.

Short-term measures need to be founded on longer-term solutions:

- Use internal mechanisms to ensure that underage workers are not hired in the future (age verification).

- Investigate external collaboration with schools and appropriate agencies. A partnership approach to encourage development and perhaps alternative economic opportunities may also be the best instrument to tackle the poverty underlying most instances of child labour.

- Seek to formalize work through policy, and progress towards appropriate, auditable procedures and checklists.

- Look for support through industry associations and relevant laws and regulations.

Case study

Shell

For the full company submission go to: www.unglobalcompact.org/un/gc/unweb/nsf/content/royaldutch.htm

Adherence to recognized international standards and the development of practical initiatives, for example in supplier contracting, contribute to Shell's efforts to ensure that its group companies do not employ child labour.

Shell was the first major energy company to publicly support the United Nations Universal Declaration of Human Rights and to incorporate this commitment into the organization's General Business Principles. As part of this commitment the company has embarked on an ongoing programme of internal education and external consultation to ensure that Shell companies do not exploit children either directly or indirectly in the course of their activities. A key document produced by the company is a primer on 'Child Labour' that provides background information and guidance for managers on this issue.

One example of practical changes by the company has been recognized by a local Brazilian non-government organization, ABRINQ, and by the United Nations Children's Fund (UNICEF). In Brazil, where the legal minimum age for working children is 14 years, the use of alcohol in fuel has resulted in extensive growth and harvesting of sugar cane, and to boost the income obtained from cane harvests many employers have used child labour. Shell Brasil sells gasoline and buys alcohol from distilleries. Since 1999 the company has had a clause in its contract with distilleries which states: 'The SUPPLIER is obliged to adopt and respect in full Shell's General Business Principles and to conduct its activities in total agreement with these principles. In this context and in line with applicable legislation, the use of child labour is absolutely unacceptable and the SUPPLIER is forbidden to adopt such practice.' Suppliers found using child labour will have their contracts terminated.

To date, all suppliers have supported the clause and in collaboration with other companies Shell has contributed to a fund that aims to educate those children who might otherwise have been working.

Fact file

■ The Royal Dutch/Shell Group is comprised of two parent companies, the Royal Dutch Petroleum Company and The 'Shell' Transport and Trading Company plc.

■ The group operating companies have activities in 135 countries, employing over 90,000 people.

■ Group activities include exploration and production, oil products, chemical, gas and oil and renewables.

■ UNICEF advocates the protection of children's rights worldwide, supporting basic needs and expanding the opportunity for children to fulfil their potential.

Contacts

■ www.shell.com

■ www.unicef.org/

Labour standards: Principle Six

Businesses should eliminate discrimination in respect of employment and occupation.

Understanding the principle

Non-discrimination means that employees are selected on the basis of their ability to do the job and that there is no distinction, exclusion or preference made on the grounds of race, colour, gender, sexual orientation, disability, religion, political affiliation, national extraction or social origin. Additional issues such as age and HIV status are also of growing importance in particular countries.

▪ ▪ ▪ ▪ ▪ ▪ ▪ ▪ ▪ ▪ ▪ ▪

Discrimination can take many forms, both in terms of gaining access to employment and in the treatment of employees once in work

▪ ▪ ▪ ▪ ▪ ▪ ▪ ▪ ▪ ▪ ▪ ▪

Discrimination can take many forms, both in terms of gaining access to employment and in the treatment of employees once in work. Examples include unequal access to training and career advancement, remuneration levels, hours of work, holiday entitlement and maternity leave, security of tenure, and health and safety protective measures.

Discrimination can be formalized in systems (and in some laws, which deny equal opportunity) but most frequently it exists informally in attitudes and practices, which if unchallenged can perpetuate in organizations. Discrimination may also have cultural roots that demand individual approaches.

Taking action

- Observe and respect all relevant local and national laws.
- Develop an understanding of the different types of discrimination and how it can affect the workforce. For example, women constitute a growing proportion of the world's workforce but consistently earn less than their male counterparts.
- Advance company policy on equal opportunity that applies qualification, skill and experience as the grounds for recruitment.

Strategies for implementation

- Assign clear, high-level responsibility that involves senior staff and managers leading by example.

- Support work with appropriate training, tailored to the different challenges brought by nationality or culture.

- Use systems of record keeping for recruitment and promotion that provide a transparent view of opportunity for employees and their progression within the organization.

- Where discrimination is identified, develop systems to address complaints, handle appeals and provide recourse for employees.

- Be aware of formal structures and informal cultural issues that can prevent employees from raising concerns and grievances.

Case study

Deloitte Touche Tohmatsu (DTT)

For the full company submission go to: www.unglobalcompact.org/un/gc/unweb/nsf/content/dtt.htm

Two transformational programmes at DTT South Africa are working internally to develop a multicultural workforce and externally to generate opportunity and economic empowerment for small and medium-sized enterprises.

DTT has been aware of the need to counter the cultural imbalances in its South African business since the 1970s. Formal work to recruit black trainee accountants began in 1990 and has developed significantly since the democratic elections in 1994, which signalled the beginning of accelerated political change in South Africa.

DTT has two key initiatives that address issues of discrimination. The MultiCultural Development Programme seeks to change the business into one that 'truly represents South Africa in terms of race, gender and organizational culture'. In order to do this, the company has initiated a range of activities that include diversity workshops to facilitate dialogue among employees, scholarships and bursaries to support talented black students and new recruits who need financial assistance, and partner pairing where employees receive mentoring.

In recognition of the urgent need for external change DTT established the Business Equity Initiative (BEI) in 1995, which aims to empower new business via community investment. Through BEI the company is able to offer training and mentoring that transfers skills to entrepreneurs. DTT has also sought to create alliances with other organizations such as financial institutions that can provide additional support for new businesses.

Using these initiatives DTT is working to overcome some of the challenges, such as a deficient education system and limited ownership of businesses by blacks, that have previously led to discrimination in employment.

Fact file

▪ Deloitte Touche Tohmatsu is one of the world's leading professional services firms, serving businesses that range from large multinationals to public institutions and small business.

▪ DTT services include assurance and advisory, tax and consulting.

▪ DTT employs more than 95,000 people in operations that span over 130 countries.

Contacts

▪ www.deloitte.com/

▪ www.deloitte.co.za/

Case study

Volvo Cars

'. . . The face of Volvo cars has changed dramatically during the past two decades and will continue to do so. Today, roughly 30 per cent of Volvo Cars' customers are women, and every year the company's customers become more and more international and multi-cultural – a fantastic ▶

opportunity for the company, provided that the company is equipped to cater for its customers' diverse needs.'[3]

Volvo has worked to promote diversity both internally and externally. Internally, it is working to promote women within the company, has a policy to hire the long-term unemployed in Sweden, many of whom are from diverse populations, and works in partnership with an NGO to promote the re-integration of ex-convicts into society. In addition to these internal programmes, Volvo is working within a consortium of companies from the Global Compact to promote diversity at the World Conference Against Racism, Racial Discrimination, Xenophobia and Related Intolerance, in Durban, South Africa, at the behest of Mary Robinson, the High Commissioner.

Background on Volvo

Founded in 1927, the Volvo Car Corporation is a car company whose core values are safety, quality and environment. With 27,300 employees producing 430,000 cars each year, Volvo embodies the essence of a truly global company: it is headquartered in Sweden, with manufacturing plants in Belgium, the Netherlands, South Africa, Malaysia, and Thailand. Key markets for Volvo cars include the US, UK, Germany, Sweden, and Italy. In 1999, Volvo became a subsidiary of the Ford Motor Company.

Women at Volvo

Volvo reports that one in five of its employees is female, but that only one in 12 managers is female.[4] To address this problem, Volvo has established the Business Women Advisory Board and has set goals for diversity within the company, aiming to increase the number of women managers to 20 per cent by 2005.

---

[3] www.volvocars.com

[4] The Global Compact, *Discrimination is Everybody's Business*, 'From Discrimination to Diversity – A Corporate Led Initiative in the Framework of the UN Global Compact, Invitation to Joint Action', p. 4. Also available on the Global Compact website: www.unglobalcompact.org, p. 7.

Giving opportunities to the long-term unemployed and to ex-convicts

Volvo Torslanda Plant in Gothenburg works with the local branch of the National Employment Agency to recruit staff from the following diverse backgrounds:

1 long-term unemployed, mostly non-Swedish background;
2 long-term unemployed engineers from other countries;
3 unemployed people over 40.

Volvo reports that the track record of the long-term unemployed it has hired is very good. Of 440 people hired since 1999, two-thirds remain at the company.

Volvo also works with the NGO KRIS (Kriminella Revansch I Samhallet) to support the re-integration of ex-convicts into society.

Environment

Principle Seven

Businesses should support a precautionary approach to environmental challenges.

Principle Eight

Businesses should undertake initiatives to promote greater environmental responsibility.

Principle Nine

Businesses should encourage the development and diffusion of environmentally friendly technologies.

The origin of the environment principles

Internationally co-ordinated work on the environment has been led by the United Nations Environment Programme since its inception in 1973. UNEP has provided leadership and encouraged partnerships to care for the environment, for example, through Multilateral Environmental Agreements (MEAs) which have addressed issues such as species loss and the need for conservation at a global and regional level. UNEP has created much of the international environmental law in use today.

The three environmental principles of the Global Compact are drawn from a Declaration of Principles and an International Action Plan (Agenda 21) that emerged from the United Nations Conference on Environment and Development (the Earth Summit) held in Rio de Janerio in 1992. Chapter 30 of Agenda 21 identified that the policies and operations of business and industry can play a major role in reducing impacts on resource use and the environment. In particular, business can contribute through the promotion of cleaner production and responsible entrepreneurship.

Key documents

- The Rio Declaration – a statement of 27 principles upon which nations agreed to base their actions in dealing with environmental and development issues. The Rio Declaration built on the previous Declaration of the United Nations Conference on the Human Environment which was adopted in Stockholm in 1972. The Stockholm conference was the first global environmental meeting of governments, which stated that long-term economic progress needs to be linked with environmental protection.

- Agenda 21 – a 40-chapter action blueprint on specific issues relating to sustainable development that emerged from the Rio Summit. Agenda 21 explained that population, consumption and technology were the primary driving forces of environmental change and for the first time, at an international level, explicitly linked the need for development and poverty eradication with progress towards sustainable development.

■ ■ ■ ■ ■ ■ ■ ■ ■ ■ ■ ■ ■

The environmental principles of the Global Compact provide an entry point for business to address the key environmental challenges

■ ■ ■ ■ ■ ■ ■ ■ ■ ■ ■ ■ ■

The Bruntland Report, 'Our Common Future' which was produced in 1987 by the World Commission on Environment and Development, also laid the foundations for the environment principles. This landmark document highlighted that people needed to change the way they lived and did business or face unacceptable levels of human suffering and environmental damage.

The environmental principles of the Global Compact provide an entry point for business to address the key environmental challenges. In particular, the principles direct activity to areas such as research, innovation, co-operation, education and self-regulation that can positively address the significant environmental degradation and damage to the planet's life support systems brought by human activity.

Key environmental challenges
- Loss of biodiversity and long-term damage to ecosystems.
- Pollution of the atmosphere and the consequences of climate change.
- Damage to aquatic ecosystems.
- Land degradation.
- The impacts of chemicals use and disposal
- waste production.
- Depletion of non-renewable resources.

Engaging

Environment: Principle Seven

Businesses should support a precautionary approach to environmental challenges.

Understanding the principle

A precautionary approach is outlined in the Rio Declaration as being appropriate: '. . . Where there are threats of serious or irreversible damage, lack of full scientific certainty shall not be used as a reason for postponing cost-effective measures to prevent environmental degradation.' Precaution as a concept emerged in the former West Germany in the 1970s, in association with Clean Air legislation, and has become an accepted principle in the European Union and part of international law.

Taking action

Precaution offers a common-sense approach for decision makers faced with uncertainty. While interpretation of the precautionary approach can present difficulties, organizations will be assisted in their assessment of potential environmental harm by a thorough understanding of current organizational environmental impacts and of the baseline environmental conditions within their sphere of influence.

Suggested management tools for action

- Risk assessment – establish the potential for unintended environmental damage alongside other risks.
- Life cycle assessment (LCA) – explore the opportunities for more environmentally benign inputs and outputs in product development.
- Environmental impact assessment – ensure that impacts of development are within acceptable levels and mitigated where necessary.

In the long term, precaution becomes a fundamental strategic issue where taking action involves preventing pollution from the outset. For business, this may involve investment in *clean technology* that avoids environmental damage at source. For external stakeholders, actions may be directed through *ethical investment* or *lending criteria* which favour a precautionary approach.

Case study

Aluminium Bahrain B S C (Alba)

For the full company submission go to: www.unglobalcompact.org/un/gc/unweb/nsf/contant/alubah.htm

A series of waste minimization and recycling initiatives have improved the recovery of waste and reduced the volume of hazardous material being sent for disposal following the aluminium smelting process. Alba has used the systematic implementation of a certified environmental management system (ISO 14001) to address the environmental performance of the company's operations. This work was recognized by an International Millennium Business Award for Environmental Achievement presented by the United Nations Environment Programme in conjunction with the International Chamber of Commerce (ICC) in 2000.

By addressing its environmental impacts in a co-ordinated manner, the company has been able to identify and focus more specifically on improvement projects that seek to avoid or reduce waste. Adopting this precautionary approach has led Alba to look for alternatives for the disposal of hazardous waste and, where necessary, to provide the safest possible conditions for disposal. For example, the company identified that excess 'ramming paste' which is used to re-line the electrolytic pots of the smelter could in fact be reused in another part of the process rather than being disposed of as special waste. In addition, the reuse of refractory bricks, which would previously have been treated as waste, has combined to create cost savings of $28,000.

This concerted effort to recycle materials has seen the volume of waste recycled rise from 0 cubic meters in 1999 to a projected figure of 7,077 cubic

▶

meters for 2001. The company reports that these high levels have been driven by a strong employee commitment to see environmental impacts reduced.

Fact file

■ Alba is one of the world's largest aluminium smelters, producing in excess of 500,000 tonnes per annum.

■ The company was founded in 1971 and employs 2,500 people.

■ UNEP was set up following the first UN Environment Conference in 1972 to provide leadership and encourage partnerships in caring for the environment.

■ ICC is an international business organization that represents business interests in international affairs.

Contacts

■ www.aluminiumbahrain.com

■ www.unep.org/

■ www.icc.org/

Case study

BASF

For the full company submission go to: www.unglobalcompact.org/un/gc/unweb/nsf/content/basf01.htm

BASF was one of the first companies to use the eco-efficiency model to guide its decision making. In relating its work to Principle 7, BASF considers eco-efficiency a mechanism for 'making future risks measurable and translating them into present management practices'.[5]

BASF Aktiengesellschaft (Global Compact icon)

One hundred and thirty-five years old, BASF is a German company producing chemicals, health and nutrition products, and oil and gas. With

[5] BASF's submission to the Global Compact, 2000/2001, June 22 2001, p. 5.

100,000 employees worldwide, BASF is one of the largest chemical companies in the world.[6] At BASF, the concept of *Verbund* or integration is a deeply rooted tradition. The vision of Friedrich Engelhorn, BASF's founder, was to integrate production so that any leftover material from one factory could be used as raw material in another factory. In a sense, the concept of *Verbund* can be viewed as a precursor to life-cycle analysis.

BASF has developed a Sustainability Council at board level to try to integrate sustainable development throughout the company. This group develops a vision and strategy for sustainable development and decides how to implement these policies throughout BASF. The company has also launched Values and Principles, a Compliance Program, and sustainability reporting. It has directed that each of its groups establish its own code of conduct based on an amalgam of local law and BASF Values and Principles.

BASF eco-efficiency analysis has several stages:

1 Assess environmental impact of a product or process by considering factors such as raw material, energy consumption, air and water emissions, disposal methods, potential toxity and future risks.

2 Compile economic data by calculating all costs involved in producing and using a product.

3 Compare the environmental and economic impacts by plotting them on a graph – see Figure 6.1.

The environmental impacts are viewed against costs to provide an ecological footprint of the product. For BASF, these types of eco-efficiency calculations are essential for sustainable development. 'The result of a BASF eco-efficiency analysis can guide long-term strategic decisions, since it helps to detect and exploit potential ecological and economic improvements and allows us to react carefully to today's and tomorrow's environmental challenges.'[7] The eco-efficiency model is a simplification of a

▶

---

[6] See press release 'BASF takes part in the UN's Global Compact Initiative', www.basf.de/en/corporate/environment/uno

[7] BASF's submission to the Global Compact, *op cit.*, p. 4.

FIGURE 6.1 ■ Comparing environmental and economic impacts

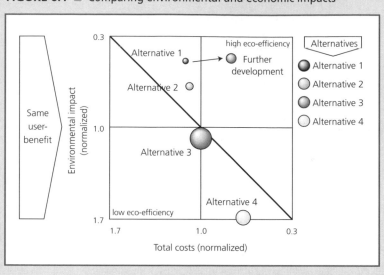

complex system that allows managers to view one product against others, based on their ecological and economic impact. Thus far, BASF has used the eco-efficiency model on 120 products.

Breakthrough icon

'But eco-efficiency is not limited to our own business: we also include our suppliers and customers in our analysis.' BASF's submission to the Global Compact provides an excellent example of the inter-connectivity between the three environmental principles, a continuum:

> Firstly, the willingness of business to support a precautionary approach to environmental protection . . . usually faces the difficult task of making future risks measurable and, just as importantly, of translating them into present management policies. A well-applied eco-efficiency scheme is able to tackle both problems, since future environmental risks are taken into account as an equal factor along with present environmental and economic determinants. Furthermore, the BASF eco-efficiency analysis provides clear results as a crucial precondition for guiding management decisions.

Secondly, as soon as the requirement of eco-efficient production is introduced into the relationship with suppliers, it serves as a tool to promote greater environmental responsibility, as stated in the Compact's eighth principle.

Thirdly, spreading the idea of eco-efficiency so as to minimize the environmental impact of products and production processes will finally lead to the development and diffusion of environmentally friendly technologies, as embodied in the last of the Compact's nine principles.[8]

BASF is working to share this change practice. The company has already developed a manual on eco-efficiency and organized a symposium on the topic for industry and NGOs.

BASF is aware of the power of change practice as it moves through the supply chain:

We believe that much of the concept of best practices builds on the multiplying effect of transnational companies in global value chains. Transnational companies reach a whole host of suppliers and customers with their best practices. Each member of the Global Compact owns specific best practices that have the potential to set benchmarks and standards in its sector for a range of suppliers in international production processes. Therefore, the members of the Global Compact Alliance should work with their suppliers towards economic, ecological and social 'value creation.'[9]

What does the future of eco-efficiency hold? BASF is seeking to integrate social issues into its eco-efficiency model.

---

[8] *Ibid.*, p. 5.
[9] *Ibid.*, p. 1.

Environment: Principle Eight

Businesses should undertake initiatives to promote greater environmental responsibility.

Understanding the principle

The imperative for business to conduct its activities in a more environmentally responsible manner has grown significantly since the 1990s. Principle Eight of the Global Compact draws on Agenda 21 to provide an outline of what environmental responsibility means for business: '[the] responsible and ethical management of products and processes from the point of view of health, safety and environmental aspects. Towards this end, business and industry should increase self-regulation, guided by appropriate codes, charters and initiatives integrated into all elements of business planning and decision making, and fostering openness and dialogue with employees and the public.'

Taking action

Business gains its legitimacy through meeting the needs of society and increasingly society is expressing a clear need for more environmentally and socially sustainable practice. In working towards environmental responsibility, business may seek to:

- develop an environmental policy appropriate to the organization;
- identify key environmental aspects – areas where the business can interact with the environment;
- formalize commitment through a management system approach.

Suggested steps towards environmental responsibility

- Establish clear environmental performance objectives that aim to take the organization beyond compliance in the long term.
- Develop and implement industry-wide codes that define acceptable behaviour and performance for (industry) association members.

■ Extend responsibility for the environmental aspects of organizational activity down the supply chain and up the product chain.

■ Monitor progress in performance and report the results of work undertaken. Use universal reporting criteria and indicators to assist with year-on-year comparisons.

■ Share experiences with other companies in the industry sector and participate in the establishment of industry codes that support the progress of other companies.

■ Build partnerships with stakeholders that support and sustain innovative projects, encourage transparency and reduce the grounds for conflict.

Case study

BP

For the full company submission go to: www.unglobalcompact.org/un/gc/unweb/nsf/content/bp.htm

The development and implementation of an in-house emissions trading scheme is assisting BP to reduce greenhouse gas (GHG) emissions to a target of 10 per cent below 1990 levels by 2010. BP's GHG emissions trading system is the first of its kind anywhere in the world. The scheme was launched in January 2000 following a year of pilot activity that involved working with the US-based NGO, Environmental Defense. Addressing an environmental issue to which contributions can be made at a global level allows 160 individual business units operating in 100 countries to take part.

Working on the basis of a group cap, each unit is allocated an allowance and can participate in the trading systems as a distinct entity. Managers are responsible for meeting their allocation and performance is measured alongside financial indicators. Emissions trading supports new innovation in abatement, without prescribing 'how' emissions are reduced. Trading also encourages business units to search for

▶

cost-effective solutions and ensures that the financial implications of GHG investments are known.

The company reports that the system has raised awareness of climate change through the engagement of a wider audience. Involving stakeholders in the developmental stages was additionally identified as a key part of the learning process.

In autumn 1998, BP's CEO Sir John Browne announced that BP would lower its GHG emissions to 10 per cent below 1990 levels by 2010.[10] This represents a rate of twice that of the target agreed upon by developed countries at Kyoto.

Trading greenhouse gases is the most cost-effective mechanism for reducing GHGs. BP sets the policy and targets at a global level but is allowing business units (BUs) to define the methods for the reductions. This 'structured flexibility' is designed to foster innovative practices. BP has 160 BUs and each is given an allowance of emissions and trades with other BUs. Each allowance translates into one metric ton of CO_2. The trades take place on the BP intranet and are registered and traded through a central broker. For example: a BU involved in deep water offshore drilling will have a higher emissions rate due to increased production. The BU decides to purchase CO_2 allowances. A BU focused on chemicals has been able to reduce emissions more quickly than expected by shutting down a furnace. Allowances are freed up and traded between the two business units.

What makes the initiative successful? A credible measurement system is paramount, as is verification. Measurement occurs at the BU level, whereas verification is conducted by KPMG, Det Norske Veritas and ICF Consulting. Incentives for co-operation are also a key part of the programme. Every business unit leader has a contract in which the GHG

---

[10] In 1999, BP merged with Amoco and Burmah Castrol. The goal set by John Browne now applies to the entire group.

allocations are stipulated. Progress is reported in the financial performance indicators for the company.

BP has also presented an environmental vision in which GHG trading is but one segment. To combat global warming, BP is taking the following actions:

1   Control greenhouse gases.
2   Conserve energy.
3   Introduce new technologies.
4   Promote flexible market instruments.
5   Participate in the policy processes.
6   Invest in research.

Lessons learned[11]

- Keep things simple.
- Engage key stakeholders at the formative stages.
- Data quality is the key to a successful trading system, particularly in the early years of a climate programme. Trading entities must understand their historical, current and future emissions.
- Understanding the cost of abatement on a project-by-project level is vital for entities to engage in emissions trading.
- Use pilot systems to maximize learning.
- Use 'structured flexibility' when you spot problems, make immediate changes to deal with serious current problems but save other changes for annual reviews. This avoids changing the rules frequently which can cause confusion.
- Link trading system compliance to managerial performance reporting.
- Establish a clear set of trading guidelines (or rulebook).

▶

---

[11] *Source:* BP's Greenhouse Gas Emissions Trading System Submission, July 2001, submission by BP to Global Compact.

Fact file

- BP is one of the world's leading energy companies.
- The company, which merged with Amoco in 1998, employs over 107,000 people.
- BP activities include oil, gas, exploration, refining, chemicals and solar energy.
- Environmental Defense is a non-profit organization dedicated to protecting the environmental rights of all people and future generations. Established in 1967, the organization has 300,000 members.

Contacts

- www.bp.com/
- www.bp.com/key_issues/environment/climate_change/index.asp
- www.edf.org/

Environment: Principle Nine

Businesses should encourage the development and diffusion of environmentally friendly technologies.

Understanding the principle

Encouraging the development and diffusion of environmentally friendly technology is a long-term challenge that will draw on both the management and research capabilities of organizations. For the purposes of engaging with the Global Compact, environmentally friendly technologies are considered to be those that are environmentally sound. Agenda 21 outlines environmentally sound technologies (ESTs) as those which '. . . protect the environment, are less polluting, use all resources in a more sustainable manner, recycle more of their wastes and products, and handle residual wastes in a more acceptable

▪ ▪ ▪ ▪ ▪ ▪ ▪ ▪ ▪ ▪ ▪ ▪

For the purposes of engaging with the Global Compact, environmentally friendly technologies are considered to be those that are environmentally sound

▪ ▪ ▪ ▪ ▪ ▪ ▪ ▪ ▪ ▪ ▪ ▪

manner than the technologies for which they were substitutes. [ESTs] are not just individual technologies but total systems which include know-how, procedures, goods and services, and equipment as well as organizational and managerial processes.'

Important here is an understanding that this is a broad definition that embraces end-of-pipe and monitoring techniques but that *explicitly encourages* more progressive pollution prevention and cleaner production technologies. The aspiration of this principle is, therefore, towards clean technology and cleaner production.

Taking action

▪ Engagement with this principle will depend to some extent on the size and nature of the business.

Suggested actions to promote the development and diffusion of ESTs

▪ Refocus research and development towards 'design for sustainability'.

▪ Employ life cycle assessment in the development of new technologies and products that take into account impacts in use as well as end-of-life aspects.

▪ Use Environmental Technology Assessment (EnTA) to ensure that decision-making processes related to technology assessment are sustainable.

▪ Examine investment criteria, source contractors that employ environmentally progressive techniques and develop tenders that stipulate minimum environmental criteria.

- Co-operate with industry partners to disseminate 'best available technology' (BAT) in other countries and to support the capacity of these countries to develop their own appropriate technologies.

In addition, many companies could benefit from the guidelines and suggested actions contained in the International Declaration on Cleaner Production. This is a voluntary initiative, developed by UNEP in consultation with stakeholders and launched in 1998, that encourages and provides support for companies engaging with cleaner production.

Case study

BMW

For the full company submission go to: www.unglobalcompact.org/un/gc/unweb/nsf/content/bmw.htm

A long-term commitment to developing more sustainable transportation has, through the 'CleanEnergy Project', resulted in the first ever production car capable of running on hydrogen.

BMW has been investigating opportunities to reduce fossil fuel consumption in motor vehicles since the 1970s. The CleanEnergy Project has been supported by an understanding that the use of finite resources and the production of carbon dioxide emissions needs to be replaced by more sustainable forms of energy. The development of the hydrogen-powered car has been driven by BMW's goal of 'closing the loop' in order to produce zero carbon dioxide emissions. Working in partnership with research institutions, industry partners and government bodies in Germany has resulted in a car that has bivalent internal combustion – able to run on hydrogen or petrol fuel.

The company recognizes that the successful development of the technology is only the first phase. There are still obstacles in terms of cost and the limitations of an infrastructure that is currently geared towards fossil fuels. However, in moves to diffuse this knowledge and inform a wider audience of the opportunities brought by hydrogen-powered vehicles, BMW conducted a CleanEnergy World Tour in 2001. This tour sought to inform international opinion leaders on the subject of hydrogen power and to promote the reality of a sustained energy supply concept.

Fact file

■ BMW is one of the world's leading automobile manufacturers and is engaged in the production, assembly, sales and distribution of cars and motorcycles.

■ The company employs over 93,000 people worldwide.

■ In 2000 BMW was chosen as the leader in sustained business operations by the Dow Jones Sustainability Group Index for the second year running.

Contacts

■ www.bmw.com; www.bmwgroup.com

■ www.bmwbw.de (Transport Energy Strategy report including hydrogen technology, sponsored by BMW)

Case study

Steelcase Inc

With 16,400 employees, Steelcase ranks 513 in the Fortune 1000.[12] The company produces a wide range of products, from filing cabinets to chairs, under the following brands: Avenir, Context, Sensor and Vecta. Design-Tex is one of the largest US fabric companies, manufacturing wall coverings and curtains for the office market. The fabrics are made without dyes and chemicals, helping to safeguard the health of workers who manufacture the fabric. The chemists who developed the new fabric have eliminated 7,962 of the 8,000 chemicals normally used to produce fabrics. There are

▶

12 www.business2.com/search?qt=Steelcase&fortune=on&x=29&y=8

38 chemicals with positive attributes involved in the production of fabric which are used to manufacture the sustainable fabric. According to its founder, William McDonough, the mill producing the sustainable fabrics uses 'no carcinogens, no mutagens, no endocrine disrupters, no heavy metals, no mercury or cadmium'.[13]

Consider the 'cradle' of this life cycle. The wool comes from free-range sheep that are treated in a humane manner. The ramie is grown without pesticides. Waste materials are recycled to form a cover for strawberry plants, replacing plastic.

Steelcase hired its first environmental engineer in 1969. Below is a list of Steelcase's eight principles. Principles 5, 6 and 8 relate to the Global Compact.

1   Business decisions are always made considering the environment.
2   All company operations are conducted so as to protect the environment and the health of our employees, neighbours and customers.
3   Environmental considerations are a priority in our product development process.
4   Environmental and employee health protection will be integrated at all levels of business decision making.
5   Environmental education and training is a corporate responsibility ensuring employee ownership and stewardship.
6   We will help to establish leading-edge standards for the healthy office environment.
7   All environmental and health laws and regulations will be complied with or exceeded.
8   We will work co-operatively with all environmental groups, our suppliers, dealers, customers and government agencies.

Steelcase also markets the Protégé chair – 'the chair that will never reach a landfill'. The chair is made of single materials, which facilitates recycling. The cushions use only water-blown foam and water-based mold releases

---

[13] Quoted by Romi Gottfried, Steelcase, Nomination for 2001 Corporate Conscience Award, Council on Economic Priorities, memorandum for judges, p. 1.

and adhesives. The paint uses a powder coat process to avoid volatile emissions. Even the shipping is taken into account so as to avoid cartons and packaging waste. Each Protégé chair is almost 100 per cent recyclable. One Steelcase subsidiary, Revest, offers to buy back furniture and remanufactures it so that it can be resold or recycled. Steelcase has eliminated all ozone-depleting substances and has cut VOC emissions by 15 per cent in 15 years – it has a goal of reducing VOC[14] emissions to zero.

The implications of environmentally friendly fabric are immense and demonstrate a potential paradigm shift. According to the company's founder: 'If the product is completely benign, there's nothing to regulate.'[15]

Steelcase is diffusing environmentally friendly practices throughout its sphere of influence, from wood suppliers (which must demonstrate that wood is sustainably harvested) to customers (who are recycling furniture and using the Internet to communicate with Steelcase, rather than using paper forms.) Companies like Procter & Gamble use the environment as a litmus test to select suppliers. Canon is working with suppliers to ensure that their procurement can be more environmentally friendly. Banks and insurers are also looking at environmental issues within their risk analysis. Even architectural firms are being called in to develop buildings which are more green. All of these layers of attention on the environment lead to many opportunities for training on environmental processes and technologies.

John Elkington, Chair of The Environment Foundation and co-founder of SustainAbility, refers to the term 'value web' in describing a company's nexus of suppliers, contractors and customers. 'Most companies have a surprisingly poor understanding of what is happening on other parts of their value web . . . The speed of globalization often means that companies are moving well ahead of the ability of current governance systems to monitor and police. Companies will be expected to fill at least some of the gap.'[16]

[14] VOC emissions are halogenated solvent emissions.
[15] Quoted in Romi Gottfried, CEP Judges Packet, p. 2.
[16] Quoted in Novartis: *Innovation and Accountability, Health, Safety, and Environment Report 2000: Sustainability and the UN Global Compact*, p. 8.

> Sharing technology, processes and systems is a mechanism for reinforcing tenuous links within a global economy. When Steelcase stipulates the kind of environmental conditions and technologies that should be used, it is cementing its relationship with its suppliers. When Novartis, through its Foundation for Sustainable Development, shares know-how on sustainable development with developing countries, it is promoting development, but it is also promoting Novartis and building social capital. Given the recent tensions between the pharmaceutical industry and developing countries over HIV and AIDS drugs, this social capital is increasingly important to the company. Promoting environmentally friendly technologies can help to raise a company's image and boost its leverage. According to Dow Chemicals Vice-President for global environment, health and safety: 'When you reduce waste and emissions, a community is a lot more willing to issue permits for other operations down the road.'[17]

The Global Compact: learning, dialogue, partnership and outreach

Introduction

This section looks at the four processes of engagement with the Compact: learning, dialogue, partnership projects and outreach. For companies which choose to commit to the Global Compact, involvement in the Learning Forum is key. This is where companies can discuss and learn from shared experience how they might translate commitment and aspiration into concrete actions. The policy dialogues are convened around a topical issue and provide a platform for the exchange of views and substantive discourse. Partnership projects involve not only the individual changes that companies choose to make but cru-

---

[17] Deutsch, Claudia (2001) 'Green – and lucrative, too, environmental projects are yielding unexpected gains,' *International Herald Tribune*, September 10, p. 9.

■ ■ ■ ■ ■ ■ ■ ■ ■ ■ ■ ■

The Learning Network helps participants share information, derive new insights and develop innovative approaches on the basis of various company experiences

■ ■ ■ ■ ■ ■ ■ ■ ■ ■ ■ ■

cially the opportunity to engage in joint working with other organizations aiming for common goals. Outreach concerns the role of the UN and partnering organizations in extending the scope and uptake of the nine principles worldwide.

This section also provides an outline of how the Global Compact relates to existing initiatives in the area of corporate citizenship. Key here is an understanding that the raft of standards and codes are continuing to evolve in line with the developing corporate citizenship agenda.

The work of the Global Compact is being promoted and disseminated through four components: learning, dialogue, partnership projects, and outreach. While each element has individual goals and a specific role to play, all four areas are linked by their use of open conversation and a 'network form' of organization.

1 Learning

The Learning Network helps participants share information, derive new insights and develop innovative approaches on the basis of various company experiences. It is a growing information bank, providing examples of company work implementing the nine principles of the Global Compact. As such, the Forum serves as a resource, highlighting actions that have worked, as well as those that have been less successful. In the long term this systematic gathering of data will provide the raw material for a deeper understanding of how company policy, structure and practice are evolving with regard to the issues embraced by corporate citizenship.

When engaging with the Network companies are asked to share, on an annual basis, an example of a concrete action or set of actions that they have undertaken to address at least one or more of the nine principles within their corporate sphere. Selected examples will, on a voluntary basis, be developed further as in-depth case studies, providing rigorous analysis and discussion of the actions taken. In addition, companies are invited to participate in an annual Learning Forum Meeting. This is an opportunity for participants to discuss their experiences of engagement and develop the work of the Forum for the future. The work of the Forum is assisted by leading academics who provide both analysis and methodological input.

2 Dialogue

The ongoing development of the Global Compact revolves around the ability of different participants to meet, debate and discuss key issues. Policy Dialogues address contemporary challenges by drawing participants from across various sectors to discuss the issues. It seeks to encourage networks and to build trust and collaboration between different parties. In 2001 the Policy Dialogue explored 'the role of the private sector in zones of conflict' and considered the opportunities for both business and civil society groups to mitigate conflict. Participants from businesses, NGOs, unions and the UN met to debate how respect for human rights and the rule of law could assist in building more constructive and stable relationships.

The deliberations included an exploration of useful methodologies, for example, multi-stakeholder processes and risk assessment. A key outcome from this Policy Dialogue was a joint agreement on the need to develop pilot projects that could both deliver progress on the ground and be of relevance to more than one participant. The pilot projects currently being considered will provide real-life examples and will be a source of inspiration for other partnerships looking to combine peace and development goals. Eventually the lessons learned will be used to inform policy makers at different levels across the sectors.

3 Partnership projects

The Global Compact has drawn on the convening power of the UN to encourage a diverse range of governmental and non-governmental groups to meet and develop practical projects that address human rights, labour and environmental issues. In particular, the initiative is seeking to harness the energy, expertise and resources of the private sector to assist in achieving UN Millennium Summit goals.

The UN Millennium Summit goals to be achieved by 2015 are:[18]

- halve extreme poverty and hunger;
- halve the proportion of people without access to safe water;
- ensure universal primary education;
- reduce maternal, infant and child mortality;
- halt and begin to reverse the spread of HIV/AIDs;
- provide universal reproductive health services including voluntary family planning;
- reverse the loss of environmental resources.

Achieving these aims requires that organizations work at a practical level to translate the nine principles into action. Actions may be taken by individual companies or through cross-sector partnerships. Examples of projects being undertaken by countries and companies covering a range of areas are available on the Global Compact website and include the development of labour accords; the reduction of carbon dioxide emissions; the provision of health care; socially responsible investment portfolios and micro-credit.

---

[18] www.un.org/millennium/

4 Outreach

A key goal of the Global Compact is not only to spread an awareness of the nine principles to all corners of the globe but also to make these issues *relevant* everywhere. The UN has a unique global presence with agencies and offices situated around the world. The Global Compact Office is, therefore, engaged in the co-ordination of an outreach programme that draws on these resources and those of the initiative partners to deliver support and encourage uptake of the nine principles. Outreach efforts have geographical spread and also seek to recognize the challenges that are faced by different industry sectors and companies of varying sizes. Key partners in this process are business leaders, business associations and employer federations.

Outreach involves:

- workshops for business leaders, on a local and regional basis;
- meetings for small and medium-sized enterprises;
- linking projects with the work of UN agencies (ILO, UNEP, UNDP, OHCHR);
- engaging cities as well as companies.

The relationship of the Global Compact to other corporate citizenship work

The Global Compact is one of the most prominent initiatives to have emerged in the field of corporate citizenship. As a signature initiative of the Secretary-General Kofi Annan it carries an authority and scope that is difficult to match. The Global Compact has a number of facets that are unique:

- First, it derives from a global institution that has chosen to state clearly through policy and action a specific position on corporate social responsibility issues.
- Second, as it stems from a representative body, this initiative has the tacit support of member states.

- ▪ Third, the genesis of the Global Compact diverges from previous voluntary initiatives which have tended to emerge through alliances of like-minded NGOs or 'think-tanks' working in the area of corporate citizenship.

- ▪ Fourth, the Global Compact is one of the few initiatives that has *explicitly sought to integrate* the issues of human rights, labour standards and the environment.

These key issues combine to differentiate the Global Compact from other initiatives. However, there are aspects of the Global Compact which intersect with existing work on corporate citizenship. It is by examining these linkages that opportunities for synergy and convergence between the different initiatives will emerge.

The Global Compact is like many of the most prominent citizenship initiatives currently in circulation in that it is voluntary. There is no compulsion beyond self-enlightened interest, stakeholder or peer pressure to become involved and it does not demand a specific standard or regulated performance achievement. The Global Compact does not seek to provide the specific, detailed directions found in other citizenship initiatives. This relatively loose composition has resulted in some criticism that organizations will be able to participate, whilst effectively avoiding some of the key concerns expressed in the Global Compact principles. However, the Global Compact architects recognize that the freedom brought by a lack of prescription has both implied strengths and weaknesses. It is accepted that organizations will approach the issues from different directions and that learning and development of the initiative will occur as a result of ongoing experiences.

The Global Compact is, nevertheless, complementary to existing initiatives and by embracing human rights, labour and environmental issues it has the potential to act as an organizing framework for companies seeking to develop policy and strategy in this area. For example, the discussion here of how organizations may engage with the nine principles includes an aspiration for companies to move towards

■ ■ ■ ■ ■ ■ ■ ■ ■ ■ ■ ■

*The Global Compact does not seek to provide the specific,
detailed directions found in other citizenship initiatives*

■ ■ ■ ■ ■ ■ ■ ■ ■ ■ ■ ■

reporting their various activities and progress in key areas. Organizations can seek to use the interconnections afforded by the Global Compact to co-ordinate and link their reporting activity in relation to each principle. One approach to achieve more integrated reporting across various organizational activities is provided by the Global Reporting Initiative (GRI) (see 'Selected corporate citizenship initiatives').

There are a huge number of initiatives, charters, codes and principles active in the area of corporate citizenship. They may be company, trade association, multi-stakeholder or inter-governmental codes. They vary in their genesis, subject focus and emphasis, spanning areas of corporate strategy, management, measurement and accounting. The Global Compact supports the reality that many companies will be engaged in one or more of these initiatives and that this work is reciprocal to the aims of the Compact.

Selected corporate citizenship initiatives

- The Global Reporting Initiative promotes the international harmonization of reporting and provides guidelines for reporting in the area of environmental, social, and economic performance – www.globalreporting.org
- The Caux Round Table provides principles for ethical and responsible corporate behaviour – www.cauxroundtable.org
- The Natural Step uses four scientifically based system conditions that form a set of operating principles for organizations – www.naturalstep.org
- The Global Sullivan Principles encourage companies to support economic, social and political justice wherever they operate – www.sullivanprinciples.org/

> ■ The Fair Labor Association has developed a workplace code of conduct and
>   working principle, in particular for the clothing industry –
>   www.fairlabor.org
> ■ The International Chamber of Commerce Business Charter for Sustainable
>   Development. Sixteen principles on environmental responsibility, appropri-
>   ate for enterprises of all sizes – www.iccwbo.org

Engaging with the Global Compact also involves developing an awareness and working understanding of key conventions. Conventions on human rights and labour standards form the foundations of the Global Compact principles and have also been instrumental in the development of other initiatives referred to in this book.

A series of environmental Conventions, for example, on global warming (Kyoto), the transboundary movement of hazardous waste (Basel) and biological diversity (Montreal) are also intrinsically linked to the aims expressed by the environmental principles. Convention secretariats provide legal and technical advice and seek to build capacity around the aims of the conventions, through engagement with business, civil society and government. The Global Compact framework can act to facilitate this engagement.

Summary

This section has discussed the four means by which companies can engage with the Global Compact. Publicly advocating the Global Compact and committing to work towards the nine principles (through a letter to the Secretary-General) are the first stages. Involvement in the learning process is a core part of engaging with the Global Compact and offers the opportunity for companies to share experience, receive feedback and stimulate new approaches on the basis of collective knowledge. Companies may also choose to broaden the scope of their involvement through focused dialogue, organized by the UN around key topics, or by entering into new action-oriented partnerships with other organizations. To support this work the UN is undertaking an expansive outreach programme to take the aims of the Global Compact to business of all sizes, globally.

The prominence and authority of the UN's Global Compact differentiate this initiative from other voluntary corporate citizenship work. However, the Global Compact shares key aims and objectives with a number of established, credible initiatives (such as the GRI, which is supported by UNEP and in 2002 was adopted by the UN) and builds on the foundations of Conventions. Increasingly the challenge will be to look for, and build on, potential synergies with these existing and emerging instruments.

Useful information

Human rights

Principles One and Two

- The full text of the Universal Declaration of Human Rights may be found at www.unq.org/Overview/rights.htm
- Translations of the UDHR are also available through the OHCHR (see below) website at www.unhchr.ch/udhr/index.htm
- The Office of the United Nations High Commissioner on Human Rights provides a summary of the key issues for businesses seeking to develop an understanding of human rights issues – www.unhchr.ch/business.htm
- The Report of the World Commission on Dams addresses key human development rights for companies – www.dams.org/
- The United States and United Kingdom governments have in association with extractive and energy companies, and non-government organizations with an interest in human rights,

developed voluntary principles on security and human rights – www.state.gov/www/global/human_rights/001220_fsdrl_ principles.html

▪ The Amnesty International Business Group encourages businesses to be aware of human rights issues and to use their influence positively – www.amnesty.org.uk/business

▪ Amnesty International and the Prince of Wales Business Leaders Forum have produced 'Human Rights: Is it any of your business?' – available from the Business and Human Rights Information Centre at www.business-human rights.org

▪ Human Rights Watch promotes the protection of human rights worldwide, monitors and reports on corporate activity – hrw.org/advocacy/corporations/index.htm

▪ The Lawyers Committee for Human Rights works to protect and promote fundamental human rights – www.lchr.org/

▪ Transparency International (TI) is an international movement devoted exclusively to the curbing of corruption – www.transparancy.de/

▪ The Danish Centre for Human Rights Business Project conducts research on key human rights questions and publishes brochures of findings and guidelines – www.humanrights.dk/humanrightsbusiness/pages/frontpage.html

▪ Amnesty International has published Human Rights Guidelines for Companies – www.amnesty.org/ailib/aipub/1998/ACT/A7000198.htm

▪ Examples of company initiatives to combat discrimination and foster diversity in the workplace and wider community may be found in 'Discrimination is Everybody's Business', a report initiated by the Volvo Car Corporation and involving the participation of six companies from five continents. It was carried out in co-ordination with the ILO, OHCHR and the

Global Compact Secretariat and facilitated by RespectEurope. The report is available via the Global Compact website, www.unglobalcompact.org

Labour

Principles Three, Four, Five and Six

- The International Labour Organisation provides extensive information on all aspects of labour law, as well as regional and global instruments. A list of ILO databases may be accessed at www.ilo.org/public/english/support/lib/ dblist.htm

- The ILOLEX is a comprehensive trilingual database on international labour standards and includes numerous related documents – www.ilolex.ilo.ch:1567/english/index.htm

- The NATLEX database is a continuously updated reference to over 55,000 national labour laws and is also available in three languages – www.natlex.ilo.org/

- The Business and Social Initiatives Database (BASI) 'includes comprehensive information on private sector initiatives which address labour and social conditions in the workplace and in the community where enterprises operate' – www.oracle02.ilo.org/dyn/basi/vpisearch.first

- The International Confederation of Free Trade Unions is a network of 221 affiliated organizations, in 148 countries, representing a membership of 156 million. This confederation of national trade union centres produces publications and annual surveys – www.icftu.org/

- The International Organisation of Employers is the only organization at an international level that represents the interests of business in the labour and social policy fields. It represents 132 national employers in 129 countries around the world – www.ioe-emp.org/

- Anti-Slavery International produces material on forced, bonded and child labour that includes useful resources for business – www.antislavery.org/

- The International Institute for Labour Studies is an autonomous facility of the ILO. Established in 1960 it is a centre for advanced study in the social and labour fields and uses research networks, policy forums, education activities and publications to promote information exchange – www.ilo.org/public/english/bureau/inst/

- The Ethical Trading Initiative was launched in the UK in 1998 as a new collaboration between industry, non-government organizations, trade unions and government. The initiative uses practical, partnership projects as a means for companies to learn and demonstrate engagement – www. ethicaltrade.org/

- SA 8000 is a global standard designed to make workplaces socially responsible. It draws on ILO conventions and was developed by business, non-government organizations and trade unions – www.cepaa.org/

- The International Programme on the Elimination of Child Labour (IPEC) defines the worst forms of all child labour and asks all governments to ban them – www.ilo/public/english/standards/ipec

Environment

Principles Seven, Eight and Nine

- The United Nations Environment Programme provides one entry point to the UN's work on the environment – www.unep.org/

- UNEP's Division of Technology Industry and Economics (DTIE) develops voluntary initiatives and partnerships with business leaders and a range of organizations focused on environmental protections, efficient resources use and innovation – www.uneptie.org/

■ A full text version of Agenda 21 may be viewed at www.unep.org/Documents/Default.asp?DocumentID:52

■ The Principles of the Rio Declaration are available at www.unep.org/Documents/Default.asp?DocumentID78& ArticleID=1163

■ The World Business Council for Sustainable Development (WBCSD) is an international business network developing links between business, government and non-government organizations on sustainable development issues – www.wbcsd.ch/

■ Business for Social Responsibility is an international business network, embracing companies of all sizes, working across a broad range of issues that include environmentally sustainable development – www.bsr.org/

■ The World Resources Institute (WRI) is a think-tank that also promotes practical ways to protect the earth – www.wri.org/

■ The World Conservation Union (IUCN) is an international body founded in 1948 to influence, encourage and assist societies in the goal of nature conservation – www.iucn.org/

■ The Coalition for Environmentally Responsible Economies is a non-profit membership organization of investors and various interest groups that developed ten principles of environmentally responsible behaviour – www.ceres.org/

■ The Greening of Industry is an international network of academic research and policy analysis focused on the relationship between industry, society and the environment – www.greeningofindustry.org/

■ UNEP's Production and Consumption Unit co-ordinates APELL – Awareness and Preparedness for Emergencies at a

Local Level. This is a modular, flexible, methodological tool for preventing accidents and failing this managing their impacts – www.uneptie.org/pc//apell/

■ UNEP's work on chemicals includes the Persistent Organic Pollutants (POPs) programme, providing information on POPs, their alternatives and alternative approaches – www.chem.unep.ch.pops/

■ UNEP has developed information and training for environmental impact assessment that include guidelines for developing countries – www.ea.gov.au/assessment/eianet/index.html

■ The LifeCycle Initiative is a joint programme developed by UNEP and the Society of Environmental Toxicology and Chemistry (SETAC) to promote best practice in life-cycle assessment – www.uneptie.org/pc//sustain/lca/lca.htm

■ The ISO 14000 series provides management tools for organizations that are aiming to demonstrate an environmentally responsible approach. For information visit the ISO 14000 Information Centre – www.iso14000.com/

■ The AA 1000 integrated management system encourages organizations to focus on the processes of managing change and to engage with stakeholders – www.accountability.org.uk/

■ The Global Reporting Initiative is a multi-stakeholder initiative that develops, promotes and disseminates a framework for integrating reporting across social, environmental and economic dimensions – www.globalreporting.org

■ The UNEP Production and Consumption Branch provides extensive information on cleaner production concepts and actions for all businesses – www.uneptie.org/pc/cp/home.htm

- Details of the International Declaration on Cleaner Production, including the 'Implementation Guidelines for Business' (downloadable as a PDF file), are available from the Production and Consumption Branch of the Division of Technology, Industry and Economics, UNEP – www.uneptie.org/pc/cp/home.htm

- Approaches to Environmental Technology Assessment are available through the International Environmental Technology Centre at UNEP – www.unep.or.jp/ietc/supportingtools/enta/index.asp

- UNEP's Division of Environmental Conventions (DEC) provides support, information and awareness raising on environmental conventions. The conventions may be accessed at www.unep.ch/conventions/

CHAPTER 7

Learning from company engagement with the Global Compact

Introduction

This chapter is based on the first phase of the Global Compact Learning Forum from July 2000 to October 2001. It draws on the theory behind the Global Compact and company engagement in the Global Compact Learning Forum, as evidenced by their submissions to the Global Compact website – www.unglobalcompact.org

The Compact is evolving, the participants are learning, and there are many beneficial spin-offs from a process that has been set in motion by this attempt to directly marry market activity and international development. As the number and scope of global corporate citizenship initiatives increases it is important to take time out to consider how these new social partnerships between private, public and civil sectors are evolving. That is the aim of this chapter, which presents the findings from phase one of the Global Compact. These findings have been presented at a number of public forums and the ensuing energetic discussion has led to a refinement of the data and lengthy debate on a number of distinct topics. It may not have been the intention of the architects of the Global Compact to focus attention on some of these topics but the learning process is possible only if all parties stand back from their entrenched positions. Here are the main topics that have arisen in open discussion:

- the varied nature of company engagement represented by quality, self-analysis, sector and topic;
- the nature of learning on the part of companies *and* the UN;
- the reaction of the UN to the findings of this research;
- the lessons drawn from the data presented by the companies in their submissions.

■ ■ ■ ■ ■ ■ ■ ■ ■ ■ ■ ■

*As the number and scope of global corporate
citizenship initiatives increases it is important
to take time out to consider how these new social partnerships
between private, public and civil sectors are evolving*

■ ■ ■ ■ ■ ■ ■ ■ ■ ■ ■ ■

It is crucial that the information presented here is taken as a starting point for discussion of one central dilemma. The UN Secretary-General in Davos, Switzerland presented this dilemma on January 31 1999. It is perhaps the leitmotif for the 21st century:

> What we need is a compact on a global scale, to underpin the
> new global economy . . . I am asking corporate leaders to
> embrace, support and enact a set of core values in the areas of
> human rights, labour standards and environmental practices.

Phase one of the Global Compact was one attempt to engage with business on these principles based on a new approach to change based on shared learning.

The Global Compact: a different approach to change

According to John Ruggie, one of the architects of the UN Global Compact, the Compact has:

> explicitly adopted a learning approach to inducing corporate
> change, as opposed to a regulatory approach; and it comprises
> a network form of organization, as opposed to the traditional
> hierarchic/bureaucratic form.[1]

It is worth spelling out this approach, which, like the original call to the business community, had received little substantive thinking

---

[1] Ruggie, John Gerard (2002) *The Theory and Practice of Learning Networks: Corporate Social Responsibility and the Global Compact*, journal of Corporate Citizenship, issue 5, Spring 2002, Sheffield: Greenleaf Publishing

before being articulated by Ruggie and others in the UN Global Compact office. First, it says that we must learn as we proceed. In effect it is saying: 'We don't know what is going to happen; we have high expectations, and we are praying that business engages fully.' Second, it sees a form of organizational learning that breaks metaphysical boundaries between business and non-business communities in order that open inquiry takes place. In doing so it suggests that an outdated mode of learning ('the hierarchic/bureaucratic form') has not taught us enough or is not adequate in a new age of globality where the challenges have new characteristics.

This has been as much of a challenge to the non-business community as to the business community. While management literature may abound with references to network organizations, horizontal organizational forms and flat management structures, in reality there still seem to be hierarchical forms of management for information and public relations.

As we have seen, supporting companies were asked to present one submission a year which indicated their implementation of one or more of the nine principles of the Compact. This chapter is an analysis of the first 33 such company submissions to arrive, prior to the first Global Compact Learning Forum conference in Denham, England in October 2001. There were several double submissions and the number of participating companies after 15 months was 30 from a possible 43 which had attended the opening session in New York on July 26 1999.

Each of the submitting companies received a written commentary from a team at Warwick Business School led by Malcolm McIntosh[2] and Ruth Thomas, which endeavoured to engage in a dialogue with each company on their submission. The intention of these commentaries was to stretch the information provided, to see clarification and to aid interpretation of the original submission. The companies were

---

2 Malcolm McIntosh is now at the University of Bath and may be contacted at malcolm.mcintosh@btinternet.com

■ ■ ■ ■ ■ ■ ■ ■ ■ ■ ■ ■ ■

The Global Compact has also proved useful globally as a convening platform, bringing together business, government and civil society organizations in regional meetings

■ ■ ■ ■ ■ ■ ■ ■ ■ ■ ■ ■ ■

asked to resubmit, having taken into account the commentaries. A few did so and some significant changes were made to their submissions. In January 2002 all the commentaries, which by that time numbered 43 from 41 companies, were posted on the unglobalcompact website with a caveat that the UN took no responsibility for the contents. In November 2001 all companies received written commentaries on their submissions to that date.

The aim of the analytical research exercise, reported here, was that companies would engage in the learning process and reassess their submissions. In reality most companies did not resubmit their reports in the light of the commentaries provided for them by the expert team. The revised and the original company submissions can be found at www.unglobalcompact.org under 'phase one', 'case studies'.

It should be mentioned that the Global Compact has also proved useful globally as a convening platform, bringing together business, government and civil society organizations in regional meetings. Many of these meetings, particularly in Brazil and Scandinavia, have encouraged companies to make submissions to the learning network such that by April 2002 many hundreds of companies had indicated their desire to make a submission to the UN.

Analysis of company submissions to the UN Global Compact (2000–2001)

The two most important findings arising from an analysis of the company submissions are:

1 There is significant information about outcomes (what had been achieved) but much less about the processes the companies went through to achieve these outcomes. There is an urgent need to study these processes and to share these stories with other companies.

2 There is a need for further research, particularly in-depth, long-term studies of processes. These would enable researchers to assemble a comparable data set which would describe the rich nuances of organizational change and learning.

Other key issues that emerged across the submissions were:

3 It was unclear in many cases whether organizations were aiming to achieve specific standards (such as ISO) rather than addressing the nine principles.

4 It was evident that many organizations faced difficulties in assessing the priority of corporate social responsibility issues in relation to their wider portfolio of activities.

5 Lessons of operating successfully in networks need to be assimilated and learned in these sample organizations. There is a great deal of research knowledge about networks which appears not to have been utilized in the present sample.

Other issues that arise from a reading of the submissions include:

6 different approaches to dealing with social and environmental issues;

7 a lack of clarity on the definitional issues;

8 convergence between different corporate citizenship initiatives;

9 the relationship between new initiatives, such as the Global Compact, and local, regional and national law;

10 creating local context for global initiatives.

There are also some problems that arise from the submissions:

11 some issues are ignored by the Global Eight;

12 there is a bias in favour of large companies;

13 the development impact is not addressed;

14 there is no analysis of compensating the losers from these new initiatives;

15 corruption is not mentioned as an issue.

Patterns and themes within and across all the cases

It is clear from the submissions that there is a concerted effort on the part of these organizations to engage in corporate social responsibility generally and to address the Global Compact's principles more specifically. However, in virtually all the submissions, there was a need for more detailed and richer information. One common theme emerging from the cases is that CSR is perceived as being closely linked to the way businesses are run in general and that companies remain highly suspicious about publicly and widely revealing how they enact CSR. As in any other form of business research, the question of business confidentiality is raised. On the more positive side, if companies are seeing CSR as integrated with their main business activities, this points to a substantial degree of integration between CSR and the perceived everyday 'business of business'.

Given the willingness to write such cases, however, one can deduce that there are great expectations around the UN Global Compact as a means to improve commercial relations, whether within the local region or at a more worldwide level. Since the UN principles are broad and far ranging, it is all the more convincing where companies are interested for 'their own sake' to address what then could be broadly labelled corporate social responsibility. The data indicates that a fundamental criterion of engaging in CSR, even at the most general levels, is predicated upon firm managerial belief and commitment. It is also worth noting that case studies alone will be unlikely fully to convince any single member of the companies participating in the UN Global Compact to implement the nine principles. To do this requires the answers to specific questions and to the broader issues of organizational design, learning and strategic change. But the cases do reveal that they are a 'good' means of building stories around what it takes to adopt mechanisms sustaining the nine principles. It is also worth noting that in none of the cases is there any evidence of organizations being critical of the nine principles.

Across-case factors and general patterns/themes

As noted above, the submissions could not provide all the data to answer all the above questions and further data collection will be needed to build richness and depth. However, some important patterns have emerged across the cases which resonate with the wider body of organization theory. In summary these patterns are:

- organizational design
- understanding processes as well as outcomes
- learning and communicating.

Organizational design

A common feature of nearly all the cases is the emphasis on working through partnerships with other organizations and agencies. Nothing, it seems, can be achieved by single organizations working alone. They have to ally themselves with others.

This resonates perfectly with changes we can observe more generally in organizations worldwide. CSR would seem to be following similar lines to the general trend towards working in networks rather than hierarchies and favouring alliances over organizations working alone. Many

■ ■ ■ ■ ■ ■ ■ ■ ■ ■ ■ ■ ■

Studies have revealed that there are broadly similar demands placed on organizations of all types when they operate in networks

■ ■ ■ ■ ■ ■ ■ ■ ■ ■ ■ ■ ■

terms have been used to describe these forms of inter-organizational working, for example 'networks',[3] 'postmodern',[4] 'federal'[5] and 'cellular'.[6] In this analysis we will use the term 'networks' for convenience, recognizing that it can cover a wide range of inter-organizational forms.

The basic premise of this radical shift in organizational design is that firms such as DuPont (one of the current submissions), General Motors and other organizations of the late 1920s had been advised that the multi-divisional from (M form) of design was the best way to achieve both efficiency and effectiveness, especially when undertaking strategic growth by expanding internationally.[7] Until the 1990s this vertical, hierarchical and firm-centric view prevailed. The advent of information technology, increased globalization, greater awareness of social values and ethics rendered this form of organization largely obsolete (that is not to say that many do not persist in retaining the M form – they do, in all countries of the world) and triggered the search for organizational designs which emphasized flexibility, knowledge

[3] Castells, M. (1996) *The Rise of the Network Society*, Oxford: Blackwell.

[4] Volberda, H. (1998) *Building the Flexible Firm*, Oxford: OUP.

[5] Handy, C. (1992) 'Balancing corporate power: a new federalist paper', *Harvard Business Review*, November–December, 59–72.

[6] Miles, R., Snow, C., Mathews, J. and Coleman, H. (1997) 'Organizing in the Knowledge Age: anticipating the cellular form,' *Academy of Management Executive*, 11, 4, 7–20.

[7] Chandler, A. (1963) *Strategy and Structure*, Cambridge, Mass.: MIT Press.

creation and collaboration. Such a design is the network form (N form) of organization and we can see strong evidence of this being put into practice in the cases described here.

However, managing in networks places different demands on organizations. Studies have revealed that there are broadly similar demands placed on organizations of all types when they operate in networks.[8] The main demand is to ensure that processes as well as structures change and inter-relate. Old, contingency perspectives on organizational design (where one variable such as organizational size was associated with another variable such as organizational structure) have made way for configurations of variables where structures, processes and boundaries have to be simultaneously managed. It has been demonstrated beyond doubt that performance benefits accrue only to those organizations which co-align structures, processes and boundaries.[9] The main features of each are briefly listed below for reference.

- *Structures:* widespread delayering and decentralization to remove the expense of hierarchy and many layers of management. Decentralization of strategic decision making and a greater emphasis on small organizational units and project-based approaches to organizing.

- *Processes:* the requirement is now for intensive interaction both vertically and horizontally in organizations. The flow of information should include all organizations in the network (such as suppliers, customers and collaborators) and requires some investment in electronic data interchange (EDI).

- *Boundaries:* the emphasis is away from the organization as a fully self-contained unit and towards a view which asks: 'What

---

[8] Whittington, R., Pettigrew, A., Peck, S., Fenton, E. and Conyon, M. (1999) 'Change and complementarities in the new competitive landscape,' *Organization Science* 10, 5, 583–600.

[9] *Ibid.*

are the core competencies of this organization?' Having defined these, organizations can redraw their boundaries around these core competencies. Outsourcing and the abandonment of non-core activities are examples of this process.

The main point about the configurational approach is that organizations will succeed to the extent that they change, adapt or pay attention to structures, processes and boundaries simultaneously rather than piecemeal. The cases reported here demonstrate that such simultaneity is a challenge for many organizations. For example, DuPont (an original M form organization in the 1920s) appears to take the view of the organization and its environment as two separate factors, rather than viewing them as integrated. Like SM Microelectronics, there is also evidence of commitment to externally set standards (such as ISO and Health and Safety) rather than to the nine principles. For other organizations in the sample (e.g. Globo), networking with other organizations is well developed but its impact upon processes (such as informing future strategies) is rather less well developed.

Organizational processes

Broadly, processes describe the various ways in which outcomes are achieved. They include the 'hard' factors of measuring performance, setting targets and financial benefits as well as the 'softer' issues of developing people as a key resource. An analysis of processes also is to 'tell the story' of how initiatives or changes were initiated, sustained and finally 'locked' into the organization's infrastructure.

This story over time is something missing from the majority of the current cases in the sample. There is a wealth of information about outcomes (what was achieved) but very little about how such outcomes were achieved. Future research will need to concentrate upon the processes. Some cases (such as Globo) come close to providing some process data, but much more detail will be needed from other cases if advances are to be made in 'knowing how' organizations implement CSR and engage with the nine principles. We would advise close consultation of the research carried out recently on both organizational change and the successful implementation of strategic initiatives.[10]

The basic findings of these investigations are as follows. Change is unlikely to happen unless it is actively locked into place in the organization. This means that, whatever the initiative, it becomes a natural way of conducting business. A great deal of effort and time may have been spent on getting changes started and keeping them alive in the organization, but successes come from ensuring that they are locked into place in the organization. Paradoxically, this means that what began as an innovative and completely new initiative becomes the everyday operation of today's actions. From the perspective of the nine principles, the challenge is to render them 'everyday' activities in organizations rather than remaining innovations or novel ways of doing business.[11]

Success in implementation is closely linked to two factors. The first is achieving high levels of acceptability amongst all stakeholders that this is the right way to proceed. The second is to ensure that strategic initiatives (such as the nine principles) are clearly prioritized in the overall strategic portfolio of the organization. There needs to be a clear indication of exactly how important this initiative is in comparison to other strategic decisions.[12]

The majority of the cases in the sample reveal little evidence of these processes, preferring instead to concentrate on reporting outcomes. For example, fostering collaboration amongst stakeholders is reported only when outcomes have already been consolidated within the organization and when the hurdles of collaboration have been largely overcome. Outcomes are important, but they do not tell the whole story.

....

[10] Wilson, D. C. (2000) *A Strategy of Change* (reprinted) London: International Thomson; Hickson, D. J., Miller, S. and Wilson, D. C. (2001/2) 'Planned or pushed: the implementation of strategy,' *Journal of Management Studies* (forthcoming).

[11] Wilson, D. C., *ibid.*

[12] Hickson *et al.*, *ibid.*

■ ■ ■ ■ ■ ■ ■ ■ ■ ■ ■ ■

From the perspective of the nine principles, the challenge is to render them 'everyday' activities in organizations rather than remaining innovations or novel ways of doing business

■ ■ ■ ■ ■ ■ ■ ■ ■ ■ ■ ■

Finally, it is a truism to say that what gets measured gets done, but the cases seem to indicate that we should not overlook the importance of assessing, specifying, measuring and resourcing these strategies.[13] For example, in cases such as Unilever, we would need to know the proportion of overall investment in the nine principles in relation to the rest of the organization's investment portfolio. We would also need to know the steps and assessment processes (measures used) in cases such as UBS, Storebrand or Statoil. These are data which a second wave of data collection could easily target.

Learning and communicating

It is clear that an immense amount of organizational learning has taken place during the time periods covered by the submissions. It also seems that organizations need to forget and 'unlearn' some of their embedded behaviours. The older organizations in the sample (not surprisingly) seem to have most need for unlearning, whilst the younger organizations have most need to build in CSR as an integral part of their strategic portfolio. In developing this work, it may be useful to sample organizations on the basis of embeddedness and/or age.

Communicating is an integral part of learning, especially when this is across networks of organizations. As far as this project is concerned, one of the primary tasks for the UN will be to maintain the discussion and the feedback on information. Otherwise, a lot of these case exam-

---

[13] *Ibid.*

ples will not gain the exposure they need. Consequently, companies will be discouraged from creating further publicity around those events. Along the same theme of communication, it is vital to examine the ways in which self-reports from companies are presented. In this book the authors have taken the data as presented at face value. A further issue of data collection would be validation and verification (in the spirit of good social science research). It will also be useful in the future to try to standardize as far as possible the ways in which data are collected and the ways in which case studies are constructed. In some of the current cases, there was something of a standardized reporting under headings such as lessons learned, costs and benefits. In others cases, such as Nexen, the whole discourse of the case is much looser and less structured. Any next phase of data collection from these and other organizations will benefit from the use of more standardized research tools and validation procedures. It is also essential, in our view, to place the changes demanded by the adoption of the nine principles in the wider context of changes taking place in the world of organizations generally.[14]

Signatories and endorsements by companies to global initiatives

Table 7.1 lists the companies participating in the Global Compact, companies using the Global Reporting Initiative and endorsing the Global Sullivan Principles and SA 8000. AA 1000 does not track the list of companies using its model. The list of signatories to ISO 14001 would take hundreds of pages.

Several interesting trends appear on this chart. First, there are very few companies that have signed more than one of the four initiatives listed below. Shell, British Airways, BT, Avon, Kesko and Ford are among the companies that signed onto two initiatives. Second, inter-

----

[14] Castells, M., *op cit.*

esting trends emerge from a sectoral point of view. Oil companies, airlines and airports and alcohol manufacturers are well represented, whereas banks, investment firms and public relations firms are not. Third, and not surprisingly, there are very few cases in which competitors appear on the same list. Fourth, the new economy is not signing onto these initiatives. It should come as no surprise that the majority of the companies listed below are large multinational enterprises, based primarily in Western Europe and the US.

See Table 7.1 on company engagement with the Global Compact in phase one, July 2000 to November 2001.

TABLE 7.1 ■ Participating companies

Company	Electronics	Extraction – oil and gas	Construction	Financial	Food	Forestry	Health and chemicals	Manufacturing and technology	Services and consultancy (including communications and financing)	Telecommunications and media
Company										
Aluminium Bahrain										
Aracruz						✓				
BASF							✓			
Bayer							✓	✓		
BP		✓								
BT										✓
Cisco								✓		
DASCH										
Deloitte Touche									✓	
DuPont							✓	✓		
Esquel										
HUDCO									✓	
Indian Oil Corporation		✓								
Ketchum Comms									✓	
Nexen		✓								
Organizacoes Globo										✓
Placer Dome										
Power Finance Corp									✓	
SAP								✓		
Shell		✓								
Skanska AB			✓							
ST Electronics	✓									
Statoil		✓								
Storebrand				✓						
UBS AG				✓						
Unilever					✓		✓			
TOTAL	1	5	1	2	1	1	4	4	4	2
SMEs										
Tammy Beauvais Designs									✓	
Regis Engineering								✓		
Bohica Medical									✓	
Mia Purwandari										
Sovitex Design Arts								✓		✓
TOTAL								2	2	1
GRAND TOTAL	1	5	1	2	1	1	4	6	6	3

Global Compact Principles

Company	Human rights		Labour standards				Environment			No. ref.
	1	2	3	4	5	6	7	8	9	
Aluminium Bahrain								✓		✓
Aracruz	✓									
BASF		✓	✓	✓		✓	✓	✓		✓
Bayer								✓	✓	✓
BP	✓	✓	✓	✓			✓	✓	✓	✓
BT										✓
Cisco										
DASCH										
Deloitte Touche						✓				
DuPont									✓	
Esquel										
HUDCO										✓
Indian Oil Corporation										✓
Ketchum Comms										
Nexen										✓ ✓
Organizacoes Globo										
Placer Dome								✓		
Power Finance Corp							✓		✓	
SAP										
Shell	✓				✓			✓		
Skanska AB		✓	✓	✓	✓	✓	✓	✓	✓	✓
ST Electronics			✓	✓	✓	✓				✓
Statoil					✓	✓		✓		✓
Storebrand										
UBS AG										✓
Unilever					✓		✓	✓	✓	✓
TOTAL	**3**	**3**	**4**	**4**	**5**	**5**	**5**	**9**	**6**	**12**
SMEs										
Tammy Beauvais Designs										
Regis Engineering								✓		✓
Bohica Medical			✓							✓
Mia Purwandari										
Sovitex Design Arts										✓
TOTAL			**1**					**1**		**3**
GRAND TOTAL	**3**	**3**	**5**	**4**	**5**	**5**	**5**	**10**	**6**	**15**

Case study focus

Company	Environmental issues				Health	Corruption	Social issues			
	Water quality	Air quality	Renewable resources (including forestry/fish)	Eco-efficiency (including waste minimization)			Labour rights and standards (including discrimination and child labour)	Infrastructure (including housing)	Education	others
Aluminium Bahrain				✓						
Aracruz			✓							
BASF				✓		✓				
Bayer		✓								
BP				✓	✓					
BT					✓					
Cisco										
DASCH										
Deloitte Touche				✓			✓		✓	
DuPont					✓					
Esquel	✓									
HUDCO								✓		
Indian Oil Corporation					✓					
Ketchum Comms										
Nexen									✓	✓
Organizacoes Globo							✓			
Placer Dome	✓					✓				
Power Finance Corp										
SAP										
Shell							✓	✓		✓
Skanska AB	✓	✓								
ST Electronics		✓								
Statoil					✓					
Storebrand										✓
UBS AG			✓							✓
Unilever	✓									
TOTAL	**4**	**3**	**2**	**4**	**5**	**2**	**3**	**2**	**2**	**4**
SMEs										
Tammy Beauvais Designs										✓
Regis Engineering				✓						
Bohica Medical										
Mia Purwandari							✓			
Sovitex Design Arts								✓		✓
TOTAL				**1**			**1**	**1**		**2**
GRAND TOTAL	**4**	**3**	**2**	**5**	**5**	**2**	**4**	**3**	**2**	**6**

Company	Country focus							
	North America	South and Central America	Europe	Asia	Africa	Australasia (including South East Asia and Australia)	Middle East	Global
Company								
Aluminium Bahrain							✓	
Aracruz		✓						
BASF			✓					
Bayer		✓						
BP								✓✓
BT								
Cisco								✓
DASCH						✓		
Deloitte Touche					✓			✓
DuPont				✓✓				
Esquel				✓✓				
HUDCO								
Indian Oil Corporation								
Ketchum Comms								
Organizacoes Globo		✓						
Placer Dome						✓		
Power Finance Corp				✓				
SAP					✓			
Shell		✓						✓
Skanska AB			✓					
ST Electronics								
Statoil			✓					✓
Storebrand								
UBS AG								
Unilever				✓				✓✓
TOTAL		4	3	5	2	2	1	10
SMEs								
Tammy Beauvais Designs	✓							
Regis Engineering								
Bohica Medical					✓			
Mia Purwandari						✓✓		
Sovitex Design Arts					✓			
TOTAL	1				2	2		
GRAND TOTAL	1	4	3	5	4	4	1	10

Systems, codes and standards

Company	EMAS ISO 14001	External certification and verification	Voluntary codes (company and external)	Sustainable development	Development targets	Stated company global standards	Awards
Company							
Aluminium Bahrain	✓						✓
Aracruz				✓		✓	
BASF							
Bayer		✓					
BP						✓	
BT			✓				
Cisco							
DASCH							
Deloitte Touche			✓				
DuPont							
Esquel							
HUDCO				✓	✓		
Indian Oil Corporation				✓	✓		
Ketchum Comms				✓	✓		
Nexen		✓	✓		✓	✓	
Organizacoes Globo							
Placer Dome							
Power Finance Corp							
SAP						✓	
Shell			✓	✓		✓	
Skanska AB	✓		✓			✓	
ST Electronics			✓			✓	
Statoil	✓		✓			✓	
Storebrand			✓			✓	
UBS AG	✓		✓			✓	
Unilever		✓	✓	✓		✓	
TOTAL	**4**	**3**	**10**	**6**	**4**	**11**	**1**
SMEs							
Tammy Beauvais Designs			✓				
Regis Engineering			✓				
Bohica Medical				✓			
Mia Purwandari							
Sovitex Design Arts							
TOTAL			**2**	**1**			
GRAND TOTAL	**4**	**3**	**12**	**7**	**4**	**11**	**1**

Relationships

Company	Academic, think-tank	Competitors (business to business)	Employees	Local communities	Non-government organizations	Government institutions (including regulators)	Supply chain	Trade unions
Aluminium		✓						
Bahrain								
Aracruz		✓		✓✓	✓✓	✓		
BASF		✓		✓	✓	✓	✓	
Bayer		✓			✓		✓	✓
BP								
BT								
Cisco								
DASCH		✓		✓	✓			✓
Deloitte Touche		✓	✓✓		✓			
DuPont			✓					
Esquel				✓		✓		
HUDCO						✓		
Indian Oil Corporation				✓✓		✓✓✓		
Ketchum Comms	✓	✓						
Nexen	✓	✓	✓✓	✓✓	✓✓	✓		✓
Organizaçoes Globo				✓	✓	✓✓		
Placer Dome		✓		✓	✓			
Power Finance Corp						✓		
SAP								
Shell			✓✓	✓	✓	✓	✓	
Skanska AB			✓			✓		✓
ST Electronics								
Statoil								
Storebrand								
UBS AG								
Unilever		✓	✓	✓	✓	✓	✓	
TOTAL	**2**	**8**	**8**	**11**	**12**	**12**	**4**	**4**
SMEs								
Tammy Beauvais Designs				✓				
Regis Engineering			✓		✓		✓	
Bohica Medical			✓	✓				
Mia Purwandari		✓✓				✓		✓
Sovitex Design Arts								
TOTAL		**2**	**2**	**2**	**1**	**1**	**1**	**1**
GRAND TOTAL	**2**	**10**	**10**	**13**	**13**	**13**	**5**	**5**

Organization and management

Company	Recruitment	Training	Quality	Business performance	Leadership	Change management	Risk management
Aluminium Bahrain							
Aracruz							
BASF		✓			✓	✓	
Bayer							
BP				✓			
BT							
Cisco							
DASCH							
Deloitte Touche	✓	✓		✓	✓	✓	
DuPont		✓	✓	✓	✓	✓	
Esquel			✓			✓	
HUDCO		✓					
Indian Oil Corporation							
Ketchum Comms							
Nexen				✓	✓	✓	✓
Organizacoes Globo	✓	✓					
Placer Dome							
Power Finance Corp							
SAP							
Shell		✓				✓	✓
Skanska AB		✓	✓				
ST Electronics	✓	✓	✓		✓	✓	
Statoil							
Storebrand							✓
UBS AG			✓				
Unilever							
TOTAL	**3**	**8**	**5**	**4**	**5**	**7**	**3**
SMEs							
Tammy Beauvais Designs							
Regis Engineering		✓					
Bohica Medical					✓		
Mia Purwandari				✓	✓	✓	
Sovitex Design Arts							
TOTAL		**1**		**1**	**2**	**1**	
GRAND TOTAL	**3**	**9**	**5**	**5**	**7**	**8**	**3**

CHAPTER 8

The future

In Chapter 1 we made several propositions. First, we said that the front-running corporate citizens, even if they are still a minority within the business community, have largely made the business case and shown that there is a possibility of 'doing well by doing good' or certainly better. Second, we asked: 'What can be learned from what is currently happening, and how can we make sense of the developments that are taking place?' Above all, the question we asked ourselves, as people whose working lives are spent surrounded by those talking the language of corporate citizenship, was: *What difference is this activity making to business outcomes and to social outcomes*? Might corporate citizenship really be seen as a new, more humanistic way of conducting business, bringing together a concern with wealth creation and a concern for the wider social good? Or is it simply a new way of *talking* about how business is conducted, a surface gloss beneath which neither business priorities nor impacts are changing?

In answer to these propositions this book has attempted to do two things. First, it has analyzed some of the current trends and thinking in corporate citizenship, and second, it has provided empirical data on a particular significant voluntary corporate citizenship initiative.

As four authors working in this field on a daily basis we understand that our readers, in the main, are coming to corporate citizenship from another place. Perhaps you are a quality or health and safety manager, or the leader of a community development project. Perhaps you are the CEO of one of the companies referred to in this book, or a worker on one of the sites profiled in a company case study. We are all consumers of corporate products and we are all interested to varying degrees in the successful outcome of the UN Secretary-General's call to business to 'join (me) in a global compact of shared values and principles, which can give a human face to the global market'. To this end we are all learning how this brave new world may turn out, aware that there are some who see any engagement between private purpose and public policy as a betrayal. This lobby argues that corporate interests are in control and that we are all victims of the market and corporate greed. They claim that in the case of the UN Global Compact the UN is being co-opted – stolen from the aspirations of its founders.

Winston Churchill said that 'the price of freedom is eternal vigilance' and we need active citizens groups to keep corporations and states on their toes. It is only those corporations and states that have power and vested interests to protect and something to hide which fear non-violent direct action from groups as diverse as the World Wide Fund for Nature and CorporateWatch. A central emphasis of this book has been on inclusivity and accountability in decision making. On this basis a cautious approach should be adopted towards those who on initial contact appear to be in the business of subverting or undermining participatory processes, who are not transparent and accountable in their decision making, and who use violence and intimidation as their weapons. But these are characteristics which can be found in businesses, governments and non-government organizations. There is variation to be found in all areas of human activity and we can find adherence to, and understanding of, the nine principles of the UN Global Compact from the local to the global, from the supra-territorial corporation to the community soccer team, and from the city to the village.

We do not suggest that the eight corporate citizenship initiatives outlined in this book deal with 'the human condition'. This book is about politics and management. It is about managing the planet in the next century and beyond, and it is about the delivery of aspirations. Looking again at the Millennium Targets, how can we deliver them? For there are few among us who do not believe that they represent *common* goals. From the UN Global Compact to the Global Reporting Initiative to AA 1000S there is a fundamental set of human values that have barely been mentioned in this book but which form the background to all the good people that we have talked to and worked with for this book and in our daily lives. These fundamental human values form the core of 'Human Values in the Workplace', inspired by Sri Sathya Sai Baba, a universal spiritual teacher, who has written and spoken about truth, righteousness, peace, love, and non-violence.[1]

Since our last book in 1998 and during the course of writing this book the four co-authors have undergone tremendous changes in their lives – as is the case with the majority of our readership. There is nowadays little peace for most people because of the way we have structured our worlds, the way we use technology and the way we hunger after everything all the time. In this context we were struck by a true story told by a vehicle recovery company executive recently. He said that when people's vehicles break down they use their mobile phones to call for help. The calls go to a central call centre, which could be anywhere in the world. The vehicle recovery company has been struck by the number of people who call and *have no idea where they are*. They are often on anonymous roads, where there may be a corporate icon glowing in the sky up ahead – McDonald's, Burger King or Shell perhaps – the weather is changeable, the cars are zipping past, and the radio is playing world hip-hop – but *they don't know where they are*. This is analogous to the state of the world at the beginning of the 21st century. We have arrived somewhere which feels very global – news from Afghanistan and New York, oranges from Israel, cars from Korea, wine from Australia – but we don't know where we are. And we can't turn off the mobile phone in case we miss something.

There are those who see the eight global corporate citizenship initiatives profiled in this book as the 'new imperialism'. This is perhaps because the words used in these initiatives, and particularly in the nine principles in the Global Compact, are not enough. Unless engagement with these and other global initiatives is underpinned by truth, right-

---

[1] www.globaldharma.org

■ ■ ■ ■ ■ ■ ■ ■ ■ ■ ■ ■ ■

***Above all there is one thing that is common to all
the corporate citizenship initiatives that we have written
about in this book, and that is a recognition of 'the other'***

■ ■ ■ ■ ■ ■ ■ ■ ■ ■ ■ ■ ■

eousness, peace, love and non-violence, they will result only in processes that undermine their intentions. If there are those who believe that we can reach the Millennium Targets without reference to these five fundamental human values, then we may fail. You have to love children to not want them to be exploited, you have to believe in peace and non-violence to engage in the lengthy process of stakeholder consultation, and you have to believe that truth is sacred to expose your decision making to scrutiny.

Above all there is one thing that is common to all the corporate citizenship initiatives that we have written about in this book, and that is a recognition of 'the other'; a recognition that I, you and we must listen if we are to hear the silence of the oppressed, the anger of the down-trodden, the exclusion of the outsider. Many of the initiatives in this book rely on listening, engaging, learning, unlearning and conversation. This is particularly true of the Global Compact, the Global Reporting Initiative, SA 8000 and AA 1000S.

The evidence presented here from phase one of the Global Compact Learning Forum is not encouraging. But such a high-profile experiment is bound to be difficult. The next phase will take note from the first and engage in more conversation round the table before it blasts off on a website. It is easy to feel frightened by global exposure and intimidated by anger from those who do not see you as you see yourself.

As we think about the future for corporate citizenship, at least three interesting questions suggest themselves to us:

One, can we show that initiatives like these deliver their promises? Two, how can we build into corporate citizenship initiatives reference and respect for fundamental human values? Three, are we all sitting round the same table, part of the same conversation?

Sometimes we wonder.

Finally we step back several hundred years. In 1790 Yorkshireman Thomas Paine, author of *The Rights of Man*, wrote to US President George Washington 'That the Rights of Man may become as universal as your Benevolence can wish, and that you may enjoy the Happiness of seeing the New World regenerate the Old'. In that pamphlet Paine wrote:

> The mutual dependence and reciprocal interest which man has upon man, and all parts of civilised community upon each other, create that great chain of connexion which holds it together.[2]

The conventions, agreements and declarations upon which the nine principles of the Global Compact are drawn owe their derivation to Paine and other civil society activists. Having established some clearly agreed principles we now have to reform our economic and multilateral institutions in order that the process of social partnership *inevitably* leads to *liberté*, *fraternité* and *egalité*.

---

[2] Paine, T. (1984) *The Rights of Man*, London: Penguin Classics, p. 163.

Appendix 1
Examples of learning from nine selected submissions

The following nine company submissions have been chosen to represent one for each of the Global Compact principles from the range of company submissions up to December 2001.

How can companies and all those interested in learning from this global dialogue learn from each other? How can we, as a global community, share lessons and move forward in the creation of a more just, sustainable world? Indeed, how can all the participants in the Global Compact conversation, whether they be from business, government or civil society, move that conversation from lobbing bricks from behind barricades to sharing the same language, the same world view, the same objectives. It may be that the UN's Millennium Objectives provide a common platform, or at least a starting point. It is also clear that the nine principles of the Global Compact have provided a convening platform for different actors to relate to each other across the world.

Given that few, if any, of the company submissions applied the criteria supplied by the Learning Forum team, they are difficult to compare, but there are some obvious areas of analysis. As commentators we had to take the companies at their word; we had to accept that the companies knew what they were doing in supplying a submission to the unglobalcompact website; we had to start with the information they had supplied. Interestingly this raises questions of the possible manipulation of data (by the companies), naivety on their part, and perhaps perfidy. More fundamentally, and perhaps more interestingly, it raises the questions about 'the other' in this sort of engagement. How do companies see themselves and how do they think they are seen by others? How do other conversants, or stakeholders, see companies?

Entry points for analysis could be references to:

- Global Compact principles;
- other corporate citizenship initiatives;
- quantitative and qualitative data that has some external reference;
- stakeholder engagement, dialogue and reporting;
- interpretation of the Global Compact principles and the Millennium Objectives in the context of the company's role, scope and purpose;
- learning through what works and what does not work;
- organizational change;
- resource allocation in financial, administrative and personnel terms to the task;

- re-evaluating the company's vision, mission and values in the light of its experiences;
- endorsement by senior management.

In this spirit, and taking nine of the company submissions at face value, we have presented the analysis in the previous chapters and here offer a further analysis of the company presentations. We are only too aware, as are many of the readers of this book, that there is much more that can be said about these companies and their operations. Here we want to provide examples of some of the more useful company statements in the hope of aiding and abetting the global dialogue that is a premise of the Global Compact Learning Forum as articulated by its main authors in the Secretary-General's office.

All the company submissions can be found on www.unglobalcompact.org so here we have just reproduced nine submissions along with a commentary on each.

Participating companies take full responsibility for both the factual content and interpretive conclusions of the submissions they make to the Global Compact Learning Forum.

Principle One

BASF's submission to the Global Compact (2000/2001)

1 Preface and context

By joining the Global Compact Alliance as one of the 44 founding members, BASF committed itself to contribute to the success of the Global Compact's nine principles.

The Global Compact aims to foster Sustainable Development, good corporate citizenship and social responsibility at a global level through cooperation in a climate of openness between the members. In the short term, the progress of the Global Compact will depend on breaking down reservations that exist between divergent partners. In the long-run, however, a crucial factor for the success will be whether the members of the Global Compact Alliance are able to implement the Compact's principles through a solution-oriented dialogue that ultimately leads to concrete projects at the operational level.

The focus of the Global Compact lies on the individual strengths that each member can contribute to the progress of the initiative as a whole. In this way, the concept of best practices is a cornerstone of the Global Compact, since it enables the partners in the Global Compact Alliance to detect potential synergies and win-win situations which best help to put the principles of the Global Compact into practice.

We believe that much of the concept of best practices builds on the multiplying effect of transnational companies in global value chains.

Transnational companies reach a whole host of suppliers and customers with their best practices. Each member of the Global Compact owns specific best practices that have the potential to set benchmarks and standards in its sector for a range of suppliers in international production processes. Therefore, the members of the Global Compact Alliance should work with their suppliers toward economic, ecological and social 'value creation'.

2 What concrete action has been taken?

In 2001, BASF's measures to make Sustainable Development part of our everyday processes and thus to promote the principles of the Global Compact culminated in the implementation of a new management structure headed by our Sustainability Council at Board level. The new structure will guide the company's activities in the area of Sustainable Development, develop strategies and decide on the Group-wide implementation of sustainability instruments.

For us, the promotion of the nine principles is part of our pledge to the concept of Sustainable Development. We undertake a wide range of activities to meet the economic, ecological and social needs of the present generation without compromising the development prospects of future generations.

Some of our recent sustainability activities with special relevance to the principles of the Global Compact are highlighted below and include:

- the implementation of new Values and Principles and a Compliance Program;
- the implementation of Group-wide sustainability reporting including the publication of BASF's first Social Responsibility Report and our Environmental Report, both forthcoming in summer 2001;
- participation in the initiative 'Remembrance, Responsibility and the Future' to help former forced laborers;
- the promotion of BASF's eco-efficiency analysis within the Global Compact Initiative.

BASF's sustainability reports, the full text of our Values and Principles and further information on the eco-efficiency analysis can be obtained via the Internet (www.basf.com).

3 Case studies

3.1 Vision, Values and Principles for BASF

BASF Group issued its new Values and Principles in 2000. Together with the 'Vision 2010', which was published a few years ago, they form the basis for our activities and provide information on BASF's goals and business practices. In addition, BASF has introduced a global Compliance Program in connection with its Values: By the end of 2001, every Group company will establish its own Code of Conduct based on the BASF Values and Principles and local laws.

Both the Values and Principles and the Compliance Program oblige all employees to act in a legal fashion. They make sure that the company is not complicit in human rights abuses. Violations will not be tolerated and may have consequences under criminal and labor law.

Our Values and Principles also clearly state that BASF Group strives to 'maintain relationships with elected employee representatives in good faith and mutual respect based on internationally recognized fundamental labor standards and orientated towards the customs of the respective countries'. The company's Social Responsibility Report provides more detailed information on BASF's employee relations.

3.2 Sustainability Reporting

In summer 2001, the BASF Group will issue its first Group-wide Social Responsibility Report. This publication completes our sustainability reporting. It focuses on the societal dimension of our activities. It provides information and statistics on the company's relations with employees, business partners, communities and other stakeholders. BASF's Social Responsibility Report is meant to foster the company's stakeholder dialogue and to form a valuable contribution to the principles 1 to 6 of the Global Compact.

The identification of key performance indicators to measure social sustainability was one of the most crucial decisions in the preparation process and one of the most difficult ones, too. The sustainability debate has recently devoted much time to discussing such key data or indicators. Non-governmental organizations (NGOs) and research institutes as well as trade associations and investors have prepared extensive lists of indicators. In order to find the most appropriate key performance indicators for BASF, we took these lists into account and focused on the questions that we are repeatedly asked in discussions with various stakeholders.

The quality of the report depends on solid data. To collect these, we had to perform a Group-wide survey. Because BASF Group companies operate under different conditions in different countries, central data collection had not seemed to make sense in many cases to date. Because the survey was carried out for the first time in this form in 2000, we are unable to make any comparisons to previous years. Other difficulties we had compiling the collected data are rooted in the different nature and size of the companies and in the special characteristics of the regions. As a result, we are not yet able to quote a global figure for all indicators. However, we have already taken steps to optimize our data basis.

Although we are aware that our sustainability reporting can still be improved, we believe that the information we present forms a good basis for the future dialogue with many of our stakeholders. We are looking forward to adding our experiences to the public debate on sustainability reporting, e.g. by taking part in the structured feedback process of the Global Reporting Initiative (GRI).

3.3 Initiative 'Remembrance, Responsibility and the Future'

During the Second World War, millions of people were forced to work for German industry, municipalities and state authorities as replacements for German citizens who had been drafted into military service. A large number of forced laborers were employed in the Ludwigshafen and Oppau works of I.G. Farbenindustrie AG, which was formed in 1925 through the merger of BASF, Bayer, Hoechst and other companies.

BASF together with 15 other major German companies founded the initiative 'Remembrance, Responsibility and the Future' (*Erinnerung, Verantwortung und Zukunft*) as a sign of reconciliation and in recognition of the historical responsibility of German industry. Funds from the initiative are paid into a Federal German Foundation to help former forced laborers and other victims of the Nazi regime. The foundation will provide approximately 5 billion DM, with half provided by German industry and half from public funds.

Dr. Jürgen F. Strube, Chairman of the Board of Directors of BASF Aktiengesellschaft, explains our company's commitment to the initiative as follows: 'Both BASF and I personally regret the suffering of forced laborers under the Nazi regime and the discrimination they were made to bear. None of us can undo past injustices, but we can ensure that they never happen again.' BASF understands the participation in the initiative as a contribution in the spirit of principle 4 of the Global Compact. See also www.stiftungsinitiative.de.

FIGURE A1.1

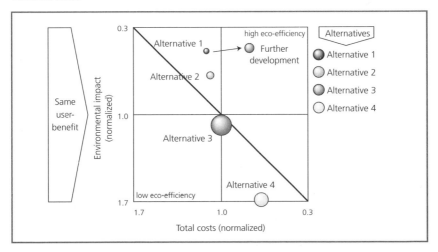

3.4 Eco-efficiency analysis

What is the BASF eco-efficiency analysis?

The purpose of BASF eco-efficiency analysis is to harmonize economy and ecology. It therefore serves as a tool for helping business activities to become sustainable. Back in 1996, BASF was one of the first chemical companies to develop this method. The company has therefore gained a wide range of experience in applying this instrument at the operational level to evaluate which business activities are worth pursuing with a view to achieving the goal of Sustainable Development.

The first stage of applying the BASF eco-efficiency analysis to a product or process is to assess its environmental impact. This takes into account the factors raw material and energy consumption, air and water emissions, disposal methods, potential toxicity and future risks. The total environmental impact of a product or production process can be calculated on the basis of these individual data. In a second step, the economic data have to be compiled by calculating all the various costs involved in manufacturing or using a product. The economic analysis and the overall environmental impact are then used to make eco-efficiency comparisons. Technically, this involves plotting the economic and ecological data on a graph, as shown above.

The costs on the horizontal axis are plotted against the environmental impact on the vertical axis. The graph reveals the eco-efficiency of a product or process compared to other products or processes. It further demonstrates that BASF eco-efficiency does not address the economical or ecological impact alone, but instead combines the two as a basis for a sustainable decision-making process. Therefore, the result of an BASF eco-efficiency analysis can guide long-term strategic decisions, since it helps to detect and exploit potential ecological and economic improvements and allows us to react carefully to today's and tomorrow's environmental challenges.

To date, some 120 of BASF's products and production processes have been analyzed using the new method. But eco-efficiency is not limited to our own business: we also include our suppliers and customers in our analysis. The eco-efficiency analysis assesses the lifecycle of a product or manufacturing process from the cradle to the grave. For example, it includes the environmental impact of products and processes, consumer behavior – by taking into account the consumption behavior of end-users – as well as various recycling and disposal options.

Finally, the BASF eco-efficiency analysis enables companies to optimize the ecological performance of their entire value chain and simultaneously obtain economic benefits from the efficient use of resources, which benefits the company and ultimately society as a whole. We believe that the BASF eco-efficiency analysis is one of our best practices that could make a valuable contribution toward putting the environmental principles of the Global Compact into practice. We are open to sharing our know-how and experience gained with the aim of enabling companies and institutions – in particular in developing countries – to enjoy the many benefits that eco-efficiency analyses are able to generate.

Which of the principles are addressed?

From our point of view, measures to foster eco-efficiency have the potential to embrace all three environmental principles contained in the Global Compact.

Firstly, the willingness of businesses *to support a precautionary approach to environmental protection* as required in the seventh principle of the Compact usually faces the difficult task of making future risks measurable and, just as importantly, of translating them into present management policies. A well-applied eco-efficiency scheme is able to tackle both problems, since future environmental risks are taken into account as an equal factor along with present environmental and economic determinants. Furthermore, the BASF eco-efficiency analysis provides clear results as a crucial precondition for guiding management decisions.

Secondly, as soon as the requirement of eco-efficient production is introduced into the relationship with suppliers, it serves as a tool *to promote greater environmental responsibility*, as stated in the Compact's eighth principle. A successful eco-efficiency analysis can be an important step to promoting environmental responsibility in a company's corporate culture. However, even a sound eco-efficiency analysis will not lead to more eco-efficient production unless the findings are implemented at the operative level. Ultimately, the success of the instrument depends entirely on the decision-makers' commitment to Sustainable Development. We believe that introducing BASF's knowledge of eco-efficiency analysis into the Global Compact can offer a living example to promote the idea of environmental responsibility.

Thirdly, spreading the idea of eco-efficiency so as to minimize the environmental impact of products and production processes will finally lead to the *development and diffusion of environmentally friendly technologies*, as embodied in the last of the Compact's nine principles.

Spreading the concept of eco-efficiency within the Global Compact

In a first step to promote its eco-efficiency analysis, BASF hosted a symposium entitled 'Eco-Efficiency – A Bridge between Economy and the Environment' in cooperation with the Wuppertal Institute on February 20 2001 in Mannheim. The event was attended by some 200 participants, including a broad spectrum of members of the Global Compact Alliance ranging from corporations to civil society organizations such as the WWF and the World Business Council on Sustainable Development. One of the aims of this symposium was to share our knowledge and experience in the field of eco-efficiency analysis and to encourage the business community to apply the BASF eco-efficiency analysis in their business practices. In addition, we sought to intensify dialogue with stakeholders on our approach to eco-efficiency.

In a second step, we are compiling a manual on the BASF eco-efficiency analysis which will contain a wealth of information on how to employ this tool and to showcase the lessons we learned in applying it. The manual will be available free of charge to all members of the Global Compact Alliance as well as to companies and organizations in developing countries. Furthermore, we encourage all interested organizations to enter into a constructive dialogue with us on how and to what extent an eco-efficiency project could be implemented within their sphere of activities.

We are currently initiating the third phase of promoting BASF's eco-efficiency analysis within the Global Compact and are discussing the possibility of organizing a training workshop on eco-efficiency together with the UNEP. The purpose of this workshop should be to highlight the benefits of eco-efficiency analysis as a management tool and to give the participants concrete instructions on how to implement the eco-efficiency analysis in practice. Again, the workshop will be hosted pro bono for all members of the Global Compact Alliance and participants from developing countries. If a specific environmental project could be identified or developed in this workshop, BASF is willing to contribute to its success by providing a comprehensive eco-efficiency analysis free of charge.

4 The road ahead

BASF is convinced that difficulties in the initial phase of the Global Compact have been overcome. We are glad that we maintain good relations with the newly established and growing UN office in New York, which provides helpful guidance for the questions arising out in our day-to-day business and we support initiatives aimed at pooling the resources on the national level available for implementing the Global Compact.

BASF is currently preparing to set up a number of projects in cooperation with UN Organizations and other members of the Global Compact. Besides the workshop on eco-efficiency these projects include:
- the promotion of employee volunteerism;
- the identification and improvement of key performance indicators, e. g. for internal audits and public reporting.

Contacts

Andreas Bluethner
Email: andreas.bluethner@basf-ag.de

Jörg Hartmann
Email: joerg.hartmann@basf-ag.de

Commentary

The BASF submission is almost unique in this sample in attempting to address all of the nine principles, albeit briefly. It is also unique in talking of economic, ecological and social 'value creation' through engagement by multinational enterprises in their supply chains. As they say: 'We believe that much of the concept of best practices builds on the multiplying effect of transnational companies in global value chains.'

Sustainability and eco-efficiency has been a significant driver of change in the company affecting the design, development and disposal of products as well as their relations with all stakeholders. But in the case of BASF and some other German companies, their growth, development and profitability in partnership with the German government and the Nazi Party in the 1930s and up to 1945 causes them to focus on human rights.

There are few companies or indeed countries that have endeavoured to engage with their tragic past in the way that Germany has. Germany's genocidal past is relatively recent history and within the lifetimes of both participants and company lives. Many of the companies that profited from close participation with the German government at that time are now global entities. As BASF points out, it was in alliance with Bayer, Hoechst and others during this period. Germany's defeat in 1945, and the subsequent restructuring of the country's economy, allows us to draw a line under company activities to that date, but how many other companies domiciled in other countries over the past 100 years or so might usefully engage in a little navel gazing? Those who do not understand history are doomed to repeat it, and learning involves unlearning and admitting mistakes. BASF and others are forced to admit grave errors of judgement and to say: 'We can ensure that (it) never happens again.'

On eco-efficiency BASF says that 'eco-efficiency analysis can guide long-term strategic decisions'. It says that its analysis includes suppliers and customers as it looks at the life cycle of the product from the cradle to the grave. This full stakeholder involvement, the company argues, supports all three of the environmental principles in the Global Compact.

This is a reflective submission and in itself an example of a more transparent and open approach to global dialogue as a corporate citizen. However, it tells us little about organisational change and is relatively light on the learning process, beyond telling us that the company has had to reflect on its past practices.

So, there are further questions that are raised by BASF's submission:

- The company says it has been closely involved with the development and application of the Global Reporting Initiative – has it been involved with, and what has it learned from, other corporate citizenship initiatives?
- What was the qualitative nature of the stakeholder engagement, who was included, and how was this exercise conducted?

- What is the resource cost of engagement with all nine principles and how has the company found itself learning and changing in the light of its experiences?
- Has the company re-evaluated any of its products or any of its operations outside Germany in the light of its engagement?

Principle Two

BT submission to Global Compact Learning Forum

The Global Compact challenges business leaders to embrace and enact nine principles covering Human Rights, Labour and the Environment. We believe that our progress against these principles, and the learning that has accompanied these developments, is best delivered by referring people to our independently verified social, economic and environmental report.

This report is only available on-line and can be found at www.groupbt. com/betterworld.

The 'Standards' section of the report (www.groupbt.com/society/ standards1.htm) sets out BT's approach to the most prominent of the different guidelines, standards and codes of practice that companies are encouraged to sign up to. Included in these is the Global Compact, where we state that 'the activities described in this report are intended to demonstrate how we apply and promote the Compact's principles'.

This submission to the Global Compact Learning Forum summarises the key sections of our report as they relate to the nine principles. Links are provided to more comprehensive information, where readers can find measures of progress, lessons learned and next steps. Consequently, these links form an important part of the submission.

For a CEO/Chairman's sign off of this submission, please see the Chairman's Introduction to our site at www.groupbt.com/society/bland. htm and the statement that 'ultimately, the report remains the responsibility of, and has been approved by, the BT Directors' in the Lloyds Register verification statement (www.groupbt.com/society/verification.htm).

Background

We have been engaged in corporate social responsibility (CSR) issues for many years and it is built into the values and principles of the company as described in the vision and values section of the site (www.groupbt. com/betterworld/vision).

We also see a strong business case for engagement in CSR (www. groupbt.com/betterworld/visionbusinesscase) and intend to strengthen this section of the site over the next few months.

Stakeholder participation

The Consultation (www.groupbt.com/betterworld/consultation) section of the site provides signposts to reports on our stakeholder dialogue activities. In the special reports produced by independent authors there were no restrictions on who they could involve as part of their research. And open, on-line debates take place through the Your Views (www.groupbt.com/betterworld/yourviews) section of the site and again there are no restrictions on who can participate in these.

Extent of report

To quote from the site (www.groupbt.com/betterworld/socialandenvironmentreport):

'Wherever possible in this report, we cover all BT's wholly-owned activities, in the UK and internationally. Wherever this is not possible, and where the data are not available or relate only to our activities in one part of the world or another, we seek to be clear about precisely what is covered.'

Certainly some items have been specific to certain business units and where this is the case we will have identified them. It is also a real time, dynamic site, so its content is continuously changing as the structure of our business changes. As you read it today it will already be different to when we first submitted our case study to the UN.

Human rights

Principles 1 and 2

www.groupbt.com./society/humanrights.htm

The human rights section of the report summarises BT's approach to Principles 1 and 2 of the Global Compact. BT's potential impact – both positive and negative – on human rights is managed by a number of departments and units throughout the business.

Links from this section provide further details on employees, suppliers, freedom of expression, privacy, intellectual property and the positive effects information and communications technology can bring to human rights.

As an example of the latter, BT has been a long-term supporter of the Oneworld network, and especially their informative and credible website (www.oneworld.org) that promotes a media gateway on human rights.

Labour

Principle 3

www.groupbt.com/society/emprel.htm
www.groupbt.com/society/sup_ethical.htm

Principles 4 and 5
www.groupbt.com/society/sup_ethical.htm

Principle 6
www.groupbt.com/society/equality.htm
www.groupbt.com/society/sup_ethical.htm

The Employees section of the report summarises BT's approach to Principles 3 and 6 in relation to our own workforce.

In the UK, BT recognises two trade unions: the Communications Workers Union (CWU), which represents 85,000 non-management grades, and Connect, which represents some 17,000 predominantly first and second-line managers and professionals.

In 2000/2001, there have been no instances of legal action taken against BT concerning anti-union practices.

A key indicator is the number of Employment Tribunal Cases judged against BT, which in 2000/01 was 2 out of 136, down from 16 out of 189 in the previous year.

Ensuring that the working conditions in our supply chain are consistent with standards based on the Universal Declaration of Human Rights and the International Labour Organisation Conventions is a more complex matter. To this end we have established *Sourcing with Human Dignity*, a supply chain initiative which seeks to promote these universal standards to our direct suppliers, and gain their support in advancing them throughout our supply chain.

This initiative covers Principles 3, 4, 5 and 6 of the Global Compact in relation to our Supply Chain, and details can be found in the Suppliers section of the report (www.groupbt.com/society/sup_ethical.htm)

We have established four key indicators for Sourcing with Human Dignity, all of which have the status of Targets in our report:

- By 31st March 2002, we will report the number and proportion of key suppliers who have signed an agreement to work towards *Sourcing with Human Dignity*.
- By 31st March 2002, we will hold at least two *Sourcing with Human Dignity* supplier forums with our key network and IT suppliers.
- By 31st March 2003, we will report the total number of suppliers and contractors who have contractually agreed to work towards the *Sourcing with Human Dignity* standard.
- By 31st March 2003, we will report the number, nature and country of identified shortfalls of the *Sourcing with Human Dignity* standard.

Implementation of *Sourcing with Human Dignity* commenced in May 2001 with a number of large multinational companies that comprise our most important first line suppliers. The need to engage the support of these companies in the first instance is paramount.

Environment

Principle 7
www.groupbt.com/society/environment/risk.htm
www.groupbt.com/society/mobiles.htm

Principle 8
www.groupbt.com/society/environment.htm

Principle 9
www.groupbt.com/society/environment/benefits.htm
www.groupbt.com/society/ebusiness.htm

Principle 7 is partly covered by the Environmental Risk section of the report (www.groupbt.com/society/environment/risk.htm). This sets out our work testing, repairing, and decommissioning of fuel tanks, a vital part of BT's major environmental improvement programme to reduce risk from the storage of diesel fuel.

A key issue affecting the telecommunications industry where a precautionary approach is required is that of Mobile Phones and Health. Consequently, we have included as part of our report an independent commentary on BT's approach to this issue, written by Green Alliance www.groupbt.com/society/mobiles.htm).

This commentary sets out BT's approach to three key challenges – public involvement, the precautionary approach and the role of scientific evidence. It highlights where BT has performed well and where improvements are required, as well as the key lessons learned and recommendations for the future.

Principle 8 is covered by the whole environmental section of the report (www.groupbt.com/society/environment.htm). This includes details of our accreditation to ISO14001 and our performance in each of the nine 'aspects' that we manage. The report includes details of 33 new environmental improvement targets that will be reported against in the future.

Principle 9 is also covered by the environment section of our report.

As we developed our environmental management system, it became increasingly clear that the creative use of information and communications technology (ICT) (including the communications products and services that BT sells) could significantly reduce the consumption of finite materials and other adverse environmental impacts. For this reason, our environmental management system includes a specific 'benefits' aspect (www.groupbt.com/society/environment/benefits.htm).

By including 'benefits' as a significant environmental effect and a focus for explicit management within the environmental management system, the positive impacts of e-business are more likely to be picked up and managed proactively.

Additionally, our E-Business Hot Topic (www.groupbt.com/society/ebusiness.htm) provides an independent commentary on BT's approach to the environmental impacts of e-business, written by UKCEED. This commentary includes a description of how BT manages the issue, key lessons learned and recommendations for the future. Highlights include audio-conferencing within BT saving around 150 million miles of travel a year, 34,000 tonnes of CO_2 and £6m, and our flexi-working programme, which has saved 424,000 miles a week of car travel and 190,000 miles a week of rail travel.

Costs and benefits

There are a number of financial figures included in specific sections of the report and significant ones are repeated in our Annual Report and Accounts (www.groupbt.com/annualreport), together with commentary on contingent risks and liabilities. However, none of these are what would be considered 'material' in the traditional accounting sense.

Similarly, the numbers of staff directly employed on managing the company's social and environmental programmes may be of interest for inter-company benchmarking but are, we propose, not critical indicators of progress towards the Global Compact vision. Rather it's the level of integration of these issues into core business activities that is critical. This is why our website includes a number of independently written hot topics that we believe give a better indication of this than would be achieved through a single project case study submission.

Overall we don't believe that special projects funded out of 'social' or 'environmental' budget lines will ever deliver the scale of relief to poverty alleviation or environmental degradation that General Secretary Kofi Annan was referring to when he made his Davos speech. This will only happen when these considerations are fully integrated into core company operations.

Next steps

We are often willing to share our experiences with others in order to learn from each other. We feel this is best done through a two-way mutual learning interaction and our door is always open to any organisation seeking to develop their own corporate social responsibility programmes.

In summary, we believe that the optimum way of demonstrating support for, and compliance with the Global Compact, is through company social and environmental reports covering all nine principles, having strong independent inputs and providing opportunities for interactive dialogue.

Contact

Dr. Chris Tuppen
Head of Sustainable Development and Corporate Accountability BT
Email: chris.tuppen@bt.com

Commentary

Like BASF's submission, this company submission addresses all nine principles. BT's submission is also of interest in three other regards. First, it directs readers to BT's website where they will find information relating to the company's social and environmental impact. Second, it states that all the company's social, economic and environmental reporting has been independently verified. Third, it challenges the UN Secretary-General's assumptions on the role of business in meeting the Millennium Summit Goals.

The challenge for companies was to present on an annual basis 'a concrete example of their implementation of one or more of the principles'. BT has an embarrassment of riches as, according to its Global Compact submission, the company is compliant on all nine principles and has evidence to prove that this is the case. It is clear from this submission that BT wishes to direct readers to numerous examples of its commitment to being a good corporate citizen. However, whilst its record may be exemplary, it would not help the learning forum if every company simply directed readers elsewhere, because as Annan, Ruggie and others have asserted, the idea was to build up a 'learning bank' of good or changed practice on each of the nine principles. But it is also true that BT's submission confronts one of the main challenges to the Global Compact, namely that company submissions are simply public relations, with no method of monitoring or verifying company statements. This perhaps points towards the future of the Learning Forum, which should contain simple statements of implementation by companies accompanied by independently written, full-length case studies on the companies. The reference in this submission and some others to engagement in one or more symbiotic corporate citizenship initiative also lends validity to the convergence and linkage model of research and dialogue suggested in chapters 5 and 6. This answers the first and second challenges in BT's submission.

The third challenge is even more fundamental and engaging. This suggests both a misunderstanding on BT's part and perhaps a misinterpretation of the Secretary-General's words. BT says in its submission:

'Overall we do not believe that special projects funded out of "social" or "environmental" budget lines will ever deliver the scale of relief to poverty alleviation or environmental degradation that General Secretary Kofi Annan was referring to when he made his Davos speech (January 1999).'

This sentiment cuts to the heart of the corporate citizenship debate. It is argued in previous chapters that to be a good corporate citizen requires an articulation of the role, scope and purpose of the company, and a justification of the public and private good created by that company. In other words, this is not just an articulation of the 'do no harm' moral argument but an understanding of the good that the company does in what it does and the way it does what it does. BT's assertion also cuts out philanthropy as an isolated criterion for being judged a responsible corporate citizen. It is arguing that what it does, and the way it operates, are integral to being a responsible company. This is a model for other companies that wish to engage in the Global Compact Learning Forum.

But questions arise that are central to the corporate citizenship debate.

- Is it for BT to judge whether the business of telecommunications is good for society as a whole?
- Can it judge whether, for instance, a particular aspect of its operations falls outside the Global Compact's nine principles? To be specific there is a real debate taking place concerning the noise pollution created by mobile phones ringing in churches, concert halls, restaurants and lecture theatres (that's a personal grump!). Whose responsibility is that – the company's or the users'?
- Why has the company chosen this high-profile route? Is it to seize the moral high ground from competitors?
- If this submission is judged to be exemplary, it would be helpful for other Global Compact companies to benefit from some understanding of the issues raised at the beginning of this chapter. What learning has taken place? What are the feedback loops between reporting on these issues and corporate governance?

Principle Three

Statoil

Good labour relations are important to Statoil. Our employees – some 16,000 people in 21 countries – are both precious assets and key stakeholders. For that reason, we have decided to focus on adherence to Global Compact principles 3, 4, 5 and 6 dealing with labour rights:

- Freedom of association and the effective recognition of the right to collective bargaining (*Principle 3*).
- The elimination of all forms of forced and compulsory labour (*Principle 4*).
- The effective abolition of child labour (*Principle 5*).
- The elimination of discrimination in respect of employment and occupation (*Principle 6*).

Statoil and labour relations

Statoil's approach to labour relations is rooted in a Norwegian tradition which emphasises dialogue and cooperation, not confrontation, between employers and employees. We aim to develop a culture of trust inside the company between management and workers and their organisations. We believe that good labour relations have to be built on open channels of communication.

Respect for the integrity of our employees lies at the heart of Statoil's approach to labour relations. We fully respect the human rights of our employees, including their freedom of association and right to collective bargaining. Conditions of employment and work in Statoil are to conform with internationally recognised standards. Remuneration systems are to be adapted to local conditions in a manner that is fair and equitable and secures the basic social needs of our employees.

Statoil's approach to labour relations has helped us build a strong and competitive national oil company by offering the following advantages:

■ a low level of conflict;
■ informed management decisions;
■ job satisfaction and employee retention.

Among the 21 countries in which Statoil currently operates, there is a large geographical spread as well as great variations in terms of socio-economic development and degree of political freedom. The extent to which labour rights are respected also varies, of course, meaning that Statoil's challenges of upholding labour standards and developing good industrial relations differ from one country to another.

However, the promotion of cooperation between workers and management remains a part of Statoil's basic approach to labour relations because we believe that it helps create a stable business environment and secure our license to operate. Statoil's agreement with the International Federation of Chemical, Energy, Mine and General Workers' Unions (ICEM) is a valuable tool in this regard.

The Statoil–ICEM Agreement

In 1998, Statoil entered into an agreement with the International Federation of Chemical, Energy, Mine and General Workers' Unions, the international trade secretariat for 20 million workers in 110 countries. This was the first agreement of its kind between a labour federation like ICEM and an individual company.

In order to create a natural link between Statoil and ICEM, the Norwegian Oil and Petrochemical Workers' Union (NOPEF) acted as intermediary and signed the agreement on their own behalf. The agreement was renewed in March 2001 and adapted to the principles of the Global Compact.

The purpose of the agreement remains '*To create an open channel of information between ICEM and Statoil Management about industrial relations issues in order to continuously improve and develop good work practise in Statoil's worldwide operations.*'

Implementation of the agreement has so far covered

■ meetings to discuss specific challenges in Statoil's international portfolio;

■ training and awareness raising, including Statoil's participation in ICEM's training of trade union representatives from SOCAR in Azerbaijan;

■ consultations whereby Statoil has been able to contribute to the resolution of labour disputes;

■ mutual support: Statoil participated at ICEM's World Congress in 1998 and recently ICEM took part in a meeting of the Scandinavian (sub-) group of Global Compact convened by Statoil.

As far as Statoil is concerned, the agreement with ICEM can contribute to improved risk management by way of increased insight into the causes of labour disputes and how to resolve them. Statoil will enhance its reputation as a socially responsible company by becoming better at managing labour relations.

A global agreement for local improvement

It is important that labour relations are managed in accordance with local conditions. Considerations of legitimacy and efficiency require that employee concerns should be handled by those closest to the issues. We believe that the ICEM agreement will help us address this requirement without interfering with established local practices.

THE STATOIL–ICEM AGREEMENT

As described on the basis of the guiding questions from the Global Compact Learning Forum.

Which of the nine principles are being addressed?

■ When renewed in March 2001, the agreement was adapted to the principles of the Global Compact. While covering human rights, labour standards and the environment, the main focus of the agreement is on the four labour principles:

• Freedom of association and the effective recognition of the right to collective bargaining (*Principle 3*).

• The elimination of all forms of forced and compulsory labour (*Principle 4*).

• The effective abolition of child labour (*Principle 5*).

- The elimination of discrimination in respect of employment and occupation (*Principle 6*).

What triggered the actions?

■ Our ambition to uphold labour standards and develop good industrial relations wherever we operate, especially in countries that tend to violate the rights of workers.

Are the actions company wide or restricted to a specific unit?

■ The ICEM agreement is a global agreement for local improvement. Considerations of legitimacy and efficiency require that employee concerns should be handled by those closest to the issues. While the agreement is company wide, the implementation of it is related to specific business units and countries. Through the ICEM agreement, Statoil hopes to improve labour relations at the local level without interfering with established local practices.

Do the actions involve other players, e.g. labour or NGOs?

■ The agreement with ICEM was the first agreement of its kind between a labour federation and an individual company. In order to create a natural link between Statoil and ICEM, the Norwegian Oil and Petrochemical Workers' Union (NOPEF) acted as intermediary and signed the agreement on their own behalf.

How is progress measured?

■ Progress is evaluated during the meetings and consultations with ICEM.

What are the costs and benefits?

■ Costs
  - There are no monetary costs related to the agreement *per se*. There are some costs related to concrete actions (i.e. training and awareness raising), but these are more than compensated for by the benefits.
■ Benefits
  - Improved risk management.
  - Enhanced reputation as a socially responsible company.

What are the factors that supported or impeded progress?

■ Support
  - A strong commitment to the rights of workers.
  - An approach to labour relations based on dialogue and cooperation between management and employees.

■ Impede
  • The challenge of assuming responsibility for upholding labour rights in countries where governance is weak or bad without overstepping the legitimate role of a commercial entity in society.

What key lessons could be useful for other companies?
■ Agreements like the one between ICEM and Statoil enable us to improve industrial relations overall without interfering with established local practices.

What are the next steps?
■ As the Statoil–ICEM relationship matures, we envision more of the same as far as practical implementation is concerned:
  • more joint training and awareness raising;
  • more frequent meetings and consultations;
  • more mutual support.

Contact

Geir Westgaard
Country Analysis and Social Responsibility
Email: gewe@statoil.com

Natalja Altermark
Country Analysis and Social Responsibility
Email: nalt@statoil.com

Commentary

As Statoil's submission states: '(Our) approach to labour relations is rooted in a Norwegian tradition which emphasises dialogue and co-operation. Not confrontation, between employers and employees.'

■ The main question arising from the company's exemplary submission is a cultural one: does this way of working translate to other parts of the world?
■ And if so, has it used it amongst its subsidiaries?
■ How has it used its global supply chains to increase 'respect for the integrity of employees' around the world in its networks?

Statoil was one of the few companies to follow the criteria laid down by the Learning Forum team for submission of a case study.

Principle Four

Skanska AB

Executive summary

Skanska is continuously working to change and improve the environment. Through our operations, we influence social developments, which makes it natural to broaden our perspective as well as establish a common approach and ambition concerning the social responsibility of the growing Skanska Group. In this work, we welcome a dialogue within world business. We regard the Global Compact as one useful way to share experience with other companies and learn from each other. By improving our expertise and working methods, we can achieve better solutions in order to protect human rights and labor as well as the environment. We are thus proud to provide a concrete example of progress made and lessons learned. The project to construct 11 bridges in Honduras after Hurricane Mitch addresses the nine principles of Global Compact in a very concrete way.

Mats Wäppling
Executive Vice President, Skanska AB

Skanska – a background

Skanska's business priorities are construction-related services and project development, with the mission to develop, build and service the physical environment for living, working and traveling. Skanska was founded in 1887 in Sweden, and started by manufacturing cement products. Today, Skanska operates in more than 60 countries around the world, and the number of employees amounts to about 85,000. The main markets are Sweden, the US, UK, Denmark, Finland, Norway, Poland, the Czech Republic, Argentina and Hong Kong. Skanska has close partnerships with many other companies, and puts together consortia to take complete responsibility for a project. Some recent and on-going projects where Skanska has had the main role are the JFK Airport in New York, the Atrium Business Center in Warsaw, the Pungwe project in Zimbabwe (providing Mutare with water) and the Öresund Bridge that links Denmark and Sweden. It is often claimed that Skanska's success can be attributed to technical competence and the ability to adapt to local cultures (for more information on Skanska, see www.skanska. com).

Implementing the nine principles at the Group level

Below, some examples are given on how Skanska endeavors to implement the nine principles of the Global Compact on the Group level. The actions are valid for all activities within the company.

Human rights

Skanska has been a member of the World Business Council for Sustainable Development (WBCSD) since 1995. Skanska is participating, among other things, in the project that is dealing with the *social responsibilities* of companies.

Labor

On February 8 2001, Skanska signed an *agreement* with the *International Federation of Building and Wood Workers*, IFBWW, an international trade secretariat that supports the organization of workers in the construction, building, wood and forestry sectors. In principle, the agreement stipulates that employment conditions offered to the employees of Skanska shall meet the minimum requirements of national legislation. Furthermore, relevant ILO conventions and recommendations concerning the company's business activities shall be respected. The agreement applies to all units and subsidiaries of the Skanska Group, and the agreement also stipulates that subcontractors should be informed of the agreement.

Environment

Skanska is working actively with environmental issues both at the policy level and in hands-on projects. For the third consecutive year, Skanska is included in the Dow Jones Sustainability Group Index. This index features companies regarded as capable of combining high sustainable profitability with long-term sustainable development (www.sustainability-index.com). Some examples of actions that regard all projects and employees are:

- Since January 1 2000, common rules for the use of *chemical substances* have applied at all companies in the Skanska Group.
- Since December 31, 2000, all of Skanska's operations have been certified according to the *ISO 14001 international standard*. Units acquired after 1998 shall have been certified within two years after acquisition.
- To decrease the contribution to the climate change, Skanska has initiated a discussion within the European Union on measures to increase *the energy efficiency of existing buildings* and is currently participating in a dialogue with the European Commission on this issue.
- During 2000, Skanska actively participated in the work of the World Commission on Dams (WCD) to develop *guidelines concerning major dam projects*. Skanska has also declared its support for the principles in the WCD's final report.
- Skanska signed the ICC Business Charter for Sustainable Development in 1995.

Internal exchange of experience takes place through the Skanska Environmental Management Forum, where all environmental managers meet annually. For a number of topics, working groups have been established at the Group level to develop best practice.

For further information, the annual environmental report of Skanska may be downloaded or ordered from www.skanska.com.

Implementing the nine principles at the Project level

The work within Skanska is largely project oriented. Besides the rules that apply to the whole Group or to a specific Business Unit, every project has its own goals, targets and programs. Consequently, the concrete actions to live up to the nine principles of the Global Compact are best demonstrated using a specific case. The on-going construction of bridges in Honduras was selected as such an example, as the project illustrates Skanska's activities in third-world countries (see also the article 'Bridge construction at record time in Honduras').

Honduras bridges – a Skanska project

At the end of October 1998, Hurricane Mitch hit Central America, and exceptional floods and erosion in the rivers caused the destruction of several large bridges and major roads. Soon afterwards, the Swedish government decided that their aid contribution would be concentrated on the re-establishment of the country's infrastructure. As a result, Skanska International Civil Engineering was awarded the contract of repairing eleven bridges. The project included:

- building temporary bypasses
- constructing new abutments
- constructing new piers
- constructing new concrete bridge decks
- reconstructing the approach roads.

The eleven bridges are being simultaneously constructed in various regions of Honduras over a very concentrated time period, which puts great demands on logistics and co-ordination. According to the Swedish International Development Cooperation Agency (Sida), the co-operation between the actors – Skanska, Sweco (a Swedish consultancy company), Sida and the Honduran National Road Administration (Soptravi) – has been very successful. On the whole, the bridge construction projects are progressing much faster than expected. For example, the Nacaome Bridge could be taken into service four months earlier than scheduled. All other projects will be finished during 2001.

Which of the nine principles are being addressed?

Human rights

■ Skanska participates in creating a waste management system in Sabá, a village near one of the sites. Skanska's role is to provide garbage bins. Skanska has also built a playground at a local school (*Principle 1*).

■ Before starting up a new site, a public meeting is held to inform and communicate with the inhabitants of the area. During the project, a local staff manager sees to the interests and rights of the locals and acts as their spokesman (*Principle 2*).

Labour

All demands on a construction project in Sweden should also be fulfilled in this project. All workers are to carry a helmet, and everyone is supplied with welding protection equipment, lifelines, working gloves, ear and eye protection. There must be first aid kits and signs stating that this is a work site and there is no admittance for unauthorised people. The Honduran staff is offered English classes and access to the Internet. A training program has been elaborated that everyone participating in the projects has to go through, followed by a written test. The salaries are automatically increased after one year of employment, and advances may be had when needed for education of children, improvement of living conditions, sudden illness in the family, etc. When new staff are recruited, those living near the site are given priority. No child labor is allowed. These actions primarily address *Principles 4 to 6* (to some extent also *Principle 8*).

The Swedish bridge projects were assessed as being of high quality when representatives of the International Federation of Building and Wood Workers paid an unexpected visit. The organization had established a contact with the Honduran government to get suggestions about a good construction site. They were then recommended to study the Swedish bridge projects in the country. The local union representatives were impressed by the order and effectiveness at the work site visited. They were also aware of Skanska's low frequency of accidents at the sites – they stated that there are considerably fewer accidents there than on the local work sites (*Principles 3 to 6*).

Environment

Environmental consideration is taken in the building of the bridges, both on sites and in the surrounding nature:

■ An environmental assessment is made for each bridge, as an obligation towards Sida (*Principle 7*).

■ Each other week, Skanska's environmental manager together with the respective site manager is performing an environmental and working environment check on each site (*Principles 7 and 8*).

- The work sites must be kept clean and proper, there must be good orderliness in storage and workshop and there must be environmentally friendly toilets, good lighting, air, battery treatment, and borders around diesel tanks and inspection pits. Information sheets regarding safe handling of chemicals are always available at each site. All local foremen must undergo a course in first aid and fire-extinguishing (*Principle7*).
- Machines in bad condition, or that are leaking, are taken out of work (*Principle 7*).
- Skanska has an agreement with Esso Standard Oil that takes care of the waste oil (*Principle 8*).
- Skanska's common rules for the use of chemical substances are applied in the purchase process, and Material Safety Data Sheets are requested from suppliers of new products (*Principle 8*).
- If feasible, the sites are connected to the existing electricity supply system to minimize use of diesel driven generators (*Principle 8)*.
- Skanska aims at using primarily local sub-contractors and suppliers. This helps to minimize the transports and to avoid delays, while giving benefit to the country. For example, previously Skanska only used own equipment but the waiting time could be long, whereas today the equipment is rented directly at site if it doesn't arrive on time. Showing the local companies which Skanska is co-operating with that it is possible to build this fast is a good way to transfer knowledge (*Principle 8*).
- Skanska is helping one of its biggest local suppliers, Conhsa Payhsa, in the process of qualifying for a ISO14001 certificate (*Principle 8*).
- All bridges are similar in design and construction, which brings about an efficient production process. The materials used for moulds may then be reused. Through prefabrication of the superstructures, the local impact on the rivers and the surrounding environment can be minimized (*Principle 9*).
- At several bridge projects, the waste water has been taken care of by connecting to the local water and sewerage system, and at the remaining projects three compartment septic tanks for treatment of the sewage have been constructed (**Principle 9**).

What triggered the actions?

High demands from the client (Sida) together with the ambitions and working methods within Skanska contributed to the actions described. Skanska's broad experience of this type of project was crucial to get the wished-for results. High motivation of the middle management at Skanska also contributed to making this project successful.

Are the actions company wide or restricted to a specific unit?

Many working methods used by Skanska are company wide, such as the commitments made through the ISO 14001 certificate, the common rules for use of chemical substances and the project plans. However, as the work within Skanska is project oriented, many issues are relevant only to the project in question. Some significant working tools applied in this project are a Mobilization manual which is used as a guideline for starting up new projects, a Logistic manual, and a Security & Emergency manual.

Do the actions involve other players, e.g. labour or NGOs?

One such involvement at the project level was the public meetings that were held with the local community. The local labor force is highly involved throughout the project

How is progress measured?

The project plan comprises eight defined targets that are based on the targets of the Business Unit and the site-specific environmental impact assessment. Of these, two targets refer to safety and two to environment:

- minimize the number of working accidents;
- minimize the number of traffic accidents;
- safe handling of chemical products;
- minimize the burden to the local community through correct handling and disposal of waste.

The targets are followed up and documented on a monthly basis. Internal project revisions are held twice a year. So far, all goals are achieved except for traffic accidents, which is partly explained by frequent transportation of equipment, material and workers to every individual bridge spread out all over Honduras.

What are the costs and benefits?

As every construction project is unique, it is hard to assess the relative costs and benefits for specific measures taken. In this project, however, obviously the activities described (keeping everything in good order, etc.) have contributed to a shortened project time leading to decreased costs for all parties involved – not to mention the benefits for the people who may take a bridge into use earlier than expected. Some of the bridges are part of the international logistic trade network between the countries, like Nacaome bridge on the Panamerican Highway, which connects El Salvador with Honduras and Nicaragua. Another benefit – although hard to quantify – is a low frequency in accidents due to continuous follow-up of quality, environment and working environment.

What are the factors that supported or impeded progress?

In general, previous experience of the Skanska organization and employees supported progress, in combination with a positive attitude from the local staff and the local community. Skanska had the opportunity to be involved at an early stage of the project, which provided the opportunity to consider efficient production methods, safety precautions and environmental aspects. The Honduran National Road Administration (Soptravi) helped voluntarily with working visas, custom clearance and required land acquisition. The Swedish Embassy opened many doors that speeded up the mobilization phase. Another example is one local city Mayor who contributed with VIP cards for all expatriates signed by him and the local police chief, to be used in case of emergency.

What key lesson could be useful to other companies?

Good and open-minded cooperation with all parties creates a favorable working climate, which often results in a successful project for all involved. Everyone is then eager to solve the problems quickly and favorably instead of antagonize tricky situations.

What are the next steps?

Skanska is currently developing a Code of Conduct that includes human rights, employee relations and environmental issues. It addresses the issues covered by the Global Compact, which thus will be integrated in the Code of Conduct.

Contact

Max Juhlin
Project Manager, Skanska International Civil Engineering AB
E-Mail: skanska.ger@mundo123.hn

Commentary

There are three features to Skanska's submission to the Global Compact Learning Forum that are useful in taking forward the corporate citizenship debate.

First, and perhaps most significant, is the style, tone and register in which the submission is written. As one would expect from a Scandinavian company there is significant reference to the building of trust and long-term relationships. This characteristic, coupled with the company's technical competence, has obviously been essential to its business success.

Second, the submission is peppered with references to the company's engagement with other initiatives. These references range from business associations to the adoption of global management systems to the inclusion of global indicators on sustainability. These references allow the reader to follow their investigative noses and develop an understanding of the larger picture on the social and environmental risks involved in running a global construction company. It is worth listing the external references in this submission as an indication of how the company sees itself in relation to its total polity:

- member of the World Business Council for Sustainable Development;
- an agreement with the International Federation of Building and Wood Workers;
- inclusion in the Dow Jones Sustainability Index;
- certification to ISO 14000 series;
- dialogue with the EU on energy efficiency;
- participation in the World Commission on Dams;
- signatory of the ICC's Business Charter on Sustainable Development.

The reader is asked to see each company submission as how the company would like to be seen. It does not presuppose that the company will necessarily be believed, but the more external reference points, the more likely it is that the company's engagement in the Learning Forum will be taken as a genuine attempt rather than disingenuousness. This leads to the third point of interest in Skanska's submission. While there are many references to its external engagements and partnerships, there is little evidence of external monitoring or verification of the many assertions that are made in the submissions with regard to health and safety and the environment. Its systems and standards mentioned are all valid and to be applauded, but the problem for any company now is that of credibility. However, companies in Scandinavia are seen in the main as active and reliable participants in society as a whole and there may be a greater reliance on trust and relationship building than in some more cynical parts of the world where business has played a greater role in social dislocation and exclusion.

Principle Five

Royal Dutch/Shell Group of Companies

Shell believes that the UN initiative to encourage a global network of values and principles agreed by all the Compact partners is an exciting opportunity. It stimulates co-operation, communication and engagement between business, policy makers, civil society organisations and other leading thinkers and actors in the global arena. And it provides a valuable forum for building a shared understanding of how important issues can be addressed realistically and responsibly.

The issues covered by the Compact are challenging. In many cases there are more dilemmas than simple global solutions. Shell certainly does not claim to have definitive answers. We are increasing our efforts to gain a deeper understanding of the issues, and to ensure that core values are applied effectively throughout our operations in more than 135 countries and a multitude of different cultures.

When the Global Compact was launched, Sir Mark Moody-Stuart, Chairman of the Royal Dutch/Shell Group, stressed that in Shell, we believe that a responsible business must justify its legitimacy in the eyes of societies and opinion leaders, and regulate itself effectively and openly. That is why, for almost 25 years, Shell companies have operated on the basis of the Shell General Business Principles (SGBP).

Over the years this statement of core values has been regularly reviewed, and when necessary revised, to reflect changing circumstances. The most recent revision, in 1997, was based on extensive consultation, both inside Shell and with external publics.

The SGBP are in line with the UN Global Compact, the Global Sullivan Principles and the recently revised OECD Guidelines for Multinational Enterprises. They are based on three fundamental values of honesty, integrity and respect for people, and they underpin all aspects of corporate behaviour.

They recognise that the Group has five areas of responsibility: to share-holders, to customers, to employees, to those with whom they do business and to society. They include commitments to support sustainable development and fundamental human rights.

Principles One and Two of the Global Compact are being addressed by the Group in accordance with its own principles governing responsibilities to employees and to society and its support for fundamental human rights.

In order to help staff understand the issues and dilemmas which may arise when applying the Business Principles in their daily working lives, the Group publishes 'primers'. One of these is an introductory guide to human rights; another deals with the complex problem of child labour. Both primers were written with the help of independent experts. They are available to the public and can be downloaded from the Shell website (www.shell.com/primers).

In addition, a special human rights site was launched on Shell's internal computer network on December 10 1998, the 50th anniversary of the United Nations Universal Declaration of Human Rights.

For this first posting, we focus specifically on our efforts with regard to Principle 5 of the Global Compact, 'the effective abolition of child labour'.

The Shell primer 'Business and Child Labour' examines the nature and causes of child labour, the major legal instruments that address the issue and how child labour affects and is affected by international businesses. It provides guidance to Shell managers, including practical examples of the measures that Shell companies are taking to address the issue.

Some key points are:

- The term 'child labour' refers to a type and intensity of work that hampers children's access to education, harms their health and development and deprives them of their childhood or their self-respect.
- The causes of child labour are complex, but are linked to poverty, the absence of basic education and the persistence of certain social structures and attitudes. Child labour is especially prevalent in the informal manufacturing sector and in domestic activities. The ILO has estimated that there are some 250 million children in paid work, with many more in unpaid activities, and that Asia accounts for more than 60% of the world's child workforce. However, the problem affects all regions and is growing in certain areas such as Eastern Europe.
- National legislation is the first point of regulation for child labour but it is also the subject of various international conventions, notably ILO 138 (The Minimum Age Convention), ILO 182 on the worst forms of child labour and the UN Convention on the Rights of the Child (especially Article 32).
- The effects of globalisation on working children can be both positive and negative. Foreign direct investment can create jobs and increase export earnings, helping to reduce the poverty associated with child labour. But increasing competition for foreign direct investment can result in greater pressure to reduce production costs, leading to the use of children as a cheap, compliant workforce.
- Company responses must be clearly thought through, taking into account the views of many stakeholders. Experience has shown that without sensitivity and broad engagement, even well meaning responses can actually have a detrimental effect on children. A broader response to child labour can be achieved through specific social investment activities.

Child labour might not seem an obvious area of concern for a global energy enterprise like Shell. But it is a problem which is affecting all regions of the world today. Our Business Principles – and the values they represent – mean that Shell companies must not exploit children in any of their activities, either directly or indirectly through joint ventures, contractors or suppliers. This is monitored, and we can report the following:

- In every Shell company, employees are above the local legal age of employment. The youngest company employee, who is 15 years old, works part time in Europe.
- Shell companies in 101 countries have a specific policy to prevent the use of child labour in any of their operations. In 112 countries, they operate a procedure to prevent the use of child labour.
- The number of Shell companies that screen contractors increased from 51 in 1998 to 63 in 1999, and those screening suppliers from 28 to 41

in the same timeframe. Such screening includes, for instance, anti-child labour clauses in contracts and notification sent to all suppliers that they should observe ILO 138. In some countries, site visits and audits have been conducted to ensure compliance.

Although we would not claim that these measures provide a complete assurance, we believe they are raising awareness of the problem and giving a clear indication to Shell companies and those they work with that the use of child labour is unacceptable.

To take one specific case, Shell Brasil has been awarded the title of 'Child Friendly Company' for its pioneering work in discouraging the use of child labour in the production of sugar cane alcohol, which it is legally obliged to sell on its forecourts and include in its gasoline.

The award was made by a local NGO called ABRINQ, supported by UNICEF. This recognition followed the participation of Shell Brasil in a broader debate with NGOs, local government and distillers to find ways to help families whose children work in the sugar cane fields and other rural industries. The legal minimum working age in Brazil is 14 years.

State governments, distillers and other producers (including producers of sisal, oranges and coal) have been working with the affected families to set up funds that can be used to educate the children who would otherwise go to work to support their families.

Shell Brasil has introduced a clause in its contracts with distillers forbidding the use of child labour and asking them to respect the Business Principles. So far, the company has not needed to enforce the clause because suppliers share these concerns.

The Shell view is that the best way to promote responsible global citizenship is to live it. We see a commitment to fundamental human rights, and a focus on issues such as child labour, as part of the 'best practice' to which Shell companies aspire. But ensuring best practice, and facing up to dilemmas posed by issues like these, is an on-going challenge. It would also be idealistic to assume that performance will automatically match aspirations unless there is effective internal and external monitoring.

That is why the Shell General Business Principles are published, and compliance with them is subject to internal checking mechanisms. But it is not enough simply to achieve internal satisfaction about the way the business is being conducted. The outside world must also be satisfied. An important step towards external verification has been the annual publication, since 1998, of The Shell Report.

These reports give detailed evidence of how Shell companies are living up to the SGBP. The Shell Report 2000 examines progress related to support for human rights, including the issue of child labour. The content of the Report can be found online throughout the Shell website www.shell.com. The Shell Reports provide a basis for dialogue, discussion

– and criticism – of performance. At the same time, work is under way to develop management systems, which will produce increasingly verifiable measures of performance.

The commitment to support fundamental human rights and the focus on the issue of child labour illustrate our belief in what the Global Compact and those associated with it are trying to achieve in these areas.

The issues are complex, and the approaches outlined here are steps along the path to a shared goal, not an end in themselves. We know there is more to be done and that others will have questions or different answers. Dialogue and debate on how best to address these issues is important in achieving the aims of the Global Compact. That is why we are happy to take this opportunity of sharing our efforts to put core values at the centre of corporate practices.

Contact

Xiaowei Liu
External Relations & Policy Development Adviser
Shell International Ltd.
Email: xiaowei.x.liu@si.shell.com

Commentary

Shell was the first company to make a submission to the Global Compact Learning Forum and as such deserves praise for engaging in this new process while other companies did so only under duress and belatedly. It was a surprise to many that this company's submission covered child labour in Brazil rather than perhaps one of its higher-profile debacles or the use of fossil fuels or its work in threatened parts of the natural world. However, in the spirit of learning the company readily accepted the UN's commentary process and was happy to address questions put to it, the answers to which have clarified some of the issues raised in the commentary.

The Shell submission does make points which are not covered by many of the other submissions. First, it refers to the company's relationship to 'policy makers, civil society organisations and other leading thinkers and actors on the global stage'. In other words it sees itself as a participant in a global conversation about the role, scope and purpose of business in the delivery of private wealth and public goods. Second, it makes reference to its General Business Principles which are founded on the personal ethical principles of 'honesty, integrity and respect for people'. As has been seen from some other high-profile cases in recent history, a statement of principles is not enough to secure either compliance with those principles or to gain credibility with external stakeholders (both Enron and Arthur Andersen had high principles and had engaged in many corporate citizenship initiatives). Shell, though, has been a leader in social and environmental reporting for many years and is light years ahead of most other oil companies, let alone most companies operating on the world stage.

However, Shell's submission raises many fundamental thoughts:

- Why did it choose this example for such a high profile initiative as the UN's Global Compact?
- How is it using its networks and supply chains to bring about a reassessment and understanding of child labour in all the 135 countries in which the company operates?
- What is the relationship between economies where exploitative child labour is common and the global fossil fuel economy? Does the latter help maintain global trading conditions that mitigate against providing basic services and education for school-age children?

Principle Six

DuPont

DuPont believes that a key aspect of human and worker rights is the right to work in an environment that is safe and healthy. A strong safety and health focus is the essential foundation for successfully implementing a culture that seeks to integrate sustainable development into the processes of the company. Safety values are also critical in the successful transferring of new technologies to developing countries. Although we believe that safety touches each of the nine principles, the specific principle being addressed is: Principle 1 – Support and respect the protection of international human rights within the sphere of influence – safe and healthy working conditions.

In 1994, as part of a process to increase transparency around DuPont policy and operations, DuPont adopted a Safety, Health, and Environmental (SHE) Commitment (whole text available at: www.dupont.com/corp/environment/commitment.html) which clearly stated the 'Goal is zero for all injuries, illnesses, and incidents' and that compliance with the Commitment is the responsibility of every employee and contractor working on behalf of DuPont. DuPont's commitment to safety and health began when the corporation was founded in 1802. Over the centuries, the products that the company produced have changed considerably, but the commitment to the value of safety, health, and environmental stewardship has remained a constant. The adoption of the SHE Commitment was a major step in publicly committing the organization to the goal of zero injuries, illnesses, and incidents any place that we operate in the world. This goal has also been extended beyond DuPont's gates to include contractors, suppliers, distributors, and customers.

There is strong backup documentation that a safe working environment makes business sense. Estimates are that each lost work injury costs a company about $50,000 and each major incident costs a company in excess of $200 million. Enhanced business value includes such things as:

- lower worker compensation expenses
- better rates from contractors and insurers
- enhanced productivity and dependability of supply
- enhanced reputation as a safe, caring and environmentally aware corporation in the eyes of the public, the media, government regulators, and the local communities where we operate.

Although many of the benefits are difficult to measure, DuPont believes that our costs would be between $150 and $200 million higher per year if we operated at the industry average for safety performance.

In addition, DuPont believes that the focus on safety is core to the company's ability to integrate sustainable growth into the business strategies globally. The organization clearly sees that the leadership values their health and wellbeing, therefore it becomes a natural extension for the organization to take responsibility for the company's impact on our local communities and society as a whole.

Key practices necessary for a robust system:

- Top management commitment and FELT leadership for the value of safety and occupational health.
- Line management personally accountable and responsible for safety and occupational health performance.
- Expectation of zero injuries, illnesses, and incidents.
- Auditing and verification.
- Employee involvement.
- Networks to share information broadly.

Based on the belief that these practices as well as specific tools that have been developed are transferable to other companies, DuPont has established a business unit to assist other organizations adopt these practices and tools.

Examples:

1. In 1994, when DuPont's safety and health performance began to deteriorate after a significant corporate reorganization, the CEO chartered a team to 'discover' reasons for the change and to implement strategies to improve performance. Team membership included senior leadership as well as operators and mechanics from key manufacturing sites. The team met regularly and included actually working a shift at one site so that they could better understand the issues associated with working safely in today's workplace. After three months, an overall assessment and recommenda-

tions were presented to the Corporate Operating Group and were immediately implemented across the corporation. The key finding was that with the multiple distractions of reorganizations and changes in operating processes, the organization had lost its focus on operating safely. Steps were taken to emphasize top management's commitment and leadership and to refocus on line management accountability. Additional steps included strengthening the networks to share information and best practices broadly around the world. The injury/illness rating improved quickly from this action – dropping from approximately 0.9 total recordable frequency rate to a sustained rate of about 0.4.

2. In 1999, a significant effort was undertaken to more fully include all ergonomic injuries and illnesses into the safety and health management system. Training materials were developed and all key personnel were trained in each of the strategic business units in the US. In 2001, the program was rolled out to the other global regions where we operate. Objectives and targets for performance improvements were set. The success of the program is demonstrated by the 21% reduction in ergonomic related injuries between 2000 and 2001. One site in Brazil reported the cost/benefit of their ergonomic programs between 1997 and 2000 to be greater than $650,000. Initiatives to reduce ergonomic injuries and illnesses included:

■ establishment of teams which included operators, mechanics, technicians and management to operate a process to uncover unsafe and unhealthy practices and procedures in operations;

■ development of a tool to quantify the risks associated with specific work practices and consequently design the task to prevent injuries and illnesses.

3. All business units also set safety objectives and targets for contractors working on our sites. Contractor safety and health performance is reported and tracked along with employee safety and health performance. Specific examples of contractor programs include:

■ development and installation of a 'Contractor Safety Learning Laboratory' for orienting all contractors to the site safety philosophy, rules and requirements and expectations for contractor behavior while on site;

■ establishment of regular safety meetings with all main permanent contractors;

■ establishment of partnerships with key contractors.

4. The standard is global, so all sites are expected to have the same performance. As an example, when the Lycra site was built in Shanghai the goal of zero injuries and illnesses was established. As a result of the safety focus, in over 2 million man-hours of work over a two-year period, there was only one minor injury. The project was completed on time and within budget. Specific safety and health programs included:

- personal protection equipment was provided and use was required at all times;
- construction safety specialists were on site during the entire project to assure standards were followed;
- the Project Manager and Construction Manager conducted weekly site audits relative to safety procedures and performance;
- goals were set and publicized broadly. Milestones were set and celebrated when they were reached.

5. DuPont Far Eastern Petrochemicals Ltd., Taiwan created an outreach program to influence associated industries with regards to distribution, safety and transportation of dangerous goods. By utilizing DuPont standards and practices and working closely with all affected parties, there has been an increased understanding of the issue, the benefits of the goal of zero accidents, and a closer working relationship has been established between suppliers and haulers. The approach involved demonstrating the benefits, influencing, coaching and team building over several years with continuity of people in key positions within DuPont and the haulers. In 1998 and 1999 there were zero distribution accidents and injuries.

6. A team from DuPont Mexico has worked with the Mexican government for the past 15 years to create a safety and accident prevention culture within industry. The team has taken a visible leadership role at discussion forums and through sponsoring and leading emergency response drills that have helped other industries to improve their safety performance. In 2000 this included the first bi-national chemical response simulation between Matamoros, Tamaulipas Mexico and Brownsville, Texas. DuPont Mexico took a leadership role in designing, planning, executing, and evaluating the simulation. Based on the success, DuPont has participated in two additional drills and will continue to participate in these bi-national simulations. DuPont Mexico believed that they received the following positive benefits from this work:

- improved employee satisfaction at seeing their experience and knowledge valued and applied by customers and authorities;
- strengthened teamwork and cooperation between authorities and industry;
- opening the door to other bi-national cooperation opportunities covered by the North American Free Trade Agreement (NAFTA).

7. Safety at our customer locations is also important to how we view our safety commitment. Over the years there have been numerous examples where we have worked in customer operations to improve their safety performance. A recent example in Canada demonstrates this. After an operator was killed on the job, two DuPont managers worked overtime in the mills to create an in depth safety report and presented recommendations to improve their safety performance. In Brazil, a team of employees devel-

oped a safety, health, and environmental education program on the safe use of crop protection chemicals for growers, applicators, end users, students and families of those directly using crop protection products. In just two years they trained 46,000 people.

Contact

Dawn Rittenhouse
Director, Sustainable Development
Email: dawn.g.rittenhouse@usa.dupont.com

Commentary

In company with some other global organizations DuPont has a zero fatality policy on its sites worldwide. Given the number of deaths that occur on industrial sites this in itself is a significant initiative. Although in some parts of the world such a policy may be taken as an obvious commitment, it must be remembered that this policy would set high standards elsewhere. DuPont accompanies this statement of policy with an explanation of the business case in some detail. Of interest is that, despite the fact that the company says that this submission is in support of human rights (it cites Principle One, but it is more appropriate to Principle Six), the substance of the content is on the management of the policy, not on the morality of the principle.

So, in terms of the Global Compact Learning Forum it is an excellent case study in that it helps other companies to understand DuPont's management of the principle. However, there are areas of interest:

- What happened in 1994 in terms of corporate reorganization that led to a deterioration in health and safety performance?
- Does the company continue to send senior management out on site to work shifts in order to learn by doing?
- Is the company's core business dangerous to people or the environment? How does it justify its work on its range of products?

Principle seven

Power Finance Corporation's role in environment management of power sector

This case study addresses the three principles of the Global Compact relating to environment, particularly to take initiatives to promote greater environmental responsibility.

Problem area

The Indian Power Sector has to grow at the rate of 12% in order to sustain the GDP growth of 7%. Large demand for power generation in India has resulted in overexploitation of natural resources and the fallout in terms of environmental degradation and resource depletion is a cause of national concern. Thermal Power Plant is one of eighteen highly polluting industries identified by the Indian Ministry of Environment & Forests (MoEF). Large Hydro Power Projects, such as Sardar Sarovar Project, are already involved in several controversies over issues of submergence and desettlement.

India is committed to various global environmental issues and is a party to several International Conventions, such as Montreal Protocol, Biodiversity etc. Ozone depletion and global warming have emerged as the major concern in recent years. The contribution of the energy sector in the global GHG emission is 54%. The contribution of coal fired power generation in the emission of CO_2 is approximately 24% of the total CO_2 resulting from the global use of fossil fuel. However, India's contribution to global greenhouse gases has been small: with 16% of world population, India's contribution is only 2% of world fossil fuel carbon emission. However, with accelerated economic growth, increasing energy intensity and heavy dependence on coal, India's contribution could grow to up to 5% of total GHG by 2025 AD.

The high ash content and low calorific value of the coal available for power generation in India has resulted in particulate emission and ash disposal problems. Most of the old power stations designed for coal with 25–30% ash content and gross calorific of 5000 kcal/kg are presently receiving coal with ash content as high as 40% and average gross calorific value between 2500 to 3500 kcal/kg. The ash pond size required for every MW of generating capacity today stands at 0.32 ha. At present, 80 million tonnes per annum of flyash is being disposed of in the slurry form in ash dykes, which is likely to increase to 100 million tonnes per annum by 2005AD.

The Indian Ministry of Environment & Forests has prescribed several measures in its guidelines for thermal power generation regarding dry flyash collection at all plants – 100% ash utilisation within a stipulated time frame of 9 to 12 years etc. However, at present, only a small percentage (3 to 5%) of flyash generated in India is used for gainful application. In some states, several incentives/steps have been provided for entrepreneurs to set up projects with flyash as their raw material to promote flyash utilisation. This includes free dry flyash to entrepreneurs, free land/water/electricity, sales tax exemption etc. Some states are also going to impose restrictions on the use of soil for making clay bricks in the vicinity of the power plant.

Thermal power stations in India have been equipped with ESPs to reduce particulate matter concentration in the flue gases. The coal quality in terms of calorific value and ash content has deteriorated over the years, leading to poor reliability of boiler, ESPs and other auxiliaries etc. At the same time, the environmental standards prescribed for particulate matter emissions are becoming increasingly stringent, leading to operational and financial pressure on thermal generation.

The burning of fossil fuel generates large amounts of CO_2, apart from SO_2 and NOx. In India, sulphur content of coal is of the order of 0.2 to 0.6%. Even with low calorific value of coal in India, Sulphur dioxide is not a major issue except in a few areas with excessive industrial activities. Control of sulphur dioxide is achieved through atmospheric dispersion. Efforts are being made to control NOx levels by providing low NOx burners in pulverised coal boilers.

One of the major comprehensive environment upgradation project undertaken by PFC is the environmental upgradation of Durgapur Power Projects Limited which included augmentation of electrostatic precipitators, related ash handling facilities, construction of new ash pond and waste water treatment and recycling etc.

Durgapur Projects Limited (DPL), situated at Durgapur in West Bengal (India), has got a coal based thermal power plant with a capacity of 395 MW. The details of the units are:

Unit no.	Capacity (MW)	Date of commissioning
1	30	10–06–60
2	30	10–04–60
3	75	23–04–64
4	75	19–06–64
5	75	04–05–66
6	110	03–07–85

The two 30 MW unit are not functional and are undergoing life extension work. The three units of 75 MW each were having mechanical dust collectors (MDCs) along with ESPs. The design of the MDC and ESP were based on the prevailing norms/practices and with 'design coal' of low ash content of 30%. The design efficiency of this combination set was 97.5% but with deterioration in quality of coal and deterioration in the efficiency of MDCs and ESPs, the outlet dust concentration was of the order of 21–26 gm/Nm3, resulting in a tremendous amount of environmental pollution and health hazards.

The Environment Protection Act, 1986 specifies a limit of 150 mg/Nm3 for the particulate matter emission from coal based thermal power plants in India.

As a consequence of the Public Interest Litigation (PIL) of M.C. Mehta Vs. Govt. of India, the Supreme Court of India ordered DPL to renovate their ESPs of Unit 3, 4 and 5 to meet the statutory requirement of 150 mg/NM3 at the earliest.

The design emission level of Unit 6 (110 MW) was 514 mg/Nm3 which was again higher than the stipulated level of 150 mg/Nm3. The associated ash handling system was also not capable of handling additional load.

The existing ash ponds, where the ash slurry was being pumped, were inadequate to handle the entire ash production mainly due to increased ash content in the coal available for power generation. Contractors were employed to evacuate ash ponds and there was indiscriminate dumping of ash in the vicinity of Durgapur. This resulted in not only degradation in soil quality but also large amounts of fugitive dust emission were taking place. Stray cases of complaints regarding deterioration in ground water quality (may be due to leaching) were also reported.

Action taken

Power Finance Corporation gives high priority to environmental protection activities of the power sector. PFC does:

■ Ensure that environmental assessment and social impact assessment of the project are incorporated in early stages of formulation as a factor in the analysis of alternatives and design of the project.

■ Assist the borrowers as necessary in identifying major environmental and social issues associated to the project.

■ Assist in the preparation of terms of reference for socio-environmental assessments (SEAs) of different kinds of projects and keep a roster of consultants who can help in preparing assessments and impact mitigation plans.

■ Monitor execution of SEAs to ensure that they meet acceptable quality standards.

■ Ensure that costs of mitigatory actions are properly considered in selecting and costing projects.

■ Ensure that SEAs are conducted in accordance with the applicable standards.

■ Monitor implementation of mitigation plans and ensure that actions indicated by the concerned agencies for environmental clearance are carried out.

■ Assist borrowers in assessing and proposing solutions for the correction of environmental deficiencies of power plants already in operation.

■ Promote and assist utilities in the creation of units specialized in environmental aspects of power utilities (i.e. design, monitoring etc.).

So far, PFC has carried out environmental reviews of 28 thermal power plants and provided technical assistance in the preparation of Environmental Upgradation Action Plans (EUAPs) with time bound implementation schedules. This has helped in prevention and control of the pollution of air, water and land from these installations.

To give extra focus and priority in the implementation of environmental schemes, PFC has relaxed several loan conditions for environmental upgradation activities. It has sanctioned loans worth US $100 million for schemes related to the augmentation of pollution control facilities and other environment protection schemes up to the financial year 2000–01. The major environmental activities being funded by PFC are:

- augmentation of electrostatic precipitators
- augmentation of ash handling plants
- dry flyash collection systems
- ash ponds
- dust extraction and suppression systems
- waste water treatment and recycling
- environment monitoring equipment
- flyash utilisation projects.

PFC has also got a provision for financial assistance to power utilities for undertaking studies to improve the performance and to assist in the development of the power sector. PFC offers various types of grants/interest free loans/soft loans for different types of studies. A grant up to a maximum of US $0.2 million per project is available under this scheme.

Flyash management is also a key area of focus. One activity which PFC has funded very pro-actively is regarding putting up dry flyash collection facilities in the existing TPSs. Presently PFC is also appraising about ten proposals for dry flyash collection systems for MSEB, MPEB and some other SEB units. Such action is likely to result in large scale flyash utilization. PFC is also keenly evaluating flyash utilisation proposals for possible funding including demonstration of new technologies.

In all PFC funded new projects, PFC ensures that various requirements of regulatory authorities put in the form of conditionalities are built in various contract documents and adequate funding is available to implement these measures. PFC has also funded several schemes related to augmentations of ESPs and associated ash handling facilities in the old power stations of electricity boards all over the country. Typically these schemes have resulted in reduction of emissions of suspended particulate matter from thermal stations from high levels of 20–40 grams per cubic meter to 150mg/Nm3 or even less.

In the area of waste management, it has been PFC's endeavors to help the utilities appreciate and adopt the 'zero discharge concept', particularly in the thermal stations located in the water starved areas of the country. To implement these ideas PFC has been regularly funding activities related to waste water treatment and recycling as well as augmentation of ash handling plants for re-circulation of ash water, thereby reducing water pollution load from thermal power stations and creating savings on water bills. Treatment of waste water and its re-use results in reduction in the total water consumption for the station and stops the discharge of waste water containing high amounts of suspended solids, high pH etc. into the fresh water bodies near the thermal station.

In an ash water recirculation scheme being implemented at Parli thermal station of Maharastra State Electricity Board (MSEB), where PFC has been involved throughout the implementation process, total water saving is estimated at 11,000 m3/day. Besides the saving in water consumption, there are other indirect social benefits of such schemes that can be traced to reduced health costs and increased agricultural productivity due to the implementation of water recycling schemes. Similar schemes have been implemented at Koradi and Bhusawal stations of MSEB as well. Such schemes are also being promoted in other thermal stations of various electricity boards.

PFC's contribution in environment upgradation of DPL

PFC had carried out an environment review of DPL and assisted in preparation of the time bound Environmental Upgradation Action Plan (EUAP) for the plant. PFC also assisted in identifying and prioritizing the environmental upgradation schemes. Subsequently, PFC assisted DPL in formulating techno-economically effective environment upgradation schemes. PFC was also involved in preparation of bid documents, technical specifications etc. The following activities were taken up by DPL with PFC's financial assistance:

a. Unit 3,4 & 5
  - Dismantling of existing MDCs and ESPs.
  - Three new electrostatic precipitators with design efficiency of 99.73% and outlet concentration of 135 mg/Nm3.
  - On-line monitoring system for particulate matter, SO_2 and NOx.

b. Unit 6
  - Adding two retrofit ESPs in series with each of the two gas paths.
  - Adding an additional 5 fields parallel to each gas path of existing ESPs.
  - Semi-pulse controller in place of existing T/R set controller.

c. Unit 1 & 2
  - New ESPs are being put up under life extension programme of Unit 1 & 2.

d. New ash pond
  - New ash pond with holding capacity of 0.9 million m3 with a dimension of 400m x 300m x 7.5m.

e. Augmentation of associated ash handling system.

Status

The plant is undergoing major life extension work and hence is not available for generation. However, the augmentation of ESPs in Unit 3, 4 & 5 has been completed. This augmentation work would result in reduced particulate matter load of the order of 552 T/day to the environment, resulting in better environment conditions in the vicinity of the power plant. Augmentation of other ESPs is in progress. Improvement in ambient air quality due to the augmentation work would result in better visibility, less asthma problems and general improvement in the health of living beings around the plant area.

The new ash pond is being constructed. The indiscriminate dumping of ash offsite would stop, thereby improving upon soil quality, air quality and ground water quality in the vicinity of the plant. Various ash utilization proposals are also being formulated. Another proposal for treatment and re-cycling of ash pond overflow and other waste water streams has been formulated and will be implemented in the near future.

Lesson learnt

It is possible to renovate old power plants to meet the present environmental stipulation. This would lead to sustainable development of the power sector by minimizing the environmental impact of coal based power generation.

Contact:

Mr. Deepika Malik
Email: deepimalik@yahoo.com

Commentary

This company submission is significant is several ways. First, it discusses the development of energy sources in an Indian and a global context. Second, the company admits to a significant problem with the disposal of flyash – a problem not confined just to India. Third, mention is made of litigation and regulatory action on this particular issue. The context in which companies operate has not been a significant descriptor in the submissions to the Global Compact Learning Forum, so this case from Power Finance Corporation of India is welcome.

This is a largely descriptive piece and as such it presents in some clarity a learning situation for the company. Beside the fact that extensive use of acronyms makes the submission difficult for non-experts to interpret, while the company tells a story of rectification and endeavour, it fails to supply any external verification for the figures it uses. Also, it would be good to hear whether the company has been working on any other related initiatives that have external validation that would help raise the company's credibility when presenting a submission for inclusion on a UN website.

Principle Eight

Aluminium Bahrain waste minimisation programme

This case study addresses Principle no. 8 from the Global Compact which is to 'undertake initiatives to promote greater environmental responsibility'.

Introduction

Alba (Aluminium Bahrain B.S.C) is one of the world's largest aluminium smelters producing in excess of 500,000 tonnes per annum of primary aluminium. The company, which commenced operations in 1971 and has 2,500 employees, has a number of international, Gulf-wide and national awards for its excellence in industry, human resources development and commitment to the protection of the environment. Its casthouses have operated to ISO 9002 since 1994 and, in addition, Alba was certified in 2000 as complying plant-wide with the ISO14000 Environmental Management System standard.

Alba was invited to join the Global Compact initiative after it was one of only 12 companies in the world to win the International Millennium Business Award for Environmental Achievement, an award presented in 2000 by the United Nations Environment Programme in conjunction with the International Chamber of Commerce.

Background

In the mid 1980s when Alba began to plan for a major expansion, it was clear that the impact on the environment would be beyond acceptable limits unless:

- the latest environmental control technologies were utilised in the expansion;
- the existing plant was retrofitted with state-of-the-art controls.

This management decision paved the way for Alba to embark upon an environmental management initiative even though regulatory controls were not in place for many years after this. At the time, there was also no pressure from stakeholders or the supply chain to implement such an initiative.

The initiative has been adopted throughout all the company's operations and sites and was carried out in a phased manner starting with gaseous emissions, then liquid effluents and finally solid waste. The focus on solid waste began in late 1999.

The commitment to the environment company-wide was translated into a formal Environment Policy in 2000 as part of the ISO 14001 certification process. The Environment Policy, aimed to secure and maintain optimum standards of environmental performance, includes:

- the prevention of pollution
- continual improvement in environmental performance
- complying with all regulatory standards
- recycling initiatives
- setting objectives and targets
- training and awareness for all employees.

Alba now also has a system of benchmarking its environmental performance against similar smelters around the world and this reveals that the company is one of the leaders in its field.

Case study focus

This case study focuses on the environmental achievements of Alba over the last 12 months. In this time, the company achieved the Environmental Management System Standard ISO 14001 for all its operations and also won a GCC-wide award for the 'best environmental activities by an industrial establishment' presented by the GCC Environment Ministers earlier this year.

During the last year, and based on the solid platform of environmental achievements highlighted above, Alba adopted a waste minimisation and recycling initiative as one of its focused environmental improvement projects.

With its 450,000 tonnes per annum (tpa) coke calcining plant, 200,000 tpa anode manufacturing plant, 1500MW power plant and 500,000 tpa aluminium smelter, the quantities of waste products generated are significant. Accordingly, both the need for as well as the opportunities for waste elimination, minimisation and recycling abound.

Planning and strategy

Firstly, a system was put in place to classify, measure and report on the different types of solid and liquid wastes around the plant.

The well-established waste management hierarchy of:

- Elimination
- Minimisation
- Recycling and re-use
- Disposal

was adopted as the way ahead for maximising the success of this initiative. With elimination and minimisation being the cornerstone of the strategy, all the opportunities for this were explored during this phase along with the system requirements, costs and training needs.

The next step consisted of evaluating the opportunities and avenues for recycling, using segregation at source to avoid double handling wherever possible, and identifying which wastes could be recycled.

Implementation

The first phase of implementation involved the preparation of detailed procedures meeting ISO 14001 standards and the subsequent training of personnel. Objectives and targets were set for all departments within the company.

The next step was to procure additional waste handling equipment and to negotiate contracts with waste handling companies and recycling facilities.

Upon implementing the recycling initiatives, the employees became highly enthusiastic about the whole programme, requesting the extension of recycling to more items of waste and to more areas within the company.

Constant vigilance and follow-up even to CEO level in the initial stages helped immensely to make timely corrections and readjustments and thus fine-tune the programme. Such extensive communication on wastes with the workforce and external recycling facilities opened up a number of further opportunities for waste recycling and minimisation.

One example of this is the recycling of ramming paste waste that is hazardous in nature. Ramming paste is used in the re-lining of the electrolytic pots in the aluminium smelter but the leftover ramming paste was being disposed of as a waste. Through trials it is being confirmed that this waste can be used to substitute expensive alumina that is utilised for cathode bedding during re-lining. This leads to a cost saving of BD3,420 (US$9,000) per annum.

In a similar manner, waste refractory bricks are now crushed and used as a substitute for alumina to obtain a flat horizontal cathode shell surface prior to the start of laying insulation bricks for pot re-lining. This has led to a cost saving of BD7,315 (US$19,000) per annum.

The waste minimization chart (Figure A1.2) shows the waste minimization which has been measured from the reduction in the waste category termed as general waste. All the recyclable items were previously disposed of under this category of waste along with other routine non-hazardous wastes.

FIGURE A1.2 ■ Aluminium Bahrain: Waste Minimization

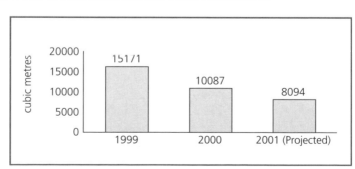

The reduction in this category of general waste and the corresponding increase in recycled wastes shown in the waste recycling chart (Figure A1.3) reflects the success of the programme.

FIGURE A1.3 ■ Aluminium Bahrain: Waste Recycling

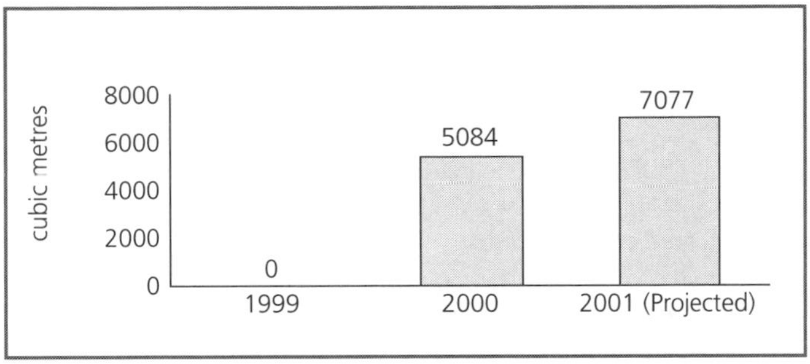

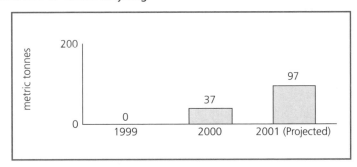

Some of the recycled materials have also brought additional revenue to the company through sales.

For example, the income from the sale of cartons, scrap steel and wood for 2001 is expected to reach US$80,000. Figure A1.4 shows the success of the recycling programme from this example of carton waste recycling.

FIGURE A1.4 ■ Carton Recycling

Hazardous waste

In parallel with the waste minimisation project, another area under focus during the last year has been the disposal of hazardous wastes.

The disposal of hazardous wastes was a major issue for Alba – and indeed other companies – since there was no facility in the country for disposal or treatment of hazardous wastes.

The Environment Ministry attained a suitable and large enough plot of land and, subsequently, Alba advanced finance for this US$1.5 million project.

The result of this partnership with the Ministry is the state-of-the-art hazardous waste disposal facility commissioned in March 2001 and now open to all industries in Bahrain. This close co-operation between the Environment Ministry and Alba continues today.

By September, several items of hazardous wastes that were being accumulated at Alba, for want of safe permanent disposal facilities, were disposed safely at this new facility. 60,000 cubic metres of spent pot lining (SPL) waste that had been generated over the past years were subjected to physical segregation at Alba. A small processing plant was set up on site and the SPL was segregated into four fractions, namely steel, carbon blocks, refractory and insulation bricks, and the fine fractions which cannot be segregated. All the steel was sold to a steel recycling furnace adjacent to Alba. The fine fraction alone was 30,000 cubic metres which was disposed of at this new facility. The carbon and refractory portions are now being recycled in ways that have been approved by the environmental authorities, and which generate a financial return, to the extent that Alba alone has saved over US$1million in the process.

Conclusion – a boost for local industry

The recycling drive at Alba has given a boost to the local waste recycling companies in Bahrain. Already there was one aluminium dross processing plant, Aluserv, which employs 25 people – operating almost exclusively to process the dross wastes from Alba and recover the aluminium content.

The paper and carton recycling company Alfa Express received a significant boost due to the introduction of a paper and carton waste recycling programme at Alba. During the last one year, 17,000 kgs of clean waste paper was given free of cost and 88,000 kgs of carton waste was given at a nominal cost of US$7.5m to this company.

Recycling companies Scrap-mould, Crown Metals and Bahrain Recycling Company are the other three companies currently benefiting from the waste minimisation and recycling initiatives of Alba.

The partnership of Alba with the five companies mentioned adjacent to the plant makes for a win-win association – enabling Alba to further improve its housekeeping, minimise wastes, save costs and, above all, prevent environmental damage.

Further details on Alba can be obtained from the company's website www.albasmelter.com

Contact

David Lloyd
Email: David.Lloyd@alba.com.bh

Commentary

This company is the recipient of a United Nations Environment Programme Award as part of the millennium celebrations and as such is seen as exemplary in the processing of aluminium.

Principle 9

Unilever

Pasig: River of Life, Philippines

Introduction

Unilever has operated in the Philippines since 1927 manufacturing packaged consumer goods including detergents, soaps, personal products and foods. Its factory in the heart of Metro Manila straddles a small tributary of the Pasig River – the 25km waterway stretching between Laguna de Bai and Manila Bay that has been a vital part of the history and fortunes of the region. The Pasig River campaign is one of Unilever's many initiatives worldwide addressed to Clean Water Stewardship and Conservation, which in turn is an important part of the company's Water Sustainability Initiative. The priority for the Pasig River project fits with company policy to focus on water and to apply the principles of local community partnership to these activities.

Summary

A practical example of how a carefully managed long-term partnership programme can start to reverse the fortunes of a dying river and improve living conditions for those depending on it. The programme addresses particularly Global Compact Principles 7, 8 and 9.

Learnings

- Although the Pasig River's problems are daunting, co-operation between government, NGOs and industry, and a step by step programme, can produce steady improvement, with benefit to the whole community.
- Leading by example in its own pioneering factory operations, Unilever Philippines is well positioned to offer advice and training to community projects supporting the Pasig campaign. Unilever's contribution works well because it focuses on problems it understands best: Clean Up, Pollution Prevention, Greening, Advocacy.

- Unilever employees and the wider community pro-actively support the Pasig project to achieve results in the community and raise environmental consciousness throughout the company.
- The ongoing Pasig experience is a key reference in the practical guidelines Unilever has developed and published on integrated water resource management. These are known around the business as the Sustainable Water and Integrated Catchment Management (SWIM) principles. These are applied in a number of places: Mersey Basin, UK; Don Watershed, Canada; and are starting in Brantas, Indonesia.

The Pasig River's problems

The Pasig River is the critical lifeline for the ecological health of Laguna de Bai to the east of Manila, one of the largest freshwater lakes in the world. The river flows from the lake westwards into Manila Bay and out to the South China Sea, and has traditionally been the source of livelihood for thousands of fishermen who depended on the migration of fish up-river to the lake.

Throughout the 20th century the Pasig's health deteriorated. By the 1930s fish were unable to make their easterly migration. By 1950 bathing or clothes washing was impossible. Ten years later the river smelled so offensive that those who could abandoned the ferry boats. By the 1980s there was almost no river tourism, and fishing was nonexistent. The Pasig River was declared biologically dead.

As a key partner in the major international multi-sector regeneration programme, Unilever Philippines has led the corporate sector in contributing to partnership projects that are working to return the Pasig to health.

The plan to save the Pasig

In 1993 the Pasig River Rehabilitation Programme (PRRP) was launched. Its aim was to improve water quality to Class C (ie with thriving aquatic life, and clean enough for boating) and to improve the environmental state of the entire river system by 2008.

Endorsed by the President, PRRP was backed by the United Nations Development Programme, government agencies, industry and business including Unilever Philippines, private organisations, the World Bank, Japan International Cooperation Agency, as well as numerous non-governmental organisations (NGOs).

PRRP's agenda is bold and spans 15 years. It includes ridding the river of solid waste, redeveloping the waterfront and renovating bridges as well as supporting community-based programmes and promoting Clean River Zones. In 1999 PRRP and other associated organisations evolved into the Pasig River Rehabilitation Commission (PRRC) which today coordinates a US$1 billion Pasig River Development Plan.

The Unilever Philippines contribution

Since 1993 Unilever Philippines' contribution to the rehabilitation programme has been in three areas:
- ensuring its own operations do not pollute;
- partnership programmes helping neighbours not to pollute;
- a wider advocacy programme, including encouraging wider participation and support for the establishment of Clean River Zones in partnership with the Sagip Pasig (Save Pasig) Movement.

Chito Macapagal, general manager corporate development, with Jika
Mendoza, corporate relations and communications manager, have led
the programme, with strong support from Howard Belton, chairman and
CEO Unilever Philippines. 'So far we have invested over US$20,000 in
cash, and many times more than that in resources. Our support is long
term,' says Chito. 'But our commitment is much more than financial
support. Our contribution comes from people who care about raising
standards. In Unilever Philippines we all care deeply about the future of
our river.'

1 Operations on the factory site

Unilever Philippines' commitment to a cleaner, greener river starts within
its plant. The factory continues to achieve reductions in amounts of water
used and wastewater generated during manufacturing processes, as well as
reductions in power use, solid waste, etc.

But perhaps its best known on-site contribution is the company's domestic sewage treatment plant – the first such plant in Metro Manila, completed in 1998. Treated sewage water (from the company's domestic water
use, ie from canteens and toilets) flows into a fishpond full of healthy freshwater fish, before discharging into the river.

The company has been pro-active in introducing new technologies in the
Philippines: for example, it introduced the first 100% biodegradable active
ingredients in powders and detergent bars in 1993. It has had a Total Quality approach since 1990, and in 1994 earned ISO 9002: the first in the
industry in the Philippines to receive this accreditation. This was followed
in 2000 by ISO 14001 accreditation.

In 2000 Unilever opened a dedicated Save Pasig Action Center within the
Unilever compound. This area is much used by numerous Pasig River advocates for debate, workshops and related events. Unilever continues to be
pro-active on site in ways that support the Pasig River project and other
environmental good practice

Learnings: the sustained company-wide initiative attracts keen support
from employees who are proud of a sewage plant which has established
new, high standards for the whole area of Metro Manila and beyond. Additionally, Unilever consumers, for whose families the river has long been

central to their existence, appreciate the investment. The Save Pasig Action Center has focused attention on the issue.

2 Partnership programmes helping neighbours not to pollute

Unilever is actively involved with a number of partnership programmes which ultimately benefit the Pasig. With the help of the NGO Sagip Pasig Movement (SPM), Unilever conducts regular clean-up drives and community-based waste management training in neighbouring communities, for example:

Paco Environment Enhancement Programme (PEEP): a project in partnership with a World Bank funded project group under the Department of Environment & Natural Resources and stall-holders of Paco Public Market – a large wet market close to the factory.

This is work with NGOs and community groups to encourage better management of market waste: discarded coconut husks and other fruit and vegetables, meat carcasses and fish, as well as packaging and other debris that stall-holders find it easier to throw into the river. Aling Diding, a campaigning stallholder in the wet market says: 'For the last 8 years Unilever has given financial support to PEEP which has been used in many practical ways to deal with market waste. These include providing drums to collect recycling materials, cleaning public comfort rooms as well as training and leaflets to encourage cleanliness and waste segregation.' The dedication of the market people is shown in the way they have put a net across their tributary and removed the floating waste even from way upstream.

The long-term aim is for the City Council of Manila with the help of Unilever Philippines and NGOs to build a facility to produce organic compost – providing an example to the city's 25 other markets.

Learnings: prevention is, obviously, better than cure but can be hard to achieve. Although clearly it is sensible to segregate waste, this is not easy to enforce when there is still an insufficient public waste disposal facility. Nevertheless people, once aware, really care about their environment, and with the support of Unilever work very hard for improvement.

Difficulties: it is taking time to see significant improvements. Patience, clarity of vision and consistent action is the way forward here. Many others would like to be involved: Unilever, with its pragmatic focus, is instrumental in finding the best avenue for effective practical contributions.

3 Wider advocacy programme

'Who Cares? . . . We do' campaign: an emotional appeal for public participation in the Pasig River rehabilitation. This initiative emphasises community clean-up, school involvement, advertising and press campaigns backed by 10 partners, all of whom have adopted the same slogan: Unilever, the Sagip Pasig Movement, Laguna Lake Development Authority, Rotary Club of Manila, Lungsod ng Maynila, Clean and Green Foundation

Inc, Piso Para Sa Pasig (A Peso for the Pasig), Department of Education, Culture & Sports, PEEP, and the Pasig River Rehabilitation Commission.

'Isang Ilog, Isang Diwa, Isang Gawa' (One River, One Thought, One Action): a programme initiated in 2000 by the Rotary Club of Manila and Unilever Philippines focusing on environmental education to raise awareness of the Pasig rehabilitation within the Clean River Zones of Manila's districts 5 & 6. Activities include inter-school competitions, community workshops on waste segregation and composting, and offering educational materials to public schools. 150,000 books on the environment have been printed for the new school year.

Tree Planting: Unilever supports government efforts to green the environment. Employees have planted 150 trees in a small public garden by the factory, and it expects to adopt a local park shortly. It supports the restoration over the next 4 years of some 25 hectares of land beside La Mesa Dam, a vital watershed.

Clean River Zones in partnership with the SPM: in 1993 Sagip Pasig Movement (SPM), with Unilever's support, launched its community-based initiative – Clean River Zones. These are finite, local communities – industrial, residential, commercial, markets and schools – who manage waste sustainably and work on cleaning and greening the river and adjacent areas. Supporters focus on community mobilisation, public information and advocacy.

The close involvement of the Unilever Philippines' chairman and the head of corporate development signals the company's determined commitment to the Clean River Zone initiative. But Unilever has extended the campaign to involve civic groups such as the Rotary Club of Manila and helped to establish further Zones supported by other major corporations. Honda Cars, Isuzu Motors, Shell and the Philippine Long Distance Telephone Company are corporate partners in the first Clean River Zone. Caltex is sponsoring the fourth Clean River Zone.

Broadening the campaign in this way follows Unilever's wider aims of working in partnership with others to maximise effectiveness. The importance of this approach was highlighted by Unilever co-chairman Niall FitzGerald in a speech to the Fourth World Congress on Detergents (Switzerland, 1998): '...the sustainability agenda brings in a wide range of other players from outside our industry, with their own interests and ideas. We could certainly benefit from co-operating more with these external parties – be it the local communities in which we operate, environmental groups, or companies in completely different industries, but who may have a relevant perspective.'

The future

Saving the Pasig is a long term programme. With a biological oxygen demand (BOD – a scientific measure of river health) down to 230 in 2001, the river is no longer classed as 'dead'. So far four Clean River Zones are identified, two of which are fully developed; reducing their BOD to 50 is the aim. Unilever's focused contribution as part of a wider programme is beginning to show improvements that benefit wider civil society as well as company employees and their families.

Unilever's next steps include supporting the application of Laguna de Bai for membership of the global Living Lakes initiative, which would help attract further international attention to the lake and river. In the words of Howard Belton: 'A body of water this important cannot wait.'

Unilever's work received the 1998 Dangal ng Pasig Award (Pride of the Pasig) from the Sagip Pasig Movement, the 1999 Mother Nature Award from the Pollution Control Association of the Philippines, and the 2001 Dangal ng Pasig Award.

Chito Macapagal comments on the initiative so far: 'Concern for the environment does not come only from policy, code or principles written in manuals. It comes from people who are committed, and from a culture where leadership encourages and practises that attitude. To be successful, company leaders must weave environmental consciousness throughout their business. This is what we try to do within Unilever.'

Contact

Unilever: www.unilever.com
Environment & Society/Case Studies for individual case studies
News/Unilever Today/Recent Speeches for Niall FitzGerald's speech
Email: Rose.Fenn@unilever.com
Living Lakes: www.livinglakes.org

Commentary

1　How much money has Unilever spent so far to implement the initiative?
2　What are the lessons learned for the other partners?
3　The case does not refer to ISEAL, an important partnership for MSC.
4　The lessons are too general since they provide little detail about what it takes to spread the word, whether in workshop, public media or communities involved. (For example, is it management only or is it the community also surrounding the fishery? Who is bringing the news and how?)

Additional material was sought where possible from relevant websites. However, websites are informative only to the extent that they report successful deeds but are superficial when it comes down to the bargaining process and the strategic actions taken in every case and depending on the different legal bodies involved in each area or country. In addition, finding and hiring independent experts seems to be a lengthy process. How expensive and sustainable *per se* such a process is are elements not mentioned in the case. It seems, however, that the general idea is simple and can be communicated directly to consumers through the identification of the MSC logo.

A recurring theme is 'otherness'. Unilever is aware of the need to create a network of organisations, whether governmental or not for profit, whether local or global, in order to lead the project.

Pasig

The case reveals a general commitment rather than a specific commitment to the nine principles. The data indicate an 'act of faith' in that Unilever takes an interest in this public good – the river – and manages to convert a non-business goal into a priority for sustaining itself. This sounds like a classic case of an 'embedded' company, where the simple equation is: dead river = dead factory. This perhaps would explain the seemingly moral imperative of '*company leaders must weave environmental consciousness throughout their business*' and make it a rhetorical statement whereby the network is more important than the river but becomes the symbolic connector for Manila.

Appendix 2
Recommended reading

Andriof, J. and McIntosh, M. (2001) *Perspectives On Corporate Citizenship*, Greenleaf.

Brown, Phillip and Lander, Hugh (2001) *Capitalism and Social Progress*, Palgrave.

Egan, J. and Wilson, D. (2002) *Private Business: Public Battleground*, Palgrave.

Fisher, R. and Ury, W. (1982) *Getting To Yes*, Hutchinson.

Giddens, A. (ed.) (2001) *The Global Third Way Debate*, Polity.

Hardt, Michael and Negri, Antonio (2001) *Empire*, Harvard University Press.

Leipziger, Deborah (2001) *SA8000*, FT Prentice Hall.

McIntosh, M. (2002) *A Ladder To The Moon*, Palgrave.

Scholte, Jan Aart (2000) *Globalisation: a critical introduction*, Macmillan.

Stead, W. and Stead, J.G. (1996) *Management For A Small Planet*, Sage.

Sunejai, Kirek (2002) *Policy Issues for Business*, Sage.

The Journal of Corporate Citizenship

Waddock, Sandra (2001) *Leading Corporate Citizens*, McGraw-Hill Irwin.

Zadek, Simon (2001) *The Civil Corporation*, Earthscan.

Appendix 3
Contacts

ABRINQ
Av. Pedroso de Moraes 2219, CEP 05419-001,
São Paulo, Brasil
Tel: +11 3816 3644 Fax: +11 3031 0226
Email: abrinq@abrinq.com.br
Website: www.fundabrinq.org.br/

ActionAid
Hamlyn House, Macdonald Road, Archway,
London N19 5PG, UK
Tel: +44 20 7561 7561
Fax: +44 20 7272 0899
Email: mail@actionaid.org.uk
Website: www.actionaid.org/

Aluminium Bahrain BSC
Website: www.aluminiumbahrain.com/

Amnesty International
99–119 Rosebery Avenue, London EC1R 4RE, UK
Tel: +44 20 7814 6200
Fax: +44 20 7833 1510
Email: info@amnesty.org.uk
Website: www.amnesty.org/

Anti-Slavery International
Thomas Clarkson House, The Stableyard,
Broomgrove Road, London SW9 9TL, UK
Tel: +44 20 7501 8920
Fax: +44 20 7738 4110
Email: info@antislavery.org
Website: www.antislavery.org/

Apparel Industry Partnership
Website:
www.users.cloud9.net/~pofn/AIPfactsheet.html

Aspen Institute
One Dupont Circle, NW Suite 700, Washington
DC 20036-1133, USA
Tel: +1 202 736 5800
Fax: +1 202 467 0790
Website: www.aspeninst.org/

Avon
Website: avon.avon.com/

**Bangladesh Garment Manufacturers and
Exporters Association (BGMEA)**
BTMC Bhaban 7-9, Kawran Bazar, Dhaka
Tel: + 880 2 8115597
Fax: + 880 2 113951
Email: info@bgmea.com
Website: www.bgmea.com/

BASF
Website: www.basf.com/

BMW
Website: www.bmw.com/

Boston College
Main Campus, 140 Commonwealth Avenue,
Chestnut Hill MA 02467, USA
Tel: +1 617 552 8000
Website: www.bc.edu/

BP
Website: www.bp.com/

British Airways (BA)
Website: http://www.british-airways.com/

British Telecom (BT)
Website: www.bt.com/

British Toy and Hobby Association,
80 Camberwell Road, London SE5 0EG, UK
Tel: +44 20 7701 7271
Fax: +44 20 7708 2437
Email: admin@btha.co.uk
Website: www.btha.co.uk/

Business for Social Responsibility
Headquarters, 609 Mission Street – 2nd Floor, San
Francisco, California 94109, USA
Tel: +1 415 537 0890
Fax: +1 415 537 0889
Email: info@bsr.org
Website: www.bsr.org/

Cable & Wireless
Website: www.cw.com/

Catholic University of Eichstätt Ingolstadt
Ostenstr. 26, 85072 Eichstätt, Germany
Tel: +49 8421 930
Website: www.ku-eichstaett.de/

Caux Round Table
RR 2, Box 239, Waterville MN 56096, USA
Tel: +1 507 362 4916
Fax: +1 507 362 4820
Email: CauxRT@aol.com

Coalition for Environmentally Responsible Economies (CERES)
11 Arlington Street, 6th Floor, Boston MA 02116, USA
Tel: +01 617 247 0700
Fax: +01 617 267 5400
Email: bakal@ceres.org
Website: www.ceres.org/

Conservation Agriculture Network
Website: www.rainforest-alliance.org/

Corporate Watch
PO Box 29344, San Francisco, CA 94129, USA
Tel: +1 415 561 6568
Fax: +1 415 561 6493
Email: corpwatch@corpwatch.org
Website: www.corpwatch.org

Danish Center for Human Rights
8 H Wilders Plads, 1403 Copenhagen, Denmark
Tel: +45 3269 8888
Fax: +45 3269 8800
Email: Center@humanrights.dk
Website: www.humanrights.dk

Deakin University
Corporate Citizenship Research Unit, Pigdons Road, Geelong, Victoria 3217, Australia
Tel: 03 5227 1100
Fax: 03 5227 2001
Website: www.deakin.edu.au/

Deloitte Touche Tahmatsu
Website: www.deloitte.com/

DuPont
Website: www.dupont.com/

Ethical Trading Initiative (ETI)
Website: www.ethicaltrade.org/

Fairtrade Labelling Organizations International (FLO)
Kaiser Friedrich Strasse 13, 53113 Bonn, Germany
Tel: +49 228 949 230
Fax: +49 228 242 1713
Website: coordination@fairtrade.net
Email: www.fairtrade.net/

Ford
Website: www.ford.com/

Foreign and Commonwealth Office
London SW1A 2AH UK
Tel: +44 20 7270 1500
Website: www.fco.gov.uk/

Global Reporting Initiative
Interim Secretariat, 11 Arlington Street, Boston MA 02116, USA
Tel: +1 617 266 9384
Fax: +1 617 267 5400
Email: info@globalreporting.org
Website: www.globalreporting.org/

Global Sullivan Principles
5040 E. Shea Boulevard – Suite 260, Scottsdale AZ 85254-4687, USA
Tel: 480 443 1800
Fax: 480 443 1824
Email: ifesh@ifesh.org
Website: www.globalsullivanprinciples.org/

Good Corporation
37 St John's Hill, Battersea, London SW11 1TT, UK
Tel: +44 20 7924 3994
Fax: +44 20 7924 7060
Email: info@goodcorporation.com
Website: www.goodcorporation.com/

Greening Industry
Website: www.worldbank.org/nipr/greening/

Greenpeace UK
Canonbury Villas, London N1 2PN, UK
Tel: +44 20 7865 8100
Fax: +44 20 7865 8200
Email: info@uk.greenpeace.org
Website: www.greenpeace.org/

Herman Miller, Inc.
855 East Main Ave, PO Box 302, Michigan 49464-0302, USA
Tel: +1 888 443 4357
Website: www.hermanmiller.com/

Human Rights Watch
350 Fifth Avenue, 34th floor, New York, NY
10118-3299, USA
Tel: +1 212 290 4700
Fax: +1 212 736 1300
Email: hrwnyc@hrw.org
Website: www.hrw.org/

Institute of Social & Ethical AccountAbility
Unit A, 137 Shepherdess Walk, London N1 7RQ,
UK
Tel: +44 20 7549 0400
Fax: +44 20 7253 7440
Website: www.accountability.org.uk/

International Chamber of Commerce
38 Cours Albert 1er, 75008 Paris, France
Tel: +33 1 49 53 28 28
Fax: +33 1 49 53 28 59
Email: webmaster@iccwbo.org

International Confederation of Free Trade
Unions
5 Boulevard du Roi Albert II, Bte 1, 1210 Brussels,
Belgium
Tel: +32 02 224 0211
Fax: +32 02 201 5815
Email: internetpo@icftu.org
Website: www.icftu.org/

International Federation of Organic
Agriculture Movements
Head Office, c/o Ökozentrum Imsbach, D-66636
Tholey-Theley, Germany
Tel: +49 6853 919890
Fax. +49 6853-919899
Email: HeadOffice@ifoam.org
Website: www.ifoam.org/

International Institute for Environment and
Development
Endsleigh Street, London WC1H 0DD, UK
Tel: +44 20 7388 2117
Fax +44 020 7388 2826
Email: mailbox@iied.org
Website: www.iied.org/

International Institute for Labour Studies
Tel: +41 22 799 6128
Fax: +41 22 799 8542
Email: inst@ilo.org
Website: www.ilo.org/public/english/bureau/inst/

International Labour Office (ILO)
4, route des Morillons, CH-1211 Geneva 22,
Switzerland
Tel: +41 22 799 7126
Fax: +41 22 799 6926
Email: Polnorm@ilo.org; normes@ilo.org
Website: www.ilo.org/

International Organic Accreditation System
Website: www.ifoam.org/

International Organization for
Standardization (ISO)
1, rue de Varembé, Case postale 56, CH-1211
Geneva 20, Switzerland
Tel: +41 22 749 01 11
Fax: +41 22 733 34 30
Email: central@iso.org
Website: www.iso.org/

International Organisation of Employers (IOE)
26 Chemin de Joinville, PO Box 68, 1216 Cointrin,
Switzerland
Tel: +41 22 798 1616
Fax: +41 22 198 8862
Email: ioe@ioe-emp.org
Website: www.ioe-emp.org/

International Programme on the Elimination
of Child Labour (IPECL)
Tel: +41 22 799 8181
Fax: +41 22 799 8771
Email: ipec@ilo.org
Website:
www.ilo.org/public/english/standards/ipec/

International Social and Environmental
Accreditation and Labelling Alliance (ISEAL)
Website: www.isealalliance.org/

Kenya Flower Council
PO Box 56325, Nairobi, Kenya
Tel: 254 2 576597
Email: Kfc@africaonline.co.ke
Website: www.kenyaflowers.co.ke/

Kesko
Website: www.kesko.fi/

Levi Strauss & Co.
Worldwide and US Headquarters, 1155 Battery
Street, San Francisco CA 94111, USA
Tel: +1 415 501 6000
Fax: +1 415 501 7112
Website: www.levistrauss.com

Lifecycle Initiative
Website: www.uneptie.org/pc/sustain/lca/lca.htm

Marine and Forest Stewardship Councils
Website:
www.panda.org/livingplanet/gttemasterpp2532.
pdf

Nike
Website: www.nike.com/

OECD
2, rue André Pascal, F-75775 Paris, Cedex 16,
France
Tel: +33 1 45 24 82 00
Website: www.oecd.org

Phillips Petroleum Company
4th and Keeler Avenue, Bartlesville OK 74004,
USA
Tel: +1 918 661 6600
Website: www.phillips66.com/

Power Finance Corporation
Website: www.pfcindia.com/

Prince of Wales Business Leaders Forum
Website: www.pwblf.org

Reebok
Website: www.reebok.com/

Rio Tinto plc
6 St James's Square, London SW1Y 4LD, UK
Tel: +44 20 7930 2399
Website: www.riotinto.com/

Royal Society for the Protection of Birds
Website: www.rspb.org.uk/

SAP Nigeria
Website: www.sap.com/contact/nigeria.htm

Save the Children
54 Wilton Road, Westport CT 06880, USA
Tel: +1 800 728 3843
Website: www.savethechildren.org/home.shtml

Shell UK Limited
Shell Centre, London SE1 7NA, UK
Tel: +44 20 7934 1234
Fax: +44 20 7934 8060
Website: www.shell.com

SIGMA Project
c/o British Standards Institution, 389 Chiswick High
Road, London W4 4AL, UK
Tel: +44 20 8996 7665
Fax: +44 20 8996 7328
Email: Fiona.Gibbons@bsi-global.com
Website: www.projectsigma.com/

Skanska
Website: www.skanska.se/

Social Accountability International
220 East 23rd Street, Suite 605, New York NY
10010, USA
Tel: +1 212 684 1414
Fax: +1 212 684 1515
Email: Info@sa-intl.org
Website: www.cepaa.org/

Statoil
N-4035 Stavanger, Norway
Tel: +47 5199 0000
Fax: +47 5199 0050
Website: www.statoil.com/

Storebrand
Website: www.storebrand.no/

Transparency International
Website: www.transparency.org/

UBS
Website: www.ubs.com/

Unilever
Website: www.unilever.com/

Union of International Associations (UIA)
rue Washingtonstraat 40, B-1050 Brussels,
Belgium
Tel: +32 2 640 18 08
Fax: + 32 2 643 61 99
Email: uia@uia.be
Website: www.uia.org/

United Nations Children's Fund (UNICEF)
Website: www.unicef.org/

United Nations Development Programme
(UNDP)
Website: www.undp.org/

United Nations Environment Programme
(UNEP)
Website: www.unep.org/

United Nations Global Compact
Executive Office of the Secretary-General, United Nations, New York NY10017, USA
Tel: +1 212 963 1490
Website: www.unglobalcompact.org/

United Nations High Commissioner for Refugees (UNHCR)
Case Postale 2500, CH-1211 Genève 2 Dépôt, Switzerland
Tel: +41 22 739 8111
Website: www.unhcr.ch/

University of Bath
Bath BA2 7AY, UK
Tel: +44 1225 388388
Website: www.bath.ac.uk/

University of Warwick
Institute for Governance and Public Management, Coventry CV4 7AL, UK
Tel: + 44 24 7652 3523
Fax: + 44 24 7646 1606
Website: www.warwick.ac.uk/

Volvo
Website: www.volvocars.com/

Wessex Water
1 Clevedon Walk, Nailsea, Bristol BS49 2QR, UK
Tel: +44 01225 526 000
Email: info@wessexwater.co.uk
Website: www.wessexwater.co.uk/

Whales and Dolphin Conservation Society
Brookfield House, 38 St Paul Street, Chippenham, Wiltshire SN15 1LY, UK
Tel: 0870 870 0027/+44 0 1249 449500
Fax: 0870 870 0028/+44 0 1249 449501
Email: info@wdcs.org
Website: www.wdcs.org/

World Business Council for Sustainable Development
4 chemin de Conches, 1231 Conches, Geneva, Switzerland
Tel: +41 22 839 3100
Fax: +1 22 839 3131
Email: info@wbcsd.org
Website: www.wbcsd.org/

World Economic Forum
91-93 route de la Capite, CH – 1223 Cologny, Geneva, Switzerland
Tel: 44 22 869 1212
Fax: 41 27 786 2744
Email: contact@weforum.org
Website: www.weforum.org/

World Resources Institute
10 G Street, NE (Suite 800), Washington DC 20002, USA
Tel: +1 202 729 7600
Fax: +1202 729 7610
Website: www.wri.org/

World Trade Organization
Rue de la Lausanne 154, CH-1211, Geneva 21, Switzerland
Website: www.wto.org/

WWF International
Avenue du Mont-Blanc, 1196 Gland, Switzerland
Tel: +41 22 364 91 11
Website: www.panda.org

Index